THE
KNACK

How Street-Smart Entrepreneurs

Learn to Handle Whatever

Comes Up

Norm Brodsky

and Bo Burlingham

Published by Random House Business Books 2008

2 4 6 8 10 9 7 5 3 1

Portions of this book first appeared in issues of *Inc.* magazine

First published in the United States in 2008 by
Portfolio, a member of the Penguin Group (USA) Inc.

First published in Great Britain in 2008 by
Random House Business Books
Random House, 20 Vauxhall Bridge Road,
London SW1V 2SA

www.rbooks.co.uk

Addresses for companies within The Random House Group Limited can be found at:
www.randomhouse.co.uk/offices.htm

The Random House Group Limited Reg. No. 954009

A CIP catalogue record for this book
is available from the British Library

ISBN 9781847940339

The Random House Group Limited supports The Forest Stewardship
Council (FSC), the leading international forest certification organisation.
All our titles that are printed on Greenpeace approved FSC certified paper
carry the FSC logo. Our paper procurement policy can be found at
www.rbooks.co.uk/environment

Mixed Sources

Product group from well-managed
forests and other controlled sources
www.fsc.org   Cert no. TT-COC-2139
© 1996 Forest Stewardship Council
FSC

Typeset in Bodoni Book

Printed and bound in Great Britain by
CPI Bookmarque, Croydon, CR0 4TD

To Elaine Jerome Brodsky

and

Lisa Meisel Burlingham

Almost eighty years of marital bliss

and counting

Contents

THE
KNACK

The Knack . . . and How to Get It

We all have mentors in business, although we're not always aware of the role they're playing. My first and best mentor was an independent businessman, a solo practitioner, in New York City. His business was custom peddling. He'd visit his customers in their homes and sell them clothing, appliances, whatever. He was like a one-man traveling department store, and he handled the full range of business functions by himself—from purchasing to bookkeeping to managing credit and collecting receivables. I sometimes went with him on his route. I'd ask him a lot of questions, and he'd explain the logic of what he was doing. That's how I learned some of the most important business concepts I use to this day.

At the time, however, I didn't appreciate the education I was getting. I was only eight years old. The custom peddler was my father.

It's ironic, I suppose, that growing up I never wanted to go into business. I had no desire to follow in my father's footsteps. After college, I went to law school, figuring I'd make my fortune in law. But life is funny, and I eventually wound up in business anyway. Only then did I begin to realize how much my father had taught me.

He was the one, for example, who first explained to me the importance of maintaining high gross margins. He called them something else—big markups—but the thought process was the same. "Always make a good sale with a big markup," he'd say. "Make sure your customer is someone you can collect from." "Don't take advantage of people." "Be fair." Those are fabulous business lessons embedded in my mind, and they came straight from my father.

Then there were his expressions. "Don't worry twice," he'd tell me when I'd get anxious about an upcoming event—a final exam, for instance. He'd ask, "Have you done your homework? Are you prepared?" I usually was. "So don't worry twice." In other words, don't waste time and energy on problems that may never arise.

Or when I complained about not knowing what to do with my life, he'd say, "There's a million dollars under your shoe; you just have to find it." It wasn't until I became an entrepreneur that I understood what he meant.

Or when I talked about things I'd like to have, he'd say, "You don't ask, you don't get," whereupon I'd request a bigger allowance. He'd smile and say, "Nice try, but just because you ask doesn't mean you're going to get it." Much later I came to understand that he'd been giving me my first lesson in selling.

Lessons like these sunk in when I wasn't looking. They became habits of mind that led me to do certain things reflexively, without even noticing what I was doing. One of my best habits, for example, grew out of my father's practice of breaking down problems and challenges into their basic components. He believed that most issues in business—and in life—are fundamentally simple, even though they may appear complicated at first. He taught me that, to deal with them, you have to examine the underlying elements and figure out what's really going on. Never assume, moreover, that the real issues are those you see on the surface. That way of thinking has been one of my most powerful business tools over the years.

Indeed, I believe it's such mental habits that allow people to become successful entrepreneurs. I myself have been an entrepreneur for three decades. I've built more than eight companies, including a messenger business that made the Inc. 500 list of fastest-growing private companies for three straight years and a records storage company that I sold for $110 million in a leveraged buyout. Along the way, I've had the privilege of meeting many other successful men and women company builders, and I've noticed that most of us share these mental habits. They are the secrets of our success. (Well, one of the them. It certainly helps to have a life partner like my wife of thirty-nine years,

Elaine, without whom I would not have achieved anywhere near the amount of success that I've enjoyed.)

Now, I realize that not everyone wants to hear this. A lot of people starting out in business would prefer to have a step-by-step formula or a specific set of rules they could use to achieve their goals. The problem is, there aren't any. Rather, there's a way of thinking that allows someone to deal with many different situations and take advantage of many different opportunities as they arise. To be sure, having that mentality doesn't guarantee that you'll succeed at everything you do, but it does improve your chances significantly. You win more than you lose, and the longer you stay in the game, the more often you come out on top.

I believe most people can develop the habits of mind I'm talking about and use them to acquire the wherewithal to live whatever kind of life they want. Not that every person will be successful to the same degree or in the same way. In business, as elsewhere, some individuals have God-given gifts that allow them to play the game better than others. We can't all be Tiger Woods, or Picasso, or Shakespeare, but anybody can learn how to play golf, or paint, or write a sonnet, and we can all learn how to be financially self-sufficient as well.

That's an opinion, I might add, that has been repeatedly tested over the past seventeen years—ever since I began mentoring Bobby and Helene Stone, an experience I recount in chapter 1 of this book. My work with them led to an article in *Inc.* by Bo Burlingham, who later became my coauthor when we launched our column, "Street Smarts," in December 1995. Through the column, I came into contact with literally thousands of people who wanted to start a business, or who were in the process of starting a business, or who already had a business and were wrestling with one problem or another. They wrote me from all over the United States, Canada, and Mexico, as well as from countries as far away as Korea, Lithuania, Brazil, Singapore, and South Africa. They were software developers, insurance brokers, headhunters, artists, swimming pool installers, concrete road pavers, furniture builders, Web site designers, machine-tool salesmen, butchers, bakers, and candlestick makers. (All right, maybe not butchers, but the others for sure.) They had tile-making businesses, diagnostic imaging facilities, cosmetics companies, bellows-making factories, recruitment services, violin shops, investment firms, consulting practices, dot-coms, movie chains, and just about every other type of business under the sun.

I read all their e-mails and responded to as many as I could. Every year, I also chose eight to ten of the writers to mentor on an ongoing basis. Some of them you will meet in the following pages. Their goals ran the gamut from building a giant business to starting a day care center to simply achieving financial independence and having more time with the family. Everybody, after all, has a different definition of success. What we have in common is the desire to have happier, richer, fuller lives for ourselves, and create a better world for our children and grandchildren. My goal was to help the entrepreneurs develop the mental habits that would allow them to do that. Judging by what some of them have accomplished, I have to believe that my efforts were not entirely in vain—which is not to take anything away from the people themselves. Building their businesses has been their doing, not mine.

I should note, moreover, that you don't have to have a mentor like me, or a father like mine, to acquire the mental habits needed to "handle whatever comes up." Many of my own habits I've developed the old-fashioned way—by making mistakes, falling on my face, picking myself up, and figuring out how not to do it again. But you know what they say: A smart person learns from his or her mistakes. A wise person learns from other people's mistakes. I guess that makes me smart. I hope that, through this book, I can help you to be wise.

CHAPTER ONE

How to Succeed in Business

I began my career as a business mentor and teacher of entrepreneurship on a cold evening in January 1992. My wife, Elaine, and I were at a restaurant with our friends Bobby and Helene Stone. They'd suggested we eat someplace less expensive than usual. When we got there, we found out why. Bobby told us that he'd been laid off from his job as a computer equipment salesman—a job he'd had for fourteen years. He was very distraught about it, and angry. He swore he'd never work for someone else again. He said he was going into Helene's home business, selling computer supplies out of their basement in North Bellmore, New York.

"That's great, Bobby," I said. "Do you have a business plan?"

"What's a business plan?" Bobby asked.

"A business plan lays out what you expect to do," I said. "You need it so you'll know if you have a viable business."

"The business is definitely viable," he said. "It's been going for seven years with just Helene and her assistant, Paula, working part-time out of our home, and no one doing sales. And I think I'm a pretty good salesman. How could it not be a viable business?"

Helene couldn't have disagreed more. "This man is nuts," she said. "There's no money. We can't even pay our bills. We're looking for a home equity loan to pay off our biggest supplier."

Bobby said Helene was being too negative. Helene said Bobby didn't know what he was talking about. I said, "Look, do me a favor. Don't do anything rash. Bring all your paperwork to my house, and we'll sit down and see if you have a viable business here." I was thinking I'd give them a little advice, and they'd take it from there. It turned out, however, that they needed a whole education.

And that proved to be the most interesting aspect of the situation. I mean, it wasn't clear to me at that point how much you could teach people about business. Could you take a middle-aged couple who weren't businesspeople, who knew nothing, really, about creating a successful business, and show them how to do it? Or did people have to learn from experience? I wasn't sure. It had taken me a lifetime to learn what I knew about business. A lot of lessons had come from getting whacked in the head. I certainly didn't learn how to do business in a classroom—and I have degrees in both law and accounting. Indeed, I'd had to unlearn a lot of the stuff I'd been taught in school. And how much of business is instinctive, anyway? How much do you learn as a kid before you're even aware it has anything to do with business at all? I didn't know, but I was curious to find out.

First Things First

Bobby and Helene came over to our house a few days later and brought with them the information I'd asked for about the business's sales, costs, and expenses for the past year or so—in other words, everything Helene had taken in, plus her receivables, and everything she'd paid out, plus her payables. I told them we'd go over the numbers after dinner. First, however, I wanted to discuss their goals, which is where I always like to start.

Now, understand, the initial goal of every business is to survive long enough to see whether or not it's viable. I don't care what business you're talking about or how much capital you have. You never know for sure if a business is viable until you do it in the real world. But viability is just a step on the way to somewhere else, and I want to know where somewhere else is. I want to hear what people have to say. What I'm listening for are goals that can't be achieved by business, or goals that will get in the way of the business, or goals that are totally unrealistic given the particular business you're looking at. I'm listening for what's really motivating people. Usually, it's something emotional.

Bobby and Helene told me they wanted to earn a living out of the business. Fair enough. But Bobby wanted something more. At that moment, what he really wanted was revenge on his old company. That was normal, but it wasn't going to get him anywhere except maybe to burn some bridges. Revenge had nothing to do with Bobby and Helene's long-term goal, which was to become financially independent and never be in this situation again. So, by identifying the goal, we were able to get those emotions out of the way.

Once you've decided on the goal, you come right back to the issue of viability. I told Bobby and Helene, "Look, I don't know if you have a real business here, and I also don't know if you can run it like a real business. But first we have to see if it's even worth trying. We have to be sure that, on paper at least, it looks as though you have a shot at making it work."

Bobby immediately began to tell me about his marketing plan and his projections. I cut him off and asked Helene for whatever information she had. She spread it out and started explaining it. I said, "You don't have to explain. I can read." I went through it, made some quick calculations, and said to Helene, "Here. I'm going to show you that your assistant, Paula, made more money last year than you did." I pointed to some numbers. "These were your sales for the year," I said, "and these were all your expenses except Paula. You subtract one from the other, and here's what you get. Would you please read that, Bobby?"

He said, "$10,000."

I said, "Right, $10,000. OK, now look over here. This is the total you paid Paula. What does that say?"

He said, "$15,000."

"Do you understand what that means?" I asked.

He said, "I think it means the business lost money."

I said, "Very good." I turned to Helene. "You lost money. Now you have some decisions to make. The business appears viable on paper. But you do have to reduce your expenses, and you're also going to have to put some money into the business. I don't know how much yet, but it will be a substantial portion of your savings. Are you willing to do that?" I knew the capital they needed would have to come out of Helene's savings account. She said she had to think about it.

The next day, they laid off her assistant, Paula, explaining that Bobby was coming into the business and it couldn't support both of them. Helene told me that she and Bobby were both in tears. "I was hysterical crying," she said, "because this was just done to him, and now we were doing it to someone else." But it was a necessary move if they really wanted to make a go of the business. As Helene put it, it was "reality smacking us in the face." There they were, just the two of them in their basement by themselves. Letting Paula go meant they were in it for the long haul.

Doing the Business Plan

Most people are scared going into their first business, which is a good reason for having a business plan. It helps to demystify the process. It takes some of the emotion out of the situation. But you can't create a business plan unless you understand cash flow, and people starting their first business seldom do. They confuse cash flow with sales or with having money in the bank. They believe that to be successful, all you have to do is generate sales. In fact, what you need is the right kind of sales. The wrong kind can drive you straight into bankruptcy.

To avoid that, you have to realize, first, that your capital is limited. That goes for everyone. Nobody starts a business with unlimited capital. The whole idea is to make sure, number one, that you have enough capital to begin with, and, number two, that it will last long enough to determine whether or not the business is viable. By viability, I mean the point at which the business is generating internally the cash it needs to pay its bills. It can survive on its own. A business plan is essentially your best guess as to how you're going to get there.

Now, when I say business plan, I don't mean anything elaborate. I'm talking about a modified, down-and-dirty income statement and cash flow statement. I just want a reasonable expectation of sales by month for a year. That's what I asked Bobby to give me. What he came up with was ridiculous. He was wildly overoptimistic, which is typical.

People on their first business venture are always overoptimistic—at the same time they're scared to death. It's weird, and it's also dangerous, because it leads them to make bad decisions about how to spend their limited capital.

With Bobby, I had to start all over again. He had based his projections more on what he thought they needed to live on than on what he could actually sell. He justified them by looking at his record with his old employer, where he'd been selling computer-cleaning equipment at $12,000 to $20,000 per unit. It never crossed his mind that it might be different selling computer supplies at, say, $40 per order. So I made him focus as narrowly as possible. This was January 1992. I said, "Let's take July. What can you do in July?"

He said, "$20,000."

I said, "There are twenty working days in a month. That's $1,000 per day. Is that realistic? Your average order is $40, so you're talking about twenty-five orders a day. In eight hours. That's three orders an hour, with phone calls. That's an order every twenty minutes. For a whole month. Can you do it?" The point was to make sure he was dealing with reality. What I wanted were reasonable projections, educated guesses. Bobby realized that his sales estimate for July was way out of whack. So he came up with a new one, and then we worked forward and backward, month by month, until we had a year's worth of sales.

Then came the most critical step: determining gross profit. Once you have reasonable sales projections, you can break them down by product category and calculate the cost of goods sold (COGS), or, in service businesses, the cost of sales. You subtract COGS from sales, and you have your gross profit or—expressed as a percentage of sales—your gross margin. In my opinion, gross profit is the single most important number in any new business. It determines everything else about your business—the amount of capital you need, the volume of sales, the overhead you can afford, the time it will take to determine viability, even viability itself.

Say you're selling an item for $1 that costs you 90¢ to produce or to buy. Your gross profit is 10¢ per item, or 10 percent of sales. Suppose you need $5,000 per month to cover your overhead. To get it, you have to do $50,000 per month in sales. Now, let's say it takes you three months to collect your receivables. You'd have to put up more than $100,000 in cash to get the $5,000 per month you need to break even. That's usually not a viable business.

And gross profit is the linchpin, the deciding factor. You have to pay all your expenses out of gross profit—your salary, your rent, the phone bill, gas, electricity, photocopying, whatever. If your gross margin is 10 percent, you need $10 in sales for every $1 of expenses just to break even. If your gross margin is 40 percent, you need only $2.50 in sales for every $1 of expenses. That difference is crucial when you're working with limited capital. The higher your gross margin, the fewer sales you need to cover expenses, and the longer your capital will last. And, for most start-ups, time is survival.

That was the most important lesson Bobby and Helene had to learn, and I made them do the math themselves. I took them through the steps. I showed them how to break down sales by category and how to calculate their cost of goods sold and their gross margin. We came up with a list of expense categories and determined their fixed overhead. With sales, COGS, and overhead expenses, they could work out the month-by-month income statement on their own. Then I took them through the process of doing monthly cash flow forecasts, from which they could put together a cash flow statement for the year. I did just enough with them to make sure they had the hang of it. The rest they did at home. With pencil and paper. No computers allowed.

It was all part of the education process. When you write out your own projections by hand, do your own calculations, and work through the numbers for a whole year, two things happen. First, you begin to get a feel for the business. Second, you start to understand reality. You see that sales don't necessarily lead to profits, and that making a sale or earning a profit is not the same as generating cash. You get a sense of the connections.

The other reason to do a business plan is to get an idea of the amount of start-up capital you need. That number comes off the cash flow statement. In most cases, you will see cumulative cash flow getting worse and worse, month after month, until the business turns a corner and cash flow starts to improve. That's assuming the business is viable on paper. If projected cash flow never improves, the business is not viable, and you should find something else to do. But if the business is viable, the amount of start-up capital you need is theoretically equal to the largest cash deficit on the statement. If you put that amount into the business, you should be able to avoid running out of cash—in theory. In practice, I always increase the number by at least 50 percent. With Bobby and Helene, for example, it looked as though they would have negative cash of about $15,000 in their worst month. I told them the business would probably require an investment of $25,000, but they had to put in only $15,000 up front.

There are two reasons for building in a reserve. First, things always cost more than you anticipate, and profits are always less. So, in fact, you probably will need more capital than appears on the projected cash flow statement. But there's also a psychological and emotional issue. It's one thing to put up additional capital down the line if you know from the start you might have to. You feel very different about it if you think you've already made the maximum investment required.

Doing the business plan leads right into the next phase because you're learning what has to happen for the business to survive. With Bobby and Helene, I was breaking survival down into terms they could understand and numbers they could monitor. They were seeing the difference between selling cleaning supplies with a gross margin of 50 percent and magnetic media with a gross margin of 10 percent. They were beginning to understand how gross margin, credit, collection, and so on would affect their cash flow, and how cash flow would determine whether or not they'd last long enough to see if the business was viable in reality as well as on paper. They were finding out where they had to focus their attention to have a decent shot at succeeding.

I should say that Helene was finding it out. She learned very quickly. Bobby took a little longer, but, then, he had more obstacles to overcome, especially the sales mentality.

Ask Norm

Dear Norm:
My home-based design business sells store fixtures and related
equipment to the retailers we work with. I try to operate on a 25
percent to 30 percent gross margin, but I don't know if that's
appropriate. I always wonder how much more revenue we could
get if we charged less.
     Norbert

Dear Norbert:
You're wondering about the wrong thing. You should be asking
yourself how much less revenue you'd get if you charged more.
Gross- and net-profit lines are far more important than sales.
I'd greatly prefer to have $20,000 in gross profit on $50,000 in
sales than to have the same gross profit on $100,000 in sales.
Why? Because I'd have fewer headaches, fewer shipments,
fewer people, and on and on. If I were you, I'd look for ways to
increase your margins, not reduce them. Maybe you can get
better deals on the products. Maybe you can cut your shipping
costs. Yes, there are circumstances when it makes sense to cut
prices, but I wouldn't do it unless you're certain that you'll get
the additional sales—and that they'll be worth it.
     —Norm

Overcoming the Sales Mentality

Almost all entrepreneurs have the sales mentality when they first go
into business. They want to see sales go up every month, every day,
every hour. I myself didn't care about anything except our weekly
sales figures. My investors were the same way, and many of them were
accountants. They never asked me about profits. All they wanted to
know about were sales. That's the sales mentality. It's the idea that you

should focus all your attention on making sales, and it's very dangerous, especially when you're operating out of your basement on a shoestring.

Why? Because sales do not equal cash, and cash is what you need to survive. You run out of cash, you go out of business. End of story. It all goes back to the fundamental reality that you are working with limited capital. If your gross profit is not enough to cover your expenses, you have to dip into your capital to make up the difference. You dip too much, and pretty soon you run out. Out of that reality comes the two most important rules for every new business. Number one, protect your capital. Spend it only on things you are certain will generate positive cash flow in the short term. Number two, maintain the highest monthly gross-profit margin you are capable of achieving. Do not go after *any* low-margin sales.

You probably think these rules sound simple enough, but it takes discipline to follow them. It's very easy to go off on tangents, mainly because of the sales mentality. Bobby Stone was a classic case. He had been trained for fourteen and a half years to think only in terms of sales. He'd never even heard of gross profit. His only job was to sell as much as he could at the prices he was given no matter how much, or how little, gross profit he generated.

So what would he do when he found himself having a bad month? Let's say that in his business plan he'd projected $20,000 in sales for the month. That was his break-even point. Now he's in the last week, and he's done just $10,000 in sales. He starts getting desperate. He calls up sales reps until he finds one who will buy $10,000 worth of supplies if Bobby will come down on price. They negotiate, and Bobby gives him a good deal. Bobby's happy. He's made his goal. He's moving a ton of product. He comes in and tells Helene, "We did it. We hit our number."

But what has he really done? First, he didn't break even. The price he negotiated left him with a 10 percent gross margin on the sale. Break-even was $20,000 at a 40 percent gross margin, or $8,000 in gross profit. He had sold $10,000 at 40 percent and $10,000 at 10 percent, for a total of $5,000 in gross profit. The margin was 25 percent, not 40 percent. That wasn't enough to cover expenses. He was short $3,000, which had to come out of capital. Five more months like that, and the business would run through the entire $15,000 Helene had put in.

Second, he'd wasted his time. He should have been using it to go after high-margin customers, which generally means smaller-volume customers. That's another rule: Spend your time developing relationships with your highest-margin customers. Let the low-margin customers come to you, and then negotiate the price up. Beyond that, Bobby had tied up $10,000 in one customer. What if the customer couldn't pay or took too long to pay or would pay only after dozens of threatening phone calls—on Bobby and Helene's nickel? It was a risk, and the risk was greater because it was a single customer. Bobby had taken a gamble without knowing it, and it came straight out of the sales mentality. Commissioned salespeople never worry about getting paid.

Don't get me wrong. I don't think the sales mentality is all bad. It's fine as long as it's balanced. Just because you have it doesn't mean you can't grasp the other parts of the business. You *must* grasp them, or you won't survive. You'll make too many costly mistakes—just to avoid having a bad month. And it's better to have a bad month, even a series of bad months, than to let your gross margins slide. I realize that's awfully hard for a salesperson—and most entrepreneurs are salespeople—to accept, but it's important. Why? Because of your goal, your long-term goal, the one you decided on before you did the business plan. Bobby and Helene wanted financial independence. The question was, would this business get them there? They needed to find out. The sales mentality gets in the way by substituting a short-term goal, making a sales target, for the long-term one: determining viability. So what if you have a series of bad months? Those results could be telling you something—that the business isn't viable, or that you're not capable of selling at a high enough gross margin to achieve your goal. If so, you should pay attention.

The usual alternative is to delude yourself with a series of high-volume, low-margin months. It's easy. You just drop your price below your competitors', and you can make all the sales you want. You'll think you're doing fine. You won't run out of cash as long as your sales keep rising and you can collect before you pay. Trouble is, you also have more payables than you can handle. You're bankrupt, and you don't know it. All of a sudden, you hit a couple of bad months, your cash disappears, and you lose everything. It happens all the time. The way to avoid that fate is to follow the rules and watch the numbers. If you watch closely enough, a picture begins to emerge. You can actually see what's going on. You can feel it. The picture gets clearer, and the feeling gets stronger, until you realize that you're going to make it—or that it's time to try something else.

Staying the course isn't easy, however. It certainly wasn't for Bobby and Helene. During the first year, they fought constantly. Helene kept telling Bobby he should get a real job. Their family and friends brought it up as well. Meanwhile, they were still getting Bobby's severance pay, and they still had his COBRA benefits. Helene was terrified about what would happen when those ran out.

My role was to help them keep everything in perspective—and to make sure that Bobby stayed focused on making high-margin sales. He and Helene were striving for an average gross margin of 40 percent, but he kept accepting sales at a 9 percent gross margin. So I made Helene the keeper of the margin. If a sale came in under 20 percent, Bobby had to ask her if they could afford it. Usually she said no. Bobby struggled with that. He'd have a chance to get a $3,000 order at 13 percent gross margin, which would put an extra $390 in the bank. Helene would tell him he couldn't do it. He'd say, "How is this business ever going to grow if we're turning away sales?" He just couldn't understand how a sale could jeopardize the business. It contradicted everything he'd learned for fourteen years.

Nevertheless, he stayed with the program. Slowly the margins improved, and the customer base expanded. At the end of the first year, we sat down and figured out that the business would have been short by about $5,000 if Bobby and Helene hadn't had his severance pay. I'd already warned them that, without the subsidy, the second year would be more difficult than the first, and they did, in fact, have a crisis when they had two bad months back-to-back. I told them they had a choice. They could put up the $10,000 they'd held in reserve, or they could go without salary for two months. They did the latter.

That blip notwithstanding, Bobby and Helene were clearly getting the hang of things. They'd been tracking the numbers month by month for a year and a half, watching sales and gross margins by product category, and following about ten categories of expenses. I'd told them, "As a business grows, it's normal to have creeping expenses. Just be aware of them. Sometimes you can't help it." But Bobby rose to the challenge, and Helene seemed more and more confident as time went along.

Ask Norm

Dear Norm:
I'm thirty-four years old, and I'm struggling to get my business up and running. I feel as though I'm riding on the edge of disaster, trying to hold the business together and build it at the same time. I've made mistakes in advertising, cash management, and just about everything else. You name it, I've blown it. I think my strongest attribute at this point is my willingness to endure pain. I'm just hoping my cash flow catches up with my stupidity before it's too late.
   Scott

Dear Scott:
Your e-mail takes me back to the first real business I started when I was thirty-three years old. I know exactly how you feel. Believe it or not, you're going through an experience that you'll look back on someday with a good deal of nostalgia. It's an experience that shows what you're really made of. I hope your business doesn't fail, but if it does, you're going to learn some important lessons, and I'm sure your next business will be a success. So hang in there.
   —Norm

Critical Mass

It's always a mistake to let yourself get too relaxed in business—to ever start thinking you're out of the woods and safe and secure. I'm not just talking about start-ups. I mean companies of any size, at any stage of development. Because fundamental shifts occur in business, and they can be good or bad. A business to me is a living thing, and living things change. People change. Trees change. So do businesses. They may change because their customers develop different needs or because they start selling to another type of customer or because a new competitor enters the market. There could be dozens of reasons. But those changes occur, and you may not be aware of them at first. They are often hidden. If the changes are bad, and you're not on top of them quickly enough, they can destroy you.

I had that in mind when I got Bobby and Helene to start tracking their numbers. I wasn't thinking only about their immediate survival. I wanted them to see from the beginning how a business changes, so they'd recognize the shifts that were bound to happen later on. And I had another purpose as well. After all, we knew their business wasn't going to be a start-up forever. We wanted to figure out when the start-up phase would end and the business would reach what I call critical mass.

By that, I mean a particular threshold that every successful start-up crosses sooner or later. It usually depends on some key factor in the business hitting a certain level. The factor may be the size of the customer base. It may be the number of active accounts. There are probably ten different types of critical mass. But however many variations there are, they all translate into the same thing for every business: self-renewing break-even cash flow. I don't mean break even on a profit-and-loss basis. I'm talking about getting to where the cash generated more or less automatically each month is enough to sustain the business and allow it to grow without going outside for new investment.

That is the major turning point for any new venture. Before critical mass, a business is a fledgling enterprise surviving on external capital. It still has its umbilical cord. After critical mass, the business is a freestanding, self-sustaining entity capable of making its own way in the world. It's your next goal after you achieve viability. The challenge is to figure out where the goal line is.

We determined, for example, that Bobby and Helene's critical mass had to do with their customer base—specifically, the number of regular customers they had. We saw that, over time, customers tended to stick with them and reorder supplies almost automatically. Some customers might have to be nudged with a fax or a phone call, but that was about all it took. Accordingly, once Bobby and Helene had a broad enough customer base, they'd know they were going to get enough sales to break even. The question was, how big a customer base did they need to get there? Well, if you know that regular customers reorder at more or less regular intervals, you can translate the number of customers you have into a specific volume of sales. That is, you can predict how many sales you're going to get from this customer base over a given period of time—say, the next year. Not that you'll get the same sales from this group month in, month out, but the good months will tend to offset the bad ones. And because we knew Bobby and Helene's gross margins, expenses, bad-debt ratio, and how long it took them to collect their receivables and pay their bills, we could also predict the cash flow those sales would generate.

If you can establish the correlation between cash flow, sales, and some other factor, you can determine critical mass very easily. You simply work backward. With Bobby and Helene, we knew the monthly cash flow they had to have, on average, to make their business self-sustaining, and we could translate that figure into average monthly sales. Then we just calculated the size of the customer base required to produce those sales. That was their critical mass. As soon as they reached it, they wouldn't be depending on Helene's savings to bail them out anymore. They'd just have to maintain their customer base, assuming there was no fundamental shift in the business.

After critical mass, growing a business becomes a matter of choice. That is clearly a huge change from before—a predictable one, and a good one, but a change that has major consequences. It opens up a whole world of possibilities that you couldn't even think about during the start-up phase. As long as you're surviving on external capital, you really have to focus on building the business you started to build. You have to be very careful, for instance, about experimenting with new products or services, at least until you've expanded your basic business as far as it can go. You can't afford to experiment. You don't have the time or the money. It goes back to those rules I talked about, all of which stem from the fundamental fact that you're living on limited capital. You have to do everything you can to reach viability before your capital runs out.

Take away that fact, and the whole picture changes. You're no longer playing with your savings or with bank loans or with capital from other investors. After critical mass, you're living off your own internally generated cash. You have profits to put in the bank. You may decide you want to invest some of them back in the business, and I think you should. It's important to explore new avenues, especially if you have a strong customer base. You might even take on some additional debt, which you can pay off out of profits. Yes, it's a little more risky, but you have the luxury to take more risks, to try some experiments, because you're playing with your own money. If you invest intelligently, you have the chance to help yourself and your customers and strengthen the business. And because you've reached critical mass, you can take the chance without putting the business in jeopardy.

Not that you can get reckless. Unfortunately, many entrepreneurs do become reckless when they hit critical mass. Often they get there by some combination of luck and instinct, without ever understanding the dynamics of their business or coming to grips with the sales mentality. They make it anyway, and the sales mentality runs wild. A whole new set of emotions comes into play. The fear fades, and they feel excitement, elation, enthusiasm bordering on euphoria. They throw caution to the wind. They want to jump on every new opportunity that arises. And if your basic business is strong enough, you can get away with that for a while. Sooner or later, though, you're going to wind up in trouble unless you stick to the rules and stay on top of the numbers. Because the numbers help you balance your emotions. They keep success from going to your head. They remind you that, while your cash may be self-generated, it is not unlimited, and it can still run out.

So you have to keep yourself from getting carried away. You have to learn how to avoid making emotional decisions. That's a very long process, but it's important. Because in business, you have to try to be objective, to be as clear as possible about what you're doing and why, and about what the likely consequences will be. You can use the tools of business to help you do that, to help you gain perspective. In the end, you may decide to go with your emotions anyway, but at least it's a choice.

And that's where Bobby and Helene were after the first two or three years. They had a bunch of choices to make. How fast did they want to grow? How big did they want to get? Did they want to keep working at home? Did they want employees? It was up to them. By that point, they had the tools they needed to make those choices wisely.

Most important, they had achieved the goal they had set for themselves when they started. In their third year of business, they did $482,000 in sales, up from $162,300 in the first year, and their average gross margin had held steady at 39 percent. They were financially independent.

"It's funny how things have changed," said Helene as she looked back. "A few months ago Bobby asked me, 'What would we say if I was offered my old job back?' I said, 'Absolutely not.' I never want to be at anybody's mercy again. Why should we give our talents away? We're smart enough to take care of ourselves. Besides, I think we have more security now than we ever had before."

"Anytime you work for someone else, it's total insecurity," said Bobby. "It really is—especially the way things are today. Look at all our friends who've been laid off. I said to her, 'That will never happen to me again.' And I felt very good about it."

"One thing Bobby always said, and he turned out to be right about it," said Helene. "He said, 'Security is not the job. It's the confidence you feel in yourself.'"

"'Yeah,' I said, 'there's no such thing as job security anymore. The only security is your own sense of self-worth and your knowledge about how to earn a living.'"

"Even when he was working for someone else, he said it," said Helene. "I always thought it was just one of his optimistic little sayings. But you know what? It turned out to be true."

The Bottom Line

Point One: Don't let your emotions lead you into hasty decisions that will make it more difficult for you to achieve your real goals.

Point Two: Make sure you understand what cash flow is and figure out in advance where it's going to come from.

Point Three: Control the sales mentality and balance it with a business mentality before it's too late.

Point Four: Learn to anticipate and recognize the changes in your business by developing a good feel for the numbers.

CHAPTER TWO

The Right Stuff

In the years since my first experience as a business mentor for Bobby and Helene Stone, I've worked with dozens of people who were trying to start a business, and dozens more who already have one. They often ask me what it takes to be a successful entrepreneur, and I tell them that the most important quality is resilience. I'm talking about the ability to bounce back from failure, to turn around a bad situation, to profit from your mistakes.

That's because everybody makes mistakes, plenty of them. What's more, we keep on making them as long as we're in business. Sure, we like to think we'll eventually get so smart we won't make mistakes anymore. Forget about it. You will never stop making mistakes. Hopefully, the new ones won't be the same as the old ones, but they'll be equally painful. They'll bug you just as much. They'll make you just as mad. As upset as you get, however, it's important to bear in mind that failure is still the best teacher around. You'll do fine as long as you're open to the lessons it's trying to teach you.

Here's a typical example from my records storage company, Citi-Storage. I still remember the moment, many years ago, when I found out we'd lost one of our biggest customers. It was five o'clock on a Friday afternoon. (Somehow these things always happen at five o'clock on a Friday afternoon.) One of my salesmen called me in my car and told me we'd just received a fax from the customer, a major law firm, announcing its intention to move its boxes out of our facility when the contract expired three months later.

Now you have to understand that, in this business, moving your boxes is a big deal. Not only is it a hassle for customers, but there are various removal fees they have to pay. So it's a real loud message when a customer leaves, and this one came completely out of the blue. I was stunned. "What are you talking about?" I said. "Man, how could we lose this account? What happened?"

The salesman didn't have an answer, and we couldn't get one from the customer. The people in charge at the law firm wouldn't see us or talk to us on the telephone. Our urgent messages brought perfunctory replies: "The decision has been made, and it is final."

Obviously, we had screwed up. The guy who had closed the account had left us five years before, and we hadn't stayed as close to the customer as we should have been. A week or so after receiving the fax, I came up with a proposal that finally got us a meeting with the firm's managing partner—to no avail. The situation was too far gone. We could offer good financial terms, but we couldn't fix problems that had been festering for years. Our competitor matched the terms and got the account.

So I called my managers and salespeople together and said, "What did we learn from this? What do we have to do differently in the future?" The real lesson, I knew, was not that we had made mistakes. You always make mistakes. We failed because we'd waited too long to find out about them. We decided that, from then on, we'd go to each customer eighteen months before the end of the contract and offer to negotiate a new one. If the customer hesitated, we'd know right away that we had a problem—while there was still time to fix it.

As soon as we began implementing the new policy, we made a very important discovery. We had unhappy customers and didn't know it. One customer was upset about our system for providing information online; we fixed it. Another customer felt it deserved a lower rate because its volume had increased dramatically; the customer was right, and we made amends. A third customer didn't like a particular aspect of our inventory system; we changed it. A fourth customer was miffed that we hadn't been sending regular monthly reports; we started sending them.

So, in four months with the new policy, we made four improvements, pleased four customers, and locked up four accounts, and all these benefits came from one failure. In the long run, that failure proved to be one of the best things that ever happened to the company.

Groundhog Day

Now, obviously, it doesn't help to be resilient if you don't learn from your mistakes. That's a challenge for some people. They suffer from what I refer to as Groundhog Day syndrome. It has to do with the tendency to fall into self-destructive patterns of behavior even though you end up getting repeatedly whacked in the head—more or less like the character Bill Murray played in the movie *Groundhog Day*.

I know one guy, for example, who put together a successful clothing business and then started taking out huge amounts of cash to build a palace for himself and his wife. When he ran into business problems, he discovered he didn't have the resources to weather them. In the end, he lost both the company and the house. So what did he do? He went out and started another clothing business, got it going, took out the cash, built another palace, ran into business problems, and lost both the company and the house. Two times in a row.

That's not as unusual as you might think. I know another guy who makes a habit of buying companies, raising tons of money from investors, and then paying himself so much in salary and perks that the company doesn't stand a chance. To be sure, he believes that each business is going to be wildly successful and that he deserves every penny he makes. But he always winds up where he started: broke. He's done that five times.

Or consider my friend Ralph (not his real name). His downfall is leverage. He's great at starting companies and getting them up and running, but then he starts leveraging them like crazy so that he can chase after business opportunities. He'll do whatever is necessary to get the credit he needs—even to the point of fooling around with his financial statements. Not that he intends to defraud anyone. He's just so focused on growing that he doesn't consider the possibility of things going wrong. Of course, when you push things too far, they do go wrong. Sooner or later, Ralph always lands in a pile of trouble.

Those cases may be somewhat extreme, but Groundhog Day syndrome is not a rare affliction. To some extent, we all have habits of mind and ways of thinking that repeatedly get us into trouble, and it's very difficult to change them. For one thing, we don't like to admit that we're the cause of our own problems. There are almost always other culprits around—people who didn't do what we wanted or factors beyond our control. It's easier to blame them for our misfortune than to take responsibility for it, and so we let ourselves off the hook. But we do ourselves a disservice in the process. The most valuable business lessons we can learn come from facing up to our weaknesses.

I'm speaking from personal experience here—specifically, the experience of my greatest business failure, the bankruptcy of my messenger business in 1988. Starting from scratch, I had built Perfect Courier to $30 million in sales, making the Inc. 500 list of fastest-growing private companies three years in a row, and then merging with a public company, CitiPostal, and landing on the Inc. 100 list of fastest-growing public companies in 1987. But I wasn't satisfied. My dream was to have a $100 million company. So when a shortcut came along, I took it, merging with a $70 million company called Sky Courier in 1987.

Sky, it turned out, had problems—big problems. For openers, it needed a quick injection of $5 million in cash. I decided to take the money out of Perfect Courier, which in itself wasn't necessarily a mistake. Even if Sky had folded and the investment had been lost, Perfect Courier would have been able to survive and keep growing at the same rate as before. But I soon realized that the $5 million wasn't going to be enough. Sky needed $2 million more in cash, which I also decided to get from Perfect Courier. In addition, I subsequently agreed to pledge several million dollars of Perfect Courier's credit to keep Sky alive.

Those two moves were very serious mistakes. They put my principal business in jeopardy. I knew that, if I lost the second round of money, Perfect Courier would be hobbled. If we got in trouble with the credit guarantee on top of that, Perfect Courier might not be able to survive.

But despite the danger, I never even considered turning back. I didn't think I had to. I was sure I could handle whatever came along. I'd been in tough situations before. I thought I was invincible. What I didn't take into account was the inevitability of unpredictable events. First came the stock market crash of October 1987. Particularly hard hit were the financial printers with which Sky did a lot of business. Overnight it lost 50 percent of its sales. Meanwhile, fax machines— which had been around for twenty years—suddenly reached a kind of critical mass, which had a devastating effect on the messenger business. Instead of sending documents by courier, more and more people were faxing them. Within a matter of months, Perfect Courier's business dropped by about 40 percent.

The combination of factors was overwhelming. In September 1988, my companies filed for protection from their creditors under Chapter 11 of the bankruptcy code. By the time we came out of Chapter 11 three years later, our workforce had shrunk from three thousand people to about fifty, and our sales from $100 million to a very shaky $2.5 million.

Believe me, that's culture shock. It took a few years before my head cleared enough for me to figure out what had really happened, and why. The process took time partly because I had such good excuses. After all, who could ever have predicted that the stock market crash and the fax machine would hit us at the same time? In my gut, however, I knew that blaming circumstances was a cop-out. The real question was, how had the company become so vulnerable to those developments?

It was extremely difficult for me to come to grips with the answer to that question. It meant admitting that the bankruptcy had a lot to do with my personality and decision-making process. Nevertheless, I eventually forced myself to acknowledge what I knew to be true. I'd taken a lovely, secure, profitable business and destroyed it by exposing it to a level of risk it should never have faced. I'd done it, moreover, because of something in my nature. I enjoy risk. I like to go to the edge of the cliff and look down. That's the personality trait behind my own Groundhog Day syndrome. This time, circumstances had pushed me over the edge of the cliff, but in fact I shouldn't have been anywhere near the edge in the first place. I'd taken a foolish risk and put everything I owned in jeopardy. As a result, hundreds of people had lost their jobs, and many others—including me—had suffered through a nightmare.

Hard as it was to admit all that, the act of facing up to it proved to be one of the most liberating experiences of my entire business career. Not that I decided to change my personality. I knew I couldn't, and I really didn't want to anyway. Rather, I began focusing on what I could do to avoid ever having to live through that Groundhog Day again. I realized, for example, that I seldom heard the advice people gave me and often wound up ignoring good advice as a result. So I trained myself to listen more closely and make sure that I at least understood the advice I was getting, whether or not I chose to accept it. I also made a point of seeking out the opinions of people whose judgment I respect but whose instincts differ from mine. And I came up with certain rules to force myself to think through the consequences of major decisions before making them.

Mainly, however, I adjusted my thinking about risk. Don't get me wrong. I'm as much of a risk taker as ever, but these days the risks I take are calculated ones. In particular, I calculate the danger that a decision of mine may cost other people their jobs. That was without doubt the most important lesson I learned from the whole episode. Through the agony of the layoffs, I developed a new understanding of the awesome responsibility CEOs have for the lives of their employees.

Out of that understanding came the cardinal rule I use in evaluating every important decision I make: always protect the pot. Once you have an ongoing, viable business, you have to put its welfare first and never do anything that would place it in jeopardy. It's all right to invest in a risky venture, provided your core business will be safe even if you lose the entire investment and some unexpected calamity comes along as well. It's a rule I've followed scrupulously thereafter. My business was healthier, and I was happier, as a result. Best of all, I could wake up every morning and know that—unless it happened to be February 2— it wasn't Groundhog Day.

Focus, Focus, Focus

Aside from resilience and the ability to learn from mistakes, what an entrepreneur needs most is a capacity for discipline and focus. People who've never built a business don't understand that. They think the secret to success lies in spotting great opportunities. I remember an old friend of mine who dropped by my records storage business one day. He hadn't seen it for years. As he looked around at the thousands and thousands of boxes in the warehouse, he could hardly believe his eyes.

"This is incredible," he said. "You saw an opportunity, and overnight you've turned it into a successful business. It's amazing!"

He should only know, I thought. The truth was that I'd spent more than a decade building my storage business by that point, but a lot of people would rather not hear about that. They like to think that successful entrepreneurs have a magical touch. All they need is the right opportunity and presto! it becomes a business.

That's one of the great myths of entrepreneurship, and it gets many would-be entrepreneurs into trouble. They waste time and money chasing after business opportunities, hoping to identify one that will guarantee success. But the world is filled with great business opportunities, and none of them guarantees success. Spotting them is the easy part. What's difficult—and essential—is developing the discipline and the stamina to stay focused on a single opportunity until you've turned it into an established business that can stand on its own.

There are two phases of the entrepreneurial process in which focus is critical and too many opportunities can be a big distraction, maybe even a fatal one. The first phase begins right when you're getting ready to take the plunge. A lot of people find they can't do it. They're mesmerized by all the opportunities they see. I'm constantly hearing from people who have ten different business ideas they're considering at the same time. They want to know which one I think is the most promising. I tell them, "You're asking the wrong question. You should be asking, 'Which business do I want to be in? Which one do I like most? Which one fits in best with what I want to do with my life?'"

If you're serious about having your own business, you need to begin by selecting one opportunity out of all those available—a single idea that, for whatever reason, strikes you as more appealing than the others. Then you need to research it thoroughly. If you can arrange to spend time working in the industry, so much the better. But you should at least find out everything you can about the current players in the industry and how the business really works. That includes getting information from trade associations, talking to people in related businesses, interviewing customers, whatever.

Bear in mind that you're preparing for a long-term commitment. I usually tell people they should plan to give the business their full attention for at least five years. Not that you should neglect the rest of your life, but at work you need to be totally dedicated to the path you've chosen until the company is firmly established, which can take a long, long time.

So it's important to determine not only whether you're going to enjoy the business but whether it's viable for you. Do you have the resources and skills you need to be successful in that particular business? Is it reasonable to think that the business will get you where you want to go? You'll find it very hard to answer those questions unless you're focusing on one specific opportunity and pushing the others out of your mind.

The bigger challenge comes in the next phase, after you've made the commitment and begun to build your new venture. You'll soon discover there are more opportunities around than you ever imagined—both inside and outside your business. You'll find them very tempting. If you're not careful, you'll lose your focus and, with it, your best shot at success.

There is only one opportunity you should be thinking about during the start-up of any business. I'm talking about the opportunity to build a customer base that will make the business viable—that is, able to sustain itself on its own internally generated cash flow. First, you have to figure out what kind of customers will give you such a base and how you can draw them in. Thereafter, you need to focus relentlessly on building the base.

That's not easy. It takes a lot of discipline, which doesn't come naturally to most people. Look at the experience of Bobby Stone, which I recounted in chapter 1. And he is typical. Most first-time entrepreneurs I know have trouble maintaining focus. They forget that in a start-up, there are two limited resources, time and money, and you can't afford to waste either one. Understand, I'm not saying you should wear blinders. Although you need to be focused, you can't be rigid. After all, your approach may not be working.

My initial approach to the records storage business didn't work. When we started out, we couldn't get much information out of people in the industry, and so we didn't know basic things, such as how to go after customers and how much to charge. In my delivery business, we'd always done well by offering competitive prices, great service, and state-of-the-art technology. I decided to use the same approach here.

Our target customers were big law firms and accounting firms. We put up display booths at the trade shows their office managers attended, and we made our pitch. We promised them service they'd never dreamed of, at the same prices our competitors were charging. Those prices were, in fact, a lot lower than we wanted, but they were high enough for us to earn an acceptable profit. Guess what. We got no bites. Not a single customer. We had to change our whole approach to selling and pricing before we found a formula that worked.

The point is that you need to be both focused and flexible. You can't let yourself be distracted by opportunities, but neither can you be so single-minded that you ignore signs of trouble. And there probably will be signs of trouble. It almost never happens that a business idea works exactly as you thought it would when you started out. You have to figure out how to make it work. You have to watch, listen, ask questions, experiment, make changes, refine your concept, and constantly develop your customer base. That's what building a business is all about, and most people can succeed at it—provided they don't lose their focus along the way. There's a big payoff at the end. Eventually, your business becomes so strong that it doesn't need you anymore. Then you can chase after other business opportunities to your heart's content.

Ask Norm

Dear Norm:
When I was in high school, my father and I made furniture pieces that we sold at craft shows. The business could easily have grown, but my father didn't want it to get bigger. Now my brother-in-law and I are talking about starting a furniture business that we'd build into a substantial company. Our problem is that we have trouble imagining ourselves doing it. How can two men from poor backgrounds get over the difficulty of visualizing themselves in a situation that's so different from anything they've ever experienced?
   Jace

Dear Jace:
It sounds as though you've already visualized the company you want to build. I think you actually have two other problems. First, you're not giving yourself enough credit. You know more about business than you realize. Second, you're looking too far ahead. Before you can have a factory, you need to have a business, and almost every business starts small. My advice would be to put together a plan about where you and your brother-in-law want to be in five years. Then figure out a good short-term goal. You might follow in your father's footsteps, selling your furniture at craft shows. As you're selling, you'll make contacts. Tell people you're thinking of starting a company. Some of them may be interested in helping you. Also look for a mentor who has built a business before. Being poor as a child is not an obstacle in business.
   —Norm

Peripheral Vision

Let me say a few more words about the flexibility part of the equation. I'm really talking about what I call "peripheral vision." By that, I mean the ability to see things out of the corners of your eyes and thereby to find solutions to problems that other people think can't be solved.

I ran into such a problem in the secure document destruction business that I started in 2000. My timing turned out to be just right. Within a couple of years, the company was growing like gangbusters, with sales increasing 150 percent from month to month. That was exciting to watch, but it highlighted a critical problem faced by every company in the industry, namely, the lack of off-the-shelf, industry-specific software for tracking the work that's been done, generating accounting reports, and automating the billing process.

We'd searched high and low for software that could handle those tasks. We'd talked to dozens of other document destruction companies and found they were all in the same boat that we were in. We'd gone outside the industry, checking out businesses we thought would have similar software needs—bottled-water distributors, for example—only to discover that the similarities were more apparent than real. We'd even contacted the software supplier for our records storage business and tried to sell its people on developing comparable software for the document destruction industry. They would work on it, they said, but it was going to take a while. The market wasn't yet big enough to justify a major investment in a document destruction product. "Wait a few years," they said.

But we couldn't wait. Without the right software, we were forced to do all of our tracking and billing by hand. The billing process alone was taking three or four days each month. Inevitably, mistakes were made. The bills weren't uniform. Customers complained. With our sales volume growing so fast, moreover, we could see that the situation would get much worse in the near future.

"We've got to do something," my partner Sam said.

"Yeah, but what?" I asked.

"I don't know," he said. "Everybody says it's impossible, but there's got to be a way."

I think that's when I decided that, come hell or high water, I was going to find the solution. What made the challenge difficult was the diversity of services a document destruction business provides. In our company, for example, about 40 percent of the revenues comes from special jobs, most of which are so-called cleanouts. We do those for customers who have accumulated a large number of sensitive documents over a long period of time and want to destroy all of them at once. We go get the material, take it out, shred it, and provide the customer with a certificate affirming that the documents have been destroyed in a secure manner.

The other 60 percent of our business is with customers we service on a regular basis. Those customers keep locked bins on their premises. Each bin has a slot through which employees can slide sensitive documents that should be destroyed. The problem is that there are two types of bin, and they're handled differently. Some of the bins look like pieces of furniture. We call them cabinets. Our service person goes in, empties the contents, and leaves the cabinet in place. Other bins look like big plastic garbage cans on wheels. We call them containers. If the customer has that type, the service person rolls the full bin out and replaces it with an empty one.

So we have some bins that stay in place, and some that are moved around, plus all the special jobs, none of which is the same as the others. In addition, we have different sizes of bins and different prices and payment terms with each customer, based on number of bins, bin sizes, type of service, pickup frequency, and other factors. We needed a tracking-and-billing system that could handle all those variables, which wasn't easy to find. If you came up with one for fixed bins, it didn't work for rolling bins, and vice versa. What's more, nothing you did with the bins could be applied to the special jobs. That's why everybody was stumped.

In my gut, however, I knew we were all approaching the problem in the wrong way. People were searching for a global solution—a system that would cover every type of job a document destruction company might handle. What if, instead, you took one piece of the problem at a time?

I can't tell you how exactly I came up with the answer, but it involved using peripheral vision. I knew that everyone else was focusing on the special jobs. I decided to start at the other end, looking at the bins. In any case, I walked into the office of Louis Weiner, my company's president, one day and announced, "OK, I've got it. We can put all the document destruction stuff on a computer, and we don't even need new software or equipment." In fact, I didn't yet have the whole solution. There was still a piece I hadn't figured out, but I had a feeling I could come up with it by talking the problem through with Louis.

He looked at me with obvious skepticism. "OK, let's hear it," he said.

"We can use the same system we have with the boxes," I said. I should explain that, in our records storage business, we track boxes with bar codes and handheld scanners. We send a sheet of bar codes to the customer, who puts one on each box. When our driver picks the boxes up, he scans their bar codes. The scanner spits out a receipt, which he gives to the customer. Back at the office, the information is downloaded to our computer, which generates the invoices and the reports.

"What are you thinking of?" Louis asked. "Putting a bar code on each bin?"

"Sort of," I said. "You can put one on each cabinet. With the containers, you can put a little plastic sleeve on the back. In the sleeve, you put a laminated bar code identifying the location, the customer, and the size and type of bin. When the service person comes in, he scans the bar code and moves it from the container he's taking out to the empty one he's leaving behind. So the bar code stays at the location."

Louis thought about it for a moment. "OK," he said, "what about the special jobs?"

"Well, what about them?" I asked. That was the part I hadn't worked out yet.

"They're 40 percent of our business," he said.

"No, they're not," I said. A thought had suddenly occurred to me. "They're 40 percent of our *revenues*. How many special jobs do we do a month?"

"I don't know," he said. "Five, six, ten at the most."

"And we have about a thousand bins, right?" I said. "Suppose we think of every bin as a separate job, and let's say we empty the bins once a month. Now we're talking about 10 jobs out of 1,010. That's not 40 percent. It's less than 1 percent. We've solved 99 percent of the problem."

Louis grunted.

"And how long could it take someone to key in the information on ten special jobs each month?" I went on. "Fifteen minutes? Half an hour? It's nothing. That's easy to do by hand."

Louis sat there thinking. Then he began slowly nodding his head. "Well, it's worth a try," he said.

The solution wasn't quite as simple, or as perfect, as it had seemed at first glance. We had to do some experimenting to figure out which type of bar code worked best. (In the records storage business, we use different types of bar code for different purposes.) In the end, we settled on one that would provide us with all the necessary information but could accommodate no more than 9,999 bins of any particular size. That would work for a few years, at which point we'd have to do some more tweaking. Meanwhile, we'd solved our tracking-and-billing problem, and we'd also created a new benefit we could offer customers: computer-generated receipts and invoices. Just as the system allowed us to track our work better, it let customers monitor what we did more closely and gave them greater confidence that our bills are accurate. That was an advantage we had over our competitors—at least until they developed their own systems.

The X Factor

There is one other quality that you must have to succeed as an entrepreneur—and it may be the most important of all. What's more, it's a quality that can't be taught or learned. Either you have it or you don't.

Ask Norm

Dear Norm:

I'm a forty-nine-year-old career changer. I started a trucking business in 1975. By the mid-1990s we'd grown to twenty-eight employees, and I decided to sell, getting an all-cash buyout in 1997. After the sale I took nine months off, built a house, and began looking for a new career. Eventually, I landed a sales job in a computer business, where I had struggles with the owner. Having never been an employee before, I didn't grasp the depth of the emperor's-new-clothes mentality. I was fired after two years for failing to toe the line. After taking some time off, I'm back in the job market. I just wonder if I'm too headstrong to work for other people. Will I ever find happiness as an employee? Is there hope, or do they shoot old horses?

   Bruce

Dear Bruce:

A lot of us are too headstrong to be long-term employees. I know I couldn't work for someone else anymore, but that doesn't mean I couldn't work with someone else. Think about becoming an independent contractor—doing outside sales, for example. If you really want to get involved in the management of a business, find a small company that wants and needs the help of an experienced entrepreneur. If that doesn't work, start a business.

   —Norm

Don't misunderstand me. I think it's possible to learn everything you need to know about starting and growing a business. Not that every start-up will become a viable company, but—as I noted earlier—there are certain habits of mind you can develop and certain principles you can follow that will maximize your chances of success and minimize your losses in case of failure. What's more, anybody can learn what those principles are.

But to apply them successfully, you need something else as well. It's more a character trait than a skill, and it lies deep within a person, hidden from view. I'm not even sure that the people who have it are aware of it until they're put to the test. But recognized or not, the quality I'm talking about is real, and it allows certain people to accomplish things that no one else would think they were capable of doing.

Consider Malki, whom I met through my wife, Elaine. A divorced mother of three, Malki was supporting herself at the time by tutoring, teaching, and doing clerical work. She wasn't happy, however. Her dream was to have her own day care center for infants and toddlers. She talked to Elaine about it, and Elaine brought her to me.

Now it so happens that a day care center is an extremely tough business to start in the state of New York unless you have a lot of money, and Malki didn't. Before you can accept your first child, you need a state license, and it takes a year to obtain one. You can obtain a license, moreover, only by passing a lot of inspections, which means you need a space that's been built out to conform to all the applicable fire, safety, and health codes. So you're paying rent and construction costs for an extended period without any income while your application is pending. If you don't get the license, you lose your investment. And even if you do get it, that's only the beginning. You still have to go through the process of building the business.

After my first meeting with Malki, it was clear to me that she had little chance of succeeding—one in ten at best. She had no money, no business experience, no partner to give her support. She'd never had an employee or a customer. She'd never negotiated a deal. She would have had a struggle establishing any type of business. A day care center seemed completely out of her reach. But I hate to discourage people from pursuing their dreams, and Malki was determined. So I agreed to advise her.

We began by figuring out what it would take to open the day care center for business. The obstacles were daunting. To minimize the

financial risk, we decided, Malki would probably be better off buying her space than renting it. That way if she failed to get her license,
she could sell the property and she wouldn't be stuck with a long-term
lease.

So somehow Malki had to find a property, work out a deal to acquire
it, make the necessary renovations, cover the mortgage payments, and
still do everything else required to launch the business successfully
when—or, rather, if—the license came through. I'm talking about
doing market research, raising working capital, figuring out her pricing, and so on. What's more, she had to do it all in her spare time. She
couldn't afford to stop working.

I thought Malki would quit when she realized what was involved,
but I was wrong. She immediately threw herself into the market
research, checking out all the day care centers in the area. She
befriended an experienced day care operator in another state who
gave her tons of invaluable advice. She obtained the various licensing
application forms that she needed and figured out the steps she had to
go through to become licensed. Meanwhile, she worked her Rolodex
tirelessly to come up with the funds she needed, eventually raising
about $150,000, almost all of it from family and friends.

But Malki's biggest coup was her real estate deal. She located a
building that was in the process of being vacated. The guys who owned
it were moving to another building and needed some flexibility on the
closing date. Malki could give them plenty of flexibility. What she
needed was time. With no business history, she couldn't get a mortgage right away, and she could afford only a small down payment, but
she thought she'd be in a better position after the day care center had
been running for a while.

So they made a deal: Malki would assume the current mortgage
on the property and pay a small amount toward the asking price. The
sellers would then give her a second mortgage to cover the balance.
After a certain period Malki would refinance the building and pay off
the second mortgage. In addition, she and the sellers agreed on a closing date that allowed her to begin the licensing process long before she

had to start making payments. As a result, her costs during the pre-start-up phase were much lower than we'd anticipated.

In the end, it took two years for Malki to put all the pieces in place. She stuck with it, and her day care center opened for business in July of 1999. It was a tremendous accomplishment. Malki felt as though she'd finally reached her goal. But in fact her biggest challenge lay ahead.

Why? Because everything changes when you open your doors and start making sales. There's a new kind of pressure and an increased sense of urgency about dealing with problems. Before you have customers, after all, a delay is not a disaster. If a piece of equipment is delivered late, you may be annoyed and frustrated, but the consequences aren't all that serious. It's a different story when you're open for business and employees don't show up for work or customers demand things you can't provide. Decisions have to be made. Actions have to be taken. Suddenly, you find yourself inundated with problems, and they all demand immediate answers. If you're a first-time entrepreneur, you tend to greet each problem with the same reaction: panic. It doesn't matter that the vast majority of the problems are actually quite manageable. To you, they all look like catastrophes.

To be successful you have to get over your panic. Not only must you develop confidence in your ability to handle problems, but your whole way of thinking about them has to change. You have to accept a never-ending flood of complications as a normal part of the business process, and you have to learn to enjoy that process. How? By getting caught up in the fun and excitement of finding solutions.

Some people can't make that transition, and I thought Malki was probably one of them. For one thing, she felt uncomfortable making decisions. She liked to get a lot of opinions and mull them over. That trait may be a virtue in some circumstances, but it doesn't make the start-up process any easier.

In fact, Malki seemed miserable for the first few months. She was frustrated. She was overwhelmed. She didn't know how to deal with the parents. She thought she'd never find the employees she needed.

The ones she had came in late or left early, forcing her to scramble to get replacements so that the ratio of adults to children remained in compliance with state regulations. Every roadblock appeared to be insurmountable. Every problem felt like the last straw.

After overcoming so many obstacles to open the center, Malki was discouraged to find she had more problems than ever. I figured she simply wasn't cut out for business. Fortunately, we'd designed an escape hatch for her. Malki could still sell the place and move on to something else without any dire financial consequences, as Elaine reminded her at one point.

But Malki kept going, and little by little her way of thinking began to change. I could see the change in the way she presented issues to Elaine and me. Instead of focusing on how bad a problem was, she started coming to us with possible solutions, asking what we thought. Meanwhile, her business was growing and so she had more problems than ever, but her sense of panic continued to dissipate. By the end of the first year, she was clearly in control.

That was almost a decade ago. The day care center has been wildly successful and today is bursting at the seams. There's a waiting list to get in. As for Malki, she's enjoying the business process more than ever. She admits that she hated it at first. There were moments when she wondered if she could last. But she held on, and her attitude gradually changed as she began to realize she could handle whatever problems came along. Was there a turning point? "Yes," she says. "It was when Elaine told me I could quit."

Malki doesn't know what kept her going, and neither do I. Call it passion, tenacity, stick-to-itiveness, true grit, or just plain stubbornness. Whatever it is and wherever it comes from, it's the most important quality an entrepreneur can have. Ultimately, it determines whether we succeed or fail.

The Bottom Line

Point One: Those who persevere win. Be resilient and welcome failure. That's how you become a better businessperson.

Point Two: You learn by refusing to make excuses and looking deep inside yourself for the reasons things have gone wrong.

Point Three: Focus and discipline are more important than identifying opportunities, but they have to be balanced with flexibility.

Point Four: The solutions are seldom right in front of you. You need to learn how to spot them out of the corner of your eye.

CHAPTER THREE

Why Start-ups Fail

People get so much bad advice when they first go into business that I sometimes wonder how any new company survives. You often hear, for example, that to be successful you need a unique product or service, something nobody else has. Or that you should choose a business with as little competition as possible, that you're better off having a market to yourself. My advice is exactly the opposite. I never want to be first in a market, and I always like to have a lot of competitors. Yes, I want to be different from them, but the more people who are making money in an industry, the better I feel about going into it. There are actually three simple criteria I use in evaluating every new business I start. I suspect they'd work for about 80 percent of the people who are going into business for the first time.

Number one, I want a concept that's been around for one hundred years or more. OK, maybe less than one hundred years. The important thing is that it's an established concept, one that everybody understands. It's not something new and revolutionary. Why? Because there is nothing more expensive than educating a market.

I found that out the hard way when I took my messenger business to Atlanta in the early 1980s. At the time, companies there handled deliveries by putting a secretary in a cab and sending her off with a package. The secretaries didn't want our service—they liked having time out of the office—and the companies didn't know they needed it. We had to do mailers, run ads, develop a whole public relations campaign. And it was a delivery service we were educating people about, not some radical new technology. I'm telling you, it was very, very expensive, and we took a beating. I'd rather be in the biggest, most competitive market in the world and go head-to-head with a hundred other companies.

Of course, if you're going to compete, you have to be able to differentiate yourself with customers. Which brings me to the second criterion: I want an industry that is antiquated. I don't necessarily mean "old-fashioned." I'm talking about a business in which most companies are out of step with the customer. Maybe the customer's needs have changed and the suppliers haven't paid attention. Maybe they're not up-to-date on the latest technology. In any case, there has been a change, and the industry hasn't followed it.

My storage company, CitiStorage, is a good example here. When I first looked into the business, I noticed that, except for a couple of big players, records storage companies were asleep. They had ancient warehouses designed to store dead files for customers. Meanwhile, the industry had completely changed. Real estate had become so expensive in major cities that customers were looking to store their active files off site—that is, files they still had to get at from time to time. The records storage business was turning into the archive retrieval business, and almost nobody seemed to notice. The two big exceptions were Iron Mountain and Pierce Leahy, the industry giants that later merged. They'd recognized the change and built huge, modern archive retrieval facilities out in the countryside. In the process, they'd become the driving force of the industry.

I sensed an opportunity here, but there was something I didn't understand. How could the other guys stay asleep? Why were they still in business? Why hadn't they lost their customer base? The answer, I discovered, was that some of the biggest customers wouldn't move their files. They didn't want their records to be so far out of town. What if they needed a particular file in an hour?

That gave me my third criterion for a successful new business: a niche. I would build a huge, modern facility in the city. I'd distinguish myself from the old records storage companies by designing the facility specifically for archive retrieval, using the latest technology. I'd distinguish myself from the giants by my location. The customers would be close to their records.

In fact, having a niche is critical to every start-up, but not for the reason most people think. It has to do with the high gross margins you must have to make sure your start-up capital lasts long enough for your business to achieve viability. If you're the new kid in town, you can't compete on price, because you'll go out of business. On the other hand, you do have to get customers. That means offering them more value at the going rate.

But how do you offer more value without increasing your direct costs, cutting your gross margins, and running through your start-up capital? The answer usually lies in the niche you've selected. I realized, for example, that the latest archive retrieval technology allowed me to cut my direct costs by building a facility with much higher ceilings than my competitors have. I could get more than 150,000 boxes in 10,000 square feet, whereas those guys were getting 40,000 or 50,000 boxes in the same space.

So those are my three criteria for starting a successful business: a one-hundred-year-old concept, an antiquated industry, and a niche. I know some people are thinking, "If everybody followed those criteria, we still wouldn't have the wheel." Well, they're right. I don't mean to discourage the visionary geniuses out there. I'm all for advances in technology and the creation of new industries. If you're another Thomas Edison, Fred Smith, or Bill Gates, forget my criteria. Go right ahead. Change the world.

But most of us go into business with more modest goals. We're happy to wind up with a company that survives and grows. If you're one of us, take my advice: Don't try to turn that revolutionary new concept into a business. Find a great old concept instead.

Buy or Start?

Here's another piece of advice to ignore: you're better off buying a business than starting one from scratch. A lot of people say you can reduce your risk, save money, and achieve your goals faster if you take over a company that's already up and running. Don't believe it. For most first-time entrepreneurs—especially those who've never run a company before—the chances of surviving are much greater if you build the business yourself, from the ground up.

There are a number of reasons. For one thing, it's harder to learn a business if you haven't been with it from the start. You miss out on all the trial-and-error education that happens in the early stages. You don't understand key relationships in the business. You don't know what to do in emergencies. You make mistakes that are much costlier than they would have been back when the company was smaller and struggling to get off the ground.

No matter how fast you learn, moreover, you're likely to find that the challenges are greater than you bargained for when you bought the business. Acquisitions are very tricky. You can do as much due diligence as you please, and you still won't know exactly what you're getting until you've already paid for it—at which point it's usually too late to go back. Even experienced businesspeople often get burned. As for inexperienced buyers, they're usually at the mercy of the seller, or the seller's representative, or the business broker (if there is one), all of whom have one thing in mind: getting the deal done. If you're not careful, you could easily wind up buying a pig in a poke.

That's what almost happened to Josh, a young fellow in his early thirties who came to me for advice a few years ago. He said he was getting ready to buy his first business, and he needed my help. He had a meeting scheduled in a few days at which he was supposed to sign some papers and put down a $100,000 deposit on the business, 60 percent of it nonrefundable. His father, a Canadian business owner, thought he was making a mistake but said Josh could go ahead if he got someone with more experience to sign off on the deal. Josh wondered if I'd be willing to look it over and give him my opinion. I agreed.

It turned out that the company he wanted to buy was a small packager of herbal lotions, which it sold through independent sales representatives to specialty stores and chains. The current owner had been running the company out of her home. She'd been in business three or four years and had done fairly well, or so it appeared from her financial statements. Now she was pregnant and wanted to cash out. She was asking for $250,000.

The company seemed to be just what Josh was looking for. It was in his price range. It had plenty of growth potential. And although it was still fairly new, it was already turning a good profit. According to the financial statements he'd received, the business had generated pretax earnings of $40,000 on sales of $201,000—a return of almost 20 percent. That was a significant improvement over the previous year, when the company had earned $17,000 on sales of $175,000. The year before that, it had lost $10,000 on $79,000 in sales.

So the numbers were moving in the right direction. Josh figured he could maintain the momentum and build a substantial business of his own—something he'd dreamed about doing for years. He could hardly wait to get started. He sent me copies of all the material the seller had given him and, a couple of days later, showed up at my office with a draft of a confidentiality agreement he'd received from the seller's lawyer. He said he had an appointment to sign the agreement—and pay the deposit—the next morning.

I told him I thought he should call the lawyer and cancel the meeting.

"What do you mean?" he said. "They want to move fast. They have another buyer in the wings."

I said, "Josh, you're not ready to sign anything. You can tell the lawyer you'll get back to him in forty-eight hours."

The problem was that he didn't have nearly enough information to answer the most basic question in any acquisition, namely, what are you buying? He *thought* he was buying a company with a good product line. But there was no way to tell how good the product line really was—or whether the price was even in the ballpark—because he didn't have any information about what was happening in the market.

He didn't know, for example, who the top ten customers were, or what percentage of sales each of them accounted for. He didn't know how their purchases changed from year to year. Were the same customers coming back, or did the company have to keep finding new customers to replace the ones who left? Did one or two customers account for a disproportionately large percentage of sales, and if so, why?

And what was going on with the sales representatives? The company was supposedly paying them each a 15 percent commission on sales. So why did total commissions amount to 15 percent of sales in one year, 12 percent the next, and 7 percent the year after that? Were sales reps leaving, turning their customers into "house accounts," or was there some other explanation? How many reps did the company have, anyway? How much business did each of them bring in, and how much were the biggest producers earning?

That was only the beginning, of course. There were dozens of other questions Josh would have to get answered before making a commitment to buy the company. But I didn't see any point in going forward until we at least got a breakdown of sales by customer and by sales representative for the past two or three years. Those numbers would show us whether or not the company did, in fact, have a product line that customers wanted to buy and sales reps wanted to sell. Without that information, it wasn't worth it for Josh to spend time investigating a possible deal, let alone hand over his money.

Josh contacted the company's owner, requesting the additional information. She responded that she wouldn't give him the names of her customers and sales representatives without a signed agreement. I told him, "Fine. She can label the customers 1, 2, 3, 4 and the sales reps A, B, C, D, but you need to see those numbers before signing anything."

I also suggested he have the seller's lawyer amend the agreement so that his deposit would be completely refundable at his whim within three weeks. Why shouldn't he be free to change his mind for any reason, as long as he acted expeditiously? The lawyer agreed and redrew the papers, but as it turned out, the change was unnecessary.

A few days later Josh received the additional information he'd asked for. It painted quite a different picture of the company. For one thing, only 15 percent of its customers, representing about 30 percent of its sales, were returning from year to year. In other words, Josh would have to replace 85 percent of the customers, and 70 percent of the sales, just to stay even. What's more, he'd have to do it with a new sales force: the company was turning over sales representatives at a rate of more than 50 percent a year.

It was hard to see what Josh would gain by acquiring the company. The products couldn't be all that great, or more customers would be reordering them. An established name? It couldn't be very strong. A dedicated sales force? He was going to have to build one anyway. As for the formulas he might need to get started, he could hire a laboratory to come up with some for a lot less than $250,000. The truth was, if he really wanted an herbal lotions company, it made more sense for him to start his own.

In the end, Josh decided he'd had his fill of herbal lotions. He told the seller he wasn't interested in pursuing the deal. He wasn't happy about letting it go, but he couldn't argue with the numbers. The last time I saw him, he was searching for another business to buy. I don't know whether he found one—or finally came to the realization that he'd be better off looking for a business to start.

Ask Norm

Dear Norm:
About a year ago I moved to Florida from the Northeast, where I had owned a few photo-processing shops. In Florida I bought a commercial printing business. I've been putting in eighty-hour weeks, learning the basics. Now I'm ready to start advertising, but I'm worried about making a major mistake, especially when it comes to pricing. Should I hire a consultant to advise me?
    Sam

Dear Sam:
I certainly wouldn't. You have business experience, and your instincts are better than those of any consultant you can find. Besides, you probably wouldn't—and shouldn't—follow a consultant's advice if you don't agree with it. So why pay somebody to give you advice that you won't listen to if it's different from what you think? Instead, I'd research the industry. Find out who your competitors are, what they're charging, what kind of quality and service they offer, and so on. Then make your own call.
    —Norm

The Wrong Kind of Business Plan

Then there's the ongoing confusion about business plans, which most people think they need in order to raise money. Granted, you do need money to get a business up and running, and you may need a business plan to raise it. But money isn't the *first* thing you need, and you're making a big mistake if you focus on raising it before you're ready to spend it intelligently.

Unfortunately, that's one mistake a lot of people make, judging by the business plans I regularly receive. I'm talking about elaborate, four-color, one-hundred-page business plans, printed on high-grade paper, with photographs, tables, graphs, pie charts, flow charts, and every kind of number you could ask for. I mean, these plans are gorgeous. There's just one problem: the numbers don't make sense. No business operating in the real world could ever produce them.

I remember one particularly professional-looking plan that I received from a husband and wife who were trying to raise $50,000 to start a cookie business. According to the plan, they were going to use that money to take the company's sales from zero to $2.9 million in just two years. Understand, it's extremely difficult to achieve such a rate of growth in any business. It's almost impossible to do it in something like the cookie business with only $50,000 in outside capital. You'd run out of cash long before you hit your sales target. And yet the numbers were all right there in black and white, and they added up perfectly, which immediately aroused my suspicions.

I gathered that the plan had been written by the husband, a guy with very little business experience, using a sophisticated business plan software package. Looking closer at the numbers, I saw how he had come up with such an outlandish projection. For one thing, he'd plugged in a ridiculously short collection period for his receivables, about twenty days, while figuring he could get away with stretching his vendor payments to sixty days. He'd also underestimated the amount of equipment he needed and assumed he'd be able to lease whatever he wanted on his own signature—without putting up any additional security. None of those assumptions were plausible. If you replaced them with more realistic ones, you'd find that the couple needed at least another $200,000 in outside capital to have a prayer of getting the company's sales to $2.9 million in the second year.

I don't mean to suggest that the guy was intentionally deceiving anybody. Frankly, I doubt he even realized what he'd done. My guess is that, like most people with an idea and a burning desire to be in business for themselves, he was thinking only about the amount of money he needed to drop everything else and get started.

So how do you raise money? With a business plan, right? He'd gone out and bought the software, which had walked him step-by-step through the plan-writing process. Then he'd tweaked the numbers until he came up with a plan that showed the business achieving its goals after two years with just the amount of capital he thought he could raise.

It was all very neat and tidy, and the final document couldn't have looked more impressive. I've been in business almost thirty years, and I've never seen such a plan, let alone produced one. What it contained, however, was not a recipe for successful cookie making. It was a recipe for disaster.

I believe strongly that the first business plan you write should be for nobody but yourself, and you don't need any special software to create it. You just need to answer four questions as honestly as you can: (1) What is the concept? (2) How are you going to market it? (3) How much do you think it will cost to produce and deliver what you're selling? (4) What do you expect will happen when you actually go out and start making sales? The idea is to spell out as clearly as possible how you think the business is going to work—what you're going to sell, how much you're going to charge, who your customers will be, how you're going to reach them, how long it will take to close a sale, and so on. You need to be completely candid with yourself. You mustn't let your own economic circumstances cloud your thinking. Put aside for the moment any concerns you may have about earning a living or raising start-up capital. You can deal with those issues when the time comes. In the beginning, what's important is to get your major assumptions down on paper.

Why? Because you need to test those assumptions *before* you go out to raise money, not afterward. You need to identify as many mistakes as possible while you still have a chance to correct them.

And, believe me, everybody makes mistakes with their first business plan. It doesn't matter how smart or how careful you are. There will be major flaws. When I started my messenger business, for example, I thought I'd collect my accounts receivable in thirty days. I found out the hard way that the actual collection time was fifty-nine days. When I started my records storage business, I thought I could charge a monthly storage fee of 35¢ a box. In fact, we learned we weren't able to land substantial accounts unless we charged about 22¢ a box—almost 40 percent less than the price in my plan.

The point is that you need to give yourself time to discover those mistakes. Not that you'll catch all of them in advance, but you can reduce them to a minimum. How? By doing research. By finding out how long companies in the industry typically take to pay their suppliers, and how long it takes them to collect their own receivables. By trying to make a few sales. By looking for cheap office space and furnishings. By visiting a leasing company to see what terms you can get. By doing everything you can think of to get as prepared as you can be. Then, and only then, are you ready to bring out the bells and whistles and start looking for money.

In the long run, that research will turn out to be the best investment you can make in your business. Having done your homework, you'll be much more likely to raise the start-up capital you're looking for. More important, you'll be able to make better decisions about how to spend it. And you'll greatly increase the odds of making it last until you don't need it anymore—that is, until the business can support itself on its own cash flow. Which is, after all, the goal.

The Most Important Resource

As important as it is to conserve start-up capital, the danger of losing it is not the biggest risk that entrepreneurs take. After all, if you work hard enough, you can eventually earn it back. There's another resource that, once you lose it, you'll never see it again. From that standpoint, it's even more important—and more valuable—than money. The loss of it can cost you your chance to realize your dream. I'm talking about time.

Ask Norm

Dear Norm:
*I'm in the process of opening an educational facility, but I can't
get anybody to sign up. I've blanketed fairs and festivals with
my information. I've run newspaper ads and held open houses.
Our prices are lower than our competitors' and we charge no
registration fee, but we have no takers. What else can I do?*
  Kathy

Dear Kathy:
Never assume a business can't succeed just because you get
nowhere with your initial marketing attempts. I started my
messenger company with a mass mailing, offering to do the
first five deliveries for free. I got zero response. I was baffled
until an office manager told me, "We do dozens of deliveries
every day. Five means nothing. What about the next fifty?" So
the market was there. I was just trying to get customers the
wrong way. In your case, price is not the main concern of parents. If they're going to send you their children, they have to
know you, trust you, think well of you. I'd try working through
community clubs, social groups, churches, and synagogues.
Do a brochure with testimonials from local people saying how
terrific you are with children. Later on, open houses will be
important, and price may become an issue, but first you have
to establish your trustworthiness.
  —Norm

Let me tell you about Rob Levin, who approached me for advice
about starting a magazine. He planned to call it *The New York Enterprise Report* and to sell it to owners and managers of small businesses
in the New York metropolitan area, offering interviews with successful

entrepreneurs and how-to articles by experts. I agreed to meet with him, although I'm not sure why. I thought starting a business magazine was a really terrible idea. The industry had been in the doldrums for years, with no relief in sight. As difficult as life was for established business magazines, I knew it would be even harder for a new publication, which would be competing not only against the big boys, but also against the providers of free information on the Internet. Besides, there were many easier, and more lucrative, ways to earn a living.

But I have an ironclad rule that I will never discourage people from pursuing their dreams. What I will do is tell them what I think of their approach. Often they're trying something that I believe, based on my business experience, is destined to fail. In that case, I'll suggest alternatives. Then again, what makes sense for one person may be a recipe for failure for someone else. So I begin by finding out as much as I can about the person I'm advising.

As first-time entrepreneurs go, Rob Levin was a fairly sophisticated businessperson. After graduating from college in 1991, he had worked for Arthur Andersen as an accountant for four years, then gone back to school to earn his MBA. Subsequently, he'd been CFO or CEO of three small companies that ranged from $1 million to $25 million in annual sales. He had parted company with his last employer the year before he contacted me and had been doing some consulting while he searched for a business to start. But although he had $300,000 of his own savings to invest and his wife had a good job, he could not go indefinitely without a steady income: his wife had recently given birth to their first child.

Rob was convinced that the magazine was his ticket to success. Not only was he passionate about it, but everything else he planned to do depended on it. He had already spent $75,000 on a Web site, and—without the magazine—it would never become viable, let alone earn a profit. He was also planning to make money from seminars and networking groups, which would be difficult if he didn't have the magazine to use as a platform. The question was, how likely was it that he could launch such a publication successfully?

Not very, I concluded, as we went through the numbers. Like all entrepreneurs starting a new business, including me, Rob was overoptimistic about the sales he could generate and the time it would take to generate them, and he drastically underestimated his expenses. One number in particular jumped out at me. He planned to sell subscriptions by direct mail and was counting on a 10 percent response rate. I don't know a lot about direct mail, but I do know that no one gets a 10 percent response rate for a new magazine. If the mailing is successful, 1 percent to 2 percent is more like it. It would therefore take him much longer, and cost much more money, than he expected to get the number of paid subscriptions he was counting on.

"This approach won't work," I told him. "You'll run out of money before you find out if your idea's viable. You have to go about it differently. Have you thought about giving the magazine away?"

I could see the shock and anger on his face. It was as if I'd insulted him. He later told me that the suggestion almost broke his heart. It was a huge blow to his ego.

The logic was simple enough, however. Rob couldn't survive without advertising revenue, and the first question of any potential advertiser would be, "How many subscribers do you have?" He wouldn't be able to make the sale until he could give the advertiser a solid number. The fastest way to get that number, and to build a subscriber base, was to offer the magazine free of charge to the members of business organizations and trade groups. Advertisers might still be cautious about spending their ad dollars in an untested publication, but at least they would have an idea of the number of people they'd be reaching, and some of them might be willing to take a chance.

If he insisted on going after paid subscriptions, Rob wouldn't have a prayer of generating the revenue he needed. He'd wind up wasting a lot of precious time, which would come back to haunt him even if he quit before spending all of his money. He would probably have to take a corporate job, and he'd have a lot of ground to make up. It would take him a year or more to get back to where he'd been before he'd left his last job. Granted, he would learn some important lessons from a failure, and he might even be able to raise enough money to give the magazine another try later on. But, in the meantime, he would have spent three or four years and ended up back where he'd started, with nothing to show for it. By giving the magazine away, he would at least have a shot at succeeding.

It wasn't what he wanted to hear. He was seething when he left. I tried to offer him an olive branch by noting that he could later convert his free subscriptions to paid. That was technically true, but I knew in my heart that—if he built a successful company around free subscriptions—he would never start charging for them. It wouldn't be necessary from a business standpoint. I doubted he would waste his time and money on something simply to boost his ego, with no benefit to the company.

In any case, the decision had to be his and his alone. "You have to go with your gut feeling because it's your money and your time," I told him as he was leaving. "I have experience, but that doesn't mean I'm right." A day or so later, he called and told me that he'd decided to take my advice. He'd done some research and realized I was correct about the direct-mail response rates. He couldn't argue with the numbers. So he was going to change his plan, basing it on free subscriptions rather than paid. I wished him luck. A couple months after that, he called again to ask if I'd be willing to let him interview me for a cover story in the magazine's premier issue. Naturally, I agreed.

In the end, it turned out that starting a business magazine in New York City wasn't such a bad idea after all. The *New York Enterprise Report* was a big success, and it's still going strong. Granted, Rob could probably have made more money by having another type of business, but he's following his passion and doing what he loves, which is far more important than getting the best possible return on his investment. On the other hand, Rob agrees that he wouldn't have gotten this far had he stuck to his original plan. "Looking back, I was overoptimistic about everything," he says. "I would definitely have run out of money, no question. I didn't know it then, but I do now. I was looking so far ahead that I wasn't focusing on the next year or so."

Most important, by adjusting his course, Rob saved three years of his life or more. Instead of spending them spinning his wheels, he used them to lay the groundwork for a business that he can stay with as long as he likes, and that can take him wherever he wants to go.

The Bottom Line

Point One: It's good to have a lot of competitors because educating a market is a very expensive proposition.

Point Two: If you're a first-time entrepreneur, it's generally better to start a business than to buy one.

Point Three: The first business plan should be simple, and you should write it for yourself, not for potential investors.

Point Four: Your time is more valuable than money, and you should be careful not to waste it.

CHAPTER FOUR

Where the Money Is

So now let's talk about money. For people who want to start a business, there's nothing more mysterious than figuring out how to raise it. I hear from them all the time. A lot of these would-be entrepreneurs have good, solid business ideas that they've researched and tested, but—try as they might—they can't find an investor. "What am I doing wrong?" they ask. "How can I find someone like you?" They don't need someone like me. What they need is a better understanding of investors.

Let me tell you about Jordan and Seth, who had a start-up that they thought could become a national provider of Internet development services to small and midsize businesses. The two of them had invested $200,000 of their own money to get the business up and running, taking sales from $42,000 in the first year to $246,000 in the second. Along the way, they'd learned a lot about the market and come up with a strategy for tapping into it, using the contacts they'd made in another company they owned, a successful print brokerage in Manhattan. They figured they needed $2 million to ramp up the new business over the next five years, and they were getting ready to approach potential investors. Jordan asked if I'd be willing to look over their business plan and offer them some advice. I said I would.

The business plan arrived the day before our meeting. It was one of the nicest I've ever seen—about thirty-five pages long with a hard cover bearing the company's name and logo. The text was succinct and to the point, providing about the right amount of background information on the business, the market, and the strategy going forward. The numbers appeared to make sense. But a couple of things jumped out at me. When I got together with Jordan and Seth, I asked them whom they were planning to go to for money. They said they had a meeting scheduled with venture capitalists in a couple of days. I said, "No venture capitalist is going to buy this plan."

There were at least three problems with it from a venture capitalist's perspective. For openers, the plan said almost nothing about how much investors could expect to make on the money they put in, or how they would eventually cash out. That's a major omission if you're going to people who invest only in businesses that promise to deliver the particular rate of return they're looking for.

Second, the plan called for using a substantial portion of the investment to buy furniture, equipment, and other fixed assets. A venture capitalist was sure to ask, "Why buy? Why not lease?" Venture capitalists like to take advantage of leverage—within reason, of course. The more debt you use to finance a start-up, the greater will be the potential increase in its equity value. It's like buying a house with the smallest possible down payment. There's a bigger risk of failing, but a bigger reward if you succeed. Jordan and Seth clearly didn't understand the investment philosophy of the people they were asking for money. Strike two.

But the biggest problem with the plan had to do with a small note on the page labeled "Projected Source and Use of Proceeds." It said that more than $200,000 of the $2 million investment would go toward "repayment of loans to officers and affiliates." I don't know anyone who'd make a substantial investment in a start-up knowing that the founders were planning to take 10 percent of the money and put it in their pockets. Venture capitalists certainly wouldn't allow it. They'd probably see it as a good reason to reject the deal.

On the other hand, they'd be impressed if Jordan and Seth said, "Look. We've financed this business ourselves for the past two years, using our own hard-earned money. Now we need your money, but ours is going to stay there at least until you get your investment out." That would have been a significant factor in their favor. So what had they done? They'd taken a big positive and turned it into a big negative. I asked if they had any other prospects besides the venture capitalists. They told me they had a lead on a group of doctors.

I don't know what it is about doctors, but people who want to raise money always seem to have access to a group of them. You'd think doctors were ready to invest any amount of money in anything that came down the pike. "How much are you looking for from each of these doctors?" I asked. They said the minimum investment amount was $250,000. I said, "You don't know these people, do you?" They admitted they didn't.

There are very few doctors willing to invest $250,000 in a start-up business. Wealthy professionals tend to approach these matters the same way that relatives, friends, or other amateur investors do. The first question they ask is, "How much do I have to put in?" Everybody has an investment plateau. It could be $10,000 or $20,000 or $100,000. Whatever it is, you won't have a chance if you come in too far above it. Even if people are kind enough to sit through your pitch, you've already lost them. They won't seriously consider investing in your deal.

So it's important to find out in advance the investment plateau of the people you're going to, especially if they're not professional money managers. If you can't ask them directly, you can talk to the contact person, or to accountants and financial advisers who know the investment habits of people like those you're planning to approach. Maybe they typically invest $25,000, in which case you'd need forty of them to raise $1 million. The point is that, once you know their investment threshold, you can tailor the offering to make it possible for them to put in an amount they're comfortable with—or you can decide it's not worth asking them at all.

But you have to do your homework. With most investors, you have just one shot. If you blow it, you're out of luck. People don't say, "Come back when you get it right." If you go in and you don't know what you're doing, it's unlikely that you'll ever get another chance. To make the most of your opportunities, you need to plan your investment strategy just as you plan your business. You need to research the market. You need to find out as much as you can about potential investors—what they want, what their criteria are, how they evaluate a deal—before you ever ask them for money.

Some research is easy. Most bankers, for example, are happy to tell you the exact criteria they use in making loans. Venture capitalists will also explain their philosophy if you approach them the right way. Alternatively, you can go to businesspeople who've received venture backing and ask them for advice. But the best research is done while you're actually out looking for the money. That's why I usually tell people to build a certain amount of failure into the process. I'm talking about including four or five long shots on your list of potential investors—and then making a point of approaching them first, knowing that you're probably going to be turned down. You're bound to learn something from each rejection. You should plan to learn as much as you can.

For example, you can draw up a questionnaire and go back to people who've rejected you. Make it clear that you aren't looking for money this time, that you respect their decision and aren't asking them to reconsider. Say that you just want to learn from the experience, and you'd be grateful if they'd explain why they said no. Urge them to be completely candid. Was it you? Was it something about the business plan? Was it the amount of money you were looking for?

The information you gather will allow you to strengthen your business plan and improve your presentation before you go to see the people most likely to give you their support. You'll get a better sense of what they're looking for, and you can make sure you're offering them what they want. Not that you should be dishonest, but there's no point in approaching them if their criteria don't mesh with your needs.

That's more or less what I told Jordan and Seth, but they had other ideas. They went ahead and met with the venture capitalists, who turned them down. A couple of weeks later, I got a call from Jordan, saying that he and Seth had decided to dissolve their partnership. Seth wanted to keep looking for investors who'd let them take their own $200,000 out of the business. Jordan thought such efforts were a waste of time. In the end, all they could agree on was to go their separate ways. Which goes to show, I suppose, that some business lessons are more expensive than others.

The Banking Choice

Getting start-up capital is certainly important, but once the company is up and running, you need to turn your attention to building another financial relationship—the one you'll have with a bank. The question then becomes, what kind of bank?

That question was on the mind of an Inc. 500 CEO who came to me for advice about securing a line of credit to finance his company's expansion. He planned to borrow against his accounts receivable. His chief financial officer wanted to use a bank, but his accountant was recommending that he go with an asset-based lender. He said he wasn't happy with his current bank and was planning to leave it anyway. Was there any reason he shouldn't use an asset-based lender for the credit line?

I told him I could think of about ten reasons. How many did he want?

I know how difficult bankers can be to deal with. I've had my full share of run-ins with them. It's amazing how poorly they sometimes treat their customers, and how hard you have to work to get them to take you on in the first place. As a group, they are just about the most inept salespeople I've ever run into. But every business needs a bank, and you should use every opportunity you have to build a relationship with one. Forget about whether or not you need a loan right now. The truth is, you're better off if you don't. What's important is to have the relationship. Why? Because the day will come when you *do* have to borrow money, and when it does, you don't want your only option to be an asset-based lender.

Please don't get me wrong here. I have nothing against asset-based lenders per se. They play an important role in our economy, lending money to companies that can't get it anywhere else. And unlike bankers, they're terrific salespeople. Yes, as they will readily admit, it's more expensive to borrow from them than from a bank, but they do so much more for you (or so they claim): monitor your collections, do credit checks on your customers, help you keep on top of your receivables. What's more, they can close a deal quickly and painlessly, in as little as two weeks, often without even requiring audited financial statements.

It can all look very tempting to a growing company with little cash and a lot of receivables, especially if you're coming off a bad experience with a bank. There's a catch, however. A loan from an asset-based lender is not the same as a loan from a bank. (By *bank*, I mean a traditional commercial lender. For the purposes of this discussion, I'm including the asset-based-lending divisions of banks with asset-based lenders.) The key difference can be summed up in one word: control.

When you borrow from an asset-based lender, you give up control of your receivables. The payments from customers no longer come to you. They go into a lockbox at the lender's bank. You get copies of the checks and a full accounting record of what happens to the money, but the lender controls the cash. If a dispute arises, or if your business gets into trouble, the lender holds all the cards. While it no doubt would prefer that your company succeed, it has no great incentive to help you get through tough times. After all, it isn't depending on you to repay the debt. It's depending on your customers. That's why asset-based lenders seldom insist that you provide them with audited financial statements. It's your customers' creditworthiness that counts, not yours.

With a bank, you're in a totally different position—because banks are not in the same business as asset-based lenders. They don't make money by managing receivables. Their profit comes from making good loans. A bank will let you borrow against receivables only if it thinks you're going to be able to repay the money with interest. It doesn't want your receivables. It's not set up to deal with them.

So the receivables remain in your hands. You're responsible for managing, monitoring, and collecting them. Granted, you're supposed to report regularly on their status, and—if things go badly—the bank can always come after them. But even then, you have much more room to maneuver and a better chance of surviving, because the bank has a vested interest in having you succeed. It cares whether or not you stay in business. It wants to get repaid, and that won't happen unless you're around.

I don't mean to suggest that the main reason to borrow from a bank is to protect yourself on the downside. It isn't. My point is that, when you borrow money, you enter a relationship, and the relationship will be a good one only if you understand what the other party is looking for. Banks look for good businesses—and good businesspeople—to invest in, whereas asset-based lenders look for good receivables to acquire.

That's why it's harder to borrow money from a bank: you have to prove yourself creditworthy. It's also why you have to do more once you get the loan. Granted, asset-based lenders provide certain services you won't get from your bank, but they're things that every business should do for itself anyway.

And therein lies the real reason to borrow from a bank, assuming you have the option. The loan gives you an opportunity to demonstrate that you understand your responsibilities as a borrower and are capable of meeting them as a businessperson. It gives you a chance to build the relationship by showing that you can hold up your end of the bargain. That is, it allows you to establish trust.

Ask Norm

Dear Norm:
I need your advice about finding investors. If I have no money to put into a business, what else might I be able to contribute as a form of personal equity to woo investors? The only idea I have is to sign a promissory note.
Dave

Dear Dave:
If sweat equity isn't enough for outside investors, I doubt that a promissory note will do the trick, either. You'll probably have to get some Rolodex funding first. By that, I mean you'll have to start calling people in your address book, including close friends and relatives. Any money you raise from them will be seen by outside investors as money from you. By asking for money from friends and family, you'll be taking a risk on your future relationships with them. That counts with outsiders who want to know you're investing something important besides your time.
—Norm

How to Lose a Loan

In the end, mutual trust is needed to cement a banking relationship, but trust is not what many entrepreneurs feel toward their bank. They live in constant fear of having their loans being called, which could happen at any moment and for almost any reason. I know one company that made a mistake with a bonus payout and was dropped by a bank it had been doing business with for fifty years, through three generations of ownership. Another was asked to leave when its bank had a change of policy and decided it would no longer do receivables financing. Yet another company was given the bum's rush because its principal customer was considered a poor credit risk. I've had my loans called twice in my career, and I wouldn't wish the experience on anyone. That said, one of the experiences was much better than the other and helped me understand what you can do to protect yourself.

The first time I got dumped was in 1985, when my messenger business was growing like crazy. The business consisted of seventeen different corporate entities, each of which had a relationship with the same bank. I thought everything was fine until one day, without warning, I received seventeen letters informing me that I had thirty days to pay off my loans. I was stunned and furious. I called my loan officer and said, "What the hell are you doing? Couldn't you at least call me before sending these letters?" He apologized and then essentially told me to get lost. The bank, he said, was getting out of receivables financing and didn't want my business anymore. I had a month to find a new lender.

The next experience, in 1995, was far more pleasant. Again, I had receivables financing from a bank that was changing its policy and getting into new lines of business. This time, however, my banker came to me and explained what was coming. "We're dividing our customers into three categories," he said. "The first group consists of those we definitely want to keep. They're good companies, and they fit into our new business plan. Second are the customers we should never have taken on in the first place. They have thirty days to get out. The third group is another story. It includes good customers like you who just don't belong here, given our new direction. We'll help you find a new bank, and you can take your time doing it. There's no pressure, but we'd like to make the transition in the next six months, if possible."

His comments were a revelation. I suddenly understood what had happened the first time: I'd landed in group two. Looking back, I realized that I could probably have gotten into group three if only I'd kept my cool. Instead of blowing my top, I should have simply asked my banker, "What's the problem? Can't we work something out?" As it was, my behavior no doubt confirmed the bank's decision to get rid of me as soon as possible. A lot of entrepreneurs make the same mistake.

In fact, I can think of seven mistakes that business owners make in dealing with their bank, often without realizing the damage they're doing to the relationship. Avoiding those blunders can save you a lot of grief. Granted, your bank may still decide to drop you someday, for reasons beyond your control, but you'll have a much better chance of winding up in group three.

Mistake #1: Submitting financial statements late. Banks are in business, too, and they have more regulations to deal with than you do. To make sure a bank is following the rules, regulators check its records at least once a year, and internal examiners look at them quarterly, or even monthly. If you don't submit your financial statements when you're supposed to, your records will be incomplete, and you'll create problems for your banker, who gets rated on the accounts he, or she, is monitoring. That's a strike against you.

Mistake #2: Running on uncollected funds. To avoid drawing down their credit line, and paying interest on it, some companies will deposit checks they receive and immediately start spending the uncollected funds, which has the side effect of keeping bank balances low. A company may save a few bucks in the process, but it does so at the cost of alienating the bank, which is deprived of income it's entitled to. That's another strike.

Mistake #3: Being unresponsive. Bankers often have questions about your financial statements, and you may not know the answers. Some people get annoyed or defensive when asked to explain their financials. Instead of having an accountant provide the necessary information, they try to talk their way out of the situation, giving lame responses that don't add up. When the examiners come in, the banker is asked the same questions, can't offer satisfactory answers, and gets hammered as a result. Another strike.

Mistake #4: Neglecting the relationship. When you don't need anything from your bank, it's easy to ignore your banker. There are always plenty of pressing matters to focus on. You figure, "Why bother with the bank? Let's leave well enough alone." But by the time you do need something, it's often too late. If you haven't already built a good relationship, the chances are you'll go away empty-handed. That's why it's important to meet regularly with your banker. My partners and I always made a point of sitting down with our bankers at least once every three months.

Mistake #5: Failing to keep the bank adequately informed. Bankers don't like big, bad surprises any more than the rest of us do. They understand that unexpected things happen in business, but many problems can be anticipated, and bankers want to have as much advance warning as possible. Bankers also need some reassurance that you're in control of your business. That's one reason they ask for annual forecasts. If your projections are way off year after year, your banker will conclude that you don't know where your business is heading—or, worse, that you're being dangerously optimistic.

Mistake #6: Ignoring the rules. Whenever a bank lends you money, it comes with strings attached, namely, the covenants contained in the loan agreement. A lot of people don't understand the covenants, or forget about them, or simply ignore them. I know one guy—let's call him Marvin—who decided, with his partners, to have their company give them a $500,000 bonus so that they could avoid having to pay taxes twice on the money. (If they'd instead taken the money as a dividend, the company would first have had to declare the $500,000 as earnings and pay corporate taxes on it, in addition to the individual taxes that would then be owed.)

Unfortunately, they overlooked the effect that the payout would have on their debt-to-equity ratio. By reducing their equity in the company, the bonus caused the ratio to soar way beyond the limits allowed by the bank. When their banker told them the company was out of ratio and they had to correct the problem, they were outraged. The company had been a loyal customer for decades. The bank, they said, had no right to tell them what to do.

Ask Norm

Dear Norm:
I'm only twenty-two years old, but I've been wanting to start a business for a long time. My passion is computers, and I've come up with a concept that has an incredible upside. I just need about $100,000 to make it a go. My father-in-law has access to that kind of money. The problem is, I have no idea how to approach him.
Brandon

Dear Brandon:
Entrepreneurs are optimistic by nature, but it's important to look at the downside risk as well as the upside potential, and let's face it: there's an inherent risk in borrowing money from in-laws. So first you need to ask yourself, What would happen if I lost all the money? If the loss would have serious personal ramifications, I'd look elsewhere. Business failure is tough enough without adding family trouble into the mix. But if losing the money would have no effect on your in-laws' lives, if your family wouldn't be torn apart, then it should be easy to approach your father-in-law. Just lay your cards on the table. Tell him you think your plan will work, but if it doesn't, there's a risk he'll lose all the money he's invested. Ask him if he's interested and assure him that, if he isn't, there will be no hard feelings. And remember there are other sources of capital around if your in-laws are not an option.
—Norm

That was an example of...

Mistake #7: Arguing when you're wrong. A lot of businesspeople think they're entitled to the money they borrow from a bank—especially if they've been good customers for a long period of time. They start to think of the bank's money as their money, and they become incensed if the bank asks for it back. But banks have the right to get their money back when borrowers violate their loan covenants. After all, those covenants are there for a reason. A bank is also required to follow certain rules. If its loans don't measure up to federal standards, it could wind up with serious regulatory problems.

Nor does it help to protest when a bank changes its lending policies, as happened in my case. Arguing won't bring the old policy back any more than outrage will make a bank forgive you for violating your loan covenants. On the contrary, by becoming a pain in the neck, you give the bank another reason to throw you out. That's exactly what happened to Marvin and his partners.

Understand, none of the mistakes I've mentioned is fatal by itself. Even Marvin could have salvaged his banking relationship if he'd stayed calm, acted reasonably, and come up with a plan for getting his company back in ratio. It takes time to build a relationship, and it takes time to break one up. One mistake compounds another. The damage is cumulative, and often invisible. You may not know exactly where you stand until it's too late. One day, the letter will arrive, or the banker will call, and you'll find out if you're in group two or group three. Perhaps you'll never get that letter or call, but if you do, let's hope you land in group three. In business, as elsewhere, it's a lot nicer to be shown gently to the door than to be unceremoniously given the boot.

Your Inner Bank

To be sure, there are times when credit gets so tight that you can't get a loan no matter what you do. Fortunately, you may have an alternative if you happen to have a business that bills its customers after delivering whatever product or service it happens to sell. Unless you've already pledged your receivables to someone else, you have your own inner bank, and you need to start thinking like a banker.

Receivables are, in effect, loans you've made to your customers, and it's always a good idea to keep an eye on the quality of your loan portfolio. It's especially important when other sources of cash dry up. You need to ask, Is it taking you more time to collect than it should? Is your average collection time increasing and, if so, why? Do customers need to be called more often? Are some of them struggling because they have problems of their own? In that case, you might need to work out new terms with them. Or are people taking advantage of you, in which case you might want to apply additional pressure—or maybe even terminate the account?

Of course, if you're borrowing against your receivables through a bank or an asset-based lender, I suspect you already have a pretty good idea of the shape they're in. Your lender is no doubt making sure that you track them closely. They're the collateral on its loan to you. If receivables go unpaid for too long, you'll stop getting the cash you need to survive. So you have a powerful incentive to find out who is paying on time and who isn't, and to go after the latter. But even without that incentive, we should all be tracking our receivables *as if* we had an asset-based lender looking over our shoulders. Unfortunately, it's easy to lose that discipline as a company grows, particularly if you have strong cash flow and money in the bank.

I discovered that danger during the due diligence process we went through when we were thinking of selling three of our companies in 2006. After looking at our receivables, the would-be buyer wanted to increase our reserve against bad debt by $200,000 to $400,000, which would have reduced the purchase price by $2 million to $4 million. "What are you talking about?" I said. "Our receivables are all good. We have the customers' boxes. They can't get their records back without paying us."

"Yeah, well, your own records show that 40 percent of your receivables are more than 120 days old," the auditor said. "That's a big number. A lot more of them may be uncollectible than you've made allowance for."

I was shocked. Even though we do a lot of business with hospitals and government agencies—which pay reliably but slowly—it was a much bigger number than I would have guessed. We had a good system in place for tracking receivables, but I hadn't been paying attention. It wasn't as if we'd been having cash flow problems, after all. We were paying our bills on time and had plenty of money left over. The thought that we might have a receivables problem never entered my mind. So monitoring collections was not very high on my list of priorities.

But the prospect of losing $2 million to $4 million got my attention real fast. I assured the buyer that almost all of the 120-day receivables were collectible, and we'd prove it. We spent the next four months doing just that.

We began by looking at the breakdown of our receivables month by month for the past three years—that is, the monthly percentage of receivables that were current, 30, 60, 90, and 120 days or more outstanding. It turned out that the 120-day number had been creeping up steadily over the entire period. The average monthly increase may have been only half a percent, but that translated into 6 percent a year. At that rate, you could start out with, say, 10 percent of your receivables in the 120-day category—the acceptable amount depends on the kind of business you're in and the type of customers you have—and wind up with 28 percent by the end of the third year. That's more or less what happened with us.

Part of the problem, we realized, was that the collections department was overworked and understaffed. So we hired an additional person, not to go after the long-term nonpayers we already had, but to keep from adding to their number in the future. That's the first step in problem solving: make sure you don't keep repeating your mistakes going forward. (See chapter 16.) Then you can go back and deal with what happened in the past. Accordingly, we next turned our attention to collecting the money we were owed by customers who hadn't paid us in more than four months.

Because we weren't in a money crunch, we were able to avoid two common mistakes made by people desperate for cash. When you absolutely must get cash right away, you naturally go to the customers most likely to pay you quickly—namely, your best accounts, those that already pay on time. You put pressure on them to pay early or you ask for favors, neither of which helps build good relationships with the people who are most important to your company's success. The second mistake is to have your accounting people do the collecting. They don't know the customer nearly as well as other employees do, and they don't have the personal relationships that they could use to avoid inadvertently antagonizing people who should be allies. A salesperson, a customer service person, or an operations person who interacts regularly with the customer may know a better way to make the request or may be able to offer a favor in return for a favor.

With that in mind, we divided up the 120-day accounts among our sales, service, and ops employees and began contacting customers. What came next was a revelation. Some people blamed us for their own failure to pay for the services that we'd performed. One customer said, "Sure, we'll pay you, but why did you wait so long to call us? You shouldn't have let it get this far. You should have let us know a lot sooner." It turned out the customer had a problem in its accounting department that was only discovered when we asked for our money. The people blamed us for not alerting them to the problem sooner. Who knows? Maybe they had a point. In any case, we apologized and moved on.

With other customers, we found that we had to modify our billing procedures. One hospital group, for example, had a purchase order system that we weren't fitting into. Without knowing it, we were forcing the group's accounting people to adapt to our system, rather than making our billing process work with their payment process. When we asked how we could get paid more quickly, they showed us what information they needed from us and in what form. We made the appropriate changes.

Then there were the instances of our bills not reaching the right people. We discovered, among other things, that we weren't updating our contact information often enough. We'd get the initial information and then check it again when the contract came up for renewal in five years. In the meantime, there could have been changes in personnel, in departments, in procedures, even in the company's name and location, and we wouldn't know about them. Or maybe our collectors knew about the change, but our billing people didn't, because—for security reasons—we don't allow anyone who handles money to make changes in our system. So we developed new procedures for coordinating the exchange of information and making sure the bills wound up where they were supposed to go.

We also came across some customers we didn't want. They were mainly small customers who had already heard from our collectors—repeatedly. We had to hound them constantly for payment. It would take six months to a year for us to collect from them, and then they would pay only because they needed to retrieve a box.

That type of customer literally takes money out of your pocket. To begin with, you don't have the use of the money that the customer owes you and promised to give you when you signed him up. Let's say his outstanding bill is for $1,000. If he doesn't pay on time, you have to borrow an extra $1,000 from the bank. Suppose you're paying 9 percent annual interest on your loans. That's $90 per year. So your $1,000 is really just $910. Meanwhile, your accounting person is spending half an hour each month calling this guy and listening to his lame excuses and false promises. That's six hours per year. If you pay the accountant $25 an hour, with benefits figured in, the slow payer costs you an additional $150 annually, meaning that the $1,000 is now down to $760.

Look at what that does to your gross margins. Normally, I would expect an account that small to have a gross margin of at least 40 percent. It wouldn't be worth accepting the business for less, even if the guy paid on time. So, on $1,000, you should be earning a gross profit of $400. But because he takes a year to pay—and makes you spend $260 on interest and labor that you wouldn't have to spend otherwise—your gross profit is $140. That's a 14 percent gross margin. I don't know about you, but if we had too many accounts like that, we'd be out of business! I don't want or need that kind of customer, and so we made those accounts pay up or leave.

In the end, we were able to reduce by more than 50 percent the share of our receivables that hadn't been paid for 120 days or more. The would-be buyers could hardly believe it. They insisted on sending in their auditors again, who confirmed that we had, in fact, shrunk the number by that amount. Not only did we address the immediate problem, but we implemented new procedures that will keep it from arising in the future. Although we didn't end up selling the company to those people, I owe them a debt of gratitude for pointing out our receivables problems and forcing us to become better bankers.

The Bottom Line

Point One: Before you ask people for money, make sure you know how much they like to invest and what they're looking for.

Point Two: Start early to build a relationship with a commercial banker and use an asset-based lender only if you can't get the money you need from a commercial bank.

Point Three: Bankers are businesspeople, too. Treat them the way you would like your customers to treat you.

Point Four: Your receivables are loans to your customers. Make sure your portfolio is in good shape.

CHAPTER FIVE

Magic Numbers

Here's the best piece of advice I can give to anyone starting a business: from day one, keep track of your monthly sales and gross margins *by hand*. Don't use a computer. Write down the numbers, broken out by product category or service type and by customer, and do the math yourself, using nothing more sophisticated than a calculator.

That's what I insisted on with Bobby and Helene Stone (see chapter 1) and what I myself do when I start a business. You can save yourself all kinds of grief—and greatly improve your chances of success—if you do the same. After all, to be successful in any business, you need to develop a feel for the numbers. You need to get a sense of the relationships between them, see the connections, figure out which ones are especially critical and have to be monitored accordingly. Numbers run businesses. They tell you how you can make the most money in the least time and with the least effort—which is, or should be, the goal of every entrepreneur. What you choose to do with the money after you've made it is another matter. You can give it all away if you want to. But first you have to earn it, and the numbers can tell you how to do that as efficiently as possible, provided you understand their language.

Tracking the numbers by hand is the best way I know of to learn that language, at least as it applies to your particular business. You can switch to computer tracking once you've mastered it, but if you let a computer do the work in the beginning, you lose something. You don't develop the same intimate connection with the numbers that you get when you track them manually. In fact, your business may never even reach viability if you don't start tracking your numbers early on.

Consider the case of Anisa Telwar, who started her business—now called Anisa International—in 1992. The business was still struggling when she contacted me four years later. She said that she had taken her cosmetics accessories business from zero to $1.5 million in sales, "...and I have nothing to show for that growth at this time." She thought what she needed were better promotional materials. I suspected her problems lay elsewhere. In any case, I agreed to meet with her.

It quickly became apparent that Anisa was lost. She realized something must be wrong because she was having trouble paying her bills every month, but she couldn't understand why. She knew her costs, and she knew how much she typically marked up the price of her products. How could she be chronically short of cash? The problem, she figured, was that she didn't have enough sales. In fact, her real problem was that she wasn't gathering simple, easy-to-get information that would have told her what was happening in her business.

That's because there were only two possible explanations for her situation. One was that she was not making enough gross profit on her sales to cover her other expenses and still get a decent return. The other was that the cash she generated was going someplace other than her bank account. The second explanation seemed unlikely, given the nature of her business. She was a packager and marketer of cosmetics brushes, sponges, bags, and gift items, which she sold to major department stores and cosmetics companies throughout the United States. Anisa would get the orders and forward them to manufacturers in the Far East, who then shipped directly to the customers. The manufacturers got paid after she got paid.

So I knew that her cash couldn't be going into inventory: she didn't have any. And I doubted that she had much of a receivables problem, given the pressure she was under to pay her own suppliers. My guess was that she was making too many low-margin sales. But which ones, and why? Was she charging too little for certain products? Was she giving too many breaks to certain customers? I couldn't find out because she hadn't kept track. I had her go back and write down her sales for the previous three months, showing me the total on every customer invoice and the cost of goods sold for each of those orders.

One look at the list, and I knew she had customer problems. She'd lost money on some of the orders. On others, she hadn't made nearly enough to survive.

Next I sent her a form on which I asked her to start tracking her sales and gross margins by product category. At the end of each month, she was to write down the sales, cost of goods, gross profit, and gross margin (that is, gross profit as a percentage of sales) on every type of product she carried, both for that month and for the year to date. Then she was to calculate the totals for the company as a whole. The whole exercise took less than thirty minutes a month and allowed her to see at a glance how much cash she was generating internally and where it was coming from. Meanwhile, she continued to track her monthly sales and gross margins by customer on a separate sheet of paper.

The reports were a revelation. Anisa later told me that it was like reality hitting her in the face. For the first time, she saw what it took to make money in business. Before, she said, she'd been winging it. Afterward, she began to understand how she could be in control. Not that she was suffering from low gross margins across the board. She was doing fine with some products and customers, but the others were dragging the average down. I told her there are basically four ways to deal with this type of situation. You can raise your prices. You can reduce your manufacturing costs. You can say no to low-margin business. Or you can find other products that you can sell at higher margins. Anisa decided to do all four.

Understand, my point here is not that Anisa was wrong to have accepted low-margin sales in the first place. When you're just starting out in business, you have to be flexible, as I noted earlier. You have to put together the pieces of the business much as you would assemble a puzzle. In the beginning, those low-margin sales may have helped Anisa build relationships with her manufacturers—by providing enough volume to make it worthwhile for them to do business with her on credit. As she soon discovered, their credit was the key to her survival.

But once she'd figured out how to earn a living from the business, she should have immediately turned her attention to increasing its profitability. She didn't because she had no idea what was going on. She wasn't even aware of the decisions that had to be made. She was operating on instinct and guesswork, rather than information, and it takes information to survive.

You need to start gathering that information from the beginning. In particular, you need to track your gross margins. High gross margins translate into high gross profit, and gross profit is the main source of the cash you'll need to support yourself and build the business.

And don't make the mistake of automating the tracking process. You have to write the numbers out by hand and calculate the percentages yourself. If you let a computer do the work, the numbers become abstract. They start to blend together. You don't focus on them. You don't absorb them. You don't get to know them as well as you must if you're really going to be in control of your business.

Don't get me wrong. I am not anticomputer. On the contrary, I began using computers in my messenger business long before anyone else in the industry. My businesses have always used the best technology available. I myself have all the state-of-the-art computer toys, not to mention a degree in accounting, and I've started several businesses. But seven years after I started my records storage business, I would still sit down every month to track the key numbers by hand—and by then the business was doing millions of dollars in sales.

It's all part of the education process, and you can't skip over it. I don't care if you're a Harvard MBA who's spent the past ten years at McKinsey. You still need to track your numbers by hand. I guarantee you'll learn something. Anisa sure did. Armed with her newfound knowledge, she took charge of her destiny and built Anisa International into one of the leading suppliers of cosmetics brushes in the country. In 2006, Target Corp. named the company Vendor of the Year in its beauty division, an award given to suppliers that demonstrate excellent business practices, innovative design, and superior customer service. Anisa could never have accomplished so much if she hadn't had a good grasp of the numbers. Tracking them by hand in the beginning helped her to develop one.

Levers of Control

I really can't emphasize enough the importance of developing a good feel for the numbers. In particular, you need to identify those that will alert you to potential problems *before* they become serious, so you can make the right decisions in time to prevent further complications.

I'll give you an example from my records storage business. In the spring of 2003, we were all geared up for a big growth spurt when I received the two-page report I get on each of my businesses every Monday morning. Among other things, the records storage report tells me how many new boxes we put away the week before. For months the number had been increasing steadily as our Manhattan-based customers—mainly law firms, accounting firms, and hospitals—struggled to get their records off-site in the wake of 9/11. In one year we grew 55 percent. But as I looked at the report that morning, I was shocked to see that, the prior week, we'd put away almost 70 percent fewer new boxes than the week before.

That stopped me dead in my tracks. The new-box count is one of my key numbers—a reliable indicator of what my overall sales for the week actually were. Although new boxes represent only one element of my total revenue, I'd learned by then that our sales rise in direct proportion to the number of new boxes we add in any given time period. Tell me on September 1 how many new boxes came in during August, and I can tell you our overall sales for August within 1 percent or 2 percent of the actual figure. If the new-box count had dropped by as much as the report indicated, we could be looking at a significant slowdown in our overall growth rate.

That was important information, and I wouldn't have gotten it so fast if I hadn't figured out a formula for calculating total sales based on new boxes. In the beginning, it was by no means obvious that there was such a formula. We get revenue from many sources, including optional services, removal charges, and special projects, not to mention storage fees for boxes we already have. New boxes account for only a small percentage of our overall sales. If I didn't have a key number, I'd have to add up sales from all the different sources to get the total. As a practical matter, that would mean waiting until we did our monthly billing.

But I didn't want to wait that long, and I knew I wouldn't have to if I could find a number that rose at the same rate as overall sales. After years of searching, I zeroed in on the new-box count and was eventually able to devise a formula that allowed me to estimate sales within 1 percent or 2 percent of the actual figure. Why the new-box count? I have no idea. It's a little like being able to determine the sales of a department store by counting the number of shoes it sells. Yet, for some reason, the formula works.

I believe every business has key numbers like that one. A restaurant owner I know can predict his evening's receipts by the length of time customers have to wait for a table at 8:30 p.m. My friend Jack Stack, the cofounder and CEO of SRC Holdings Corp. and the pioneer of open-book management, told me about a guy with a gear-making company who knows his sales by the weight of the gears that have been shipped. Not the dollars. Not the orders. Not the number or type of gears. The weight.

Indeed, the best businesspeople I know all have certain key numbers they track on a daily or weekly basis. It's an essential part of running a successful enterprise. Key numbers give you the financial information you need to take timely action. Business moves too fast to wait for the monthly, quarterly, or annual statements from your accountant. By the time you get them—weeks or months after the end of the period—you're already dealing with the consequences of whatever problems may have arisen when you weren't looking. You've probably missed out on a number of opportunities as well. You need real-time information, and the only way to get it is by coming up with a set of simple measurements you can use to figure out what's happening in your business at any given moment.

Of course, one of those measurements will relate to sales, although I hasten to add that it shouldn't be the only one. If you just track sales, you can get into serious trouble. Sales don't make a company successful. Profits and cash flow do. A lot of companies land in bankruptcy court because their owners focus so much on driving sales that profit and cash become an afterthought.

That said, it is important to have a key number for sales. What it will be varies from business to business, and it's seldom self-evident. I often have to follow the numbers for years before I can identify a single measurement I can use to tell me quickly what my sales are.

Take the document destruction business that we launched in the spring of 2000. As I noted earlier, we get our revenue from two types of services. One service involves so-called cleanouts, wherein we destroy a large volume of sensitive documents that a customer has accumulated over a long period of time. The other service is for customers who routinely produce material that needs to be destroyed on a regular basis. In those cases, we place locked bins around the customers' offices.

The revenue from the cleanouts is easy to track, since we do only a few each month. The bin business is much trickier because of the different types of bin, the different sizes of each type, the varying frequency of pickups, and so on. So there are a number of factors that go into determining overall sales. After three years of tracking them, I still couldn't identify the key number for sales in the bin business. One possibility was the number of new bins added. Another was the total number of bins outstanding. Or maybe it was the number of pickups. Then again, it could have been something else altogether. I tracked all of those numbers and several others. Finally, I decided that the number of bins scanned weekly correlated best with sales as a whole. But it was a long time before we had enough experience, and enough bins, to understand the relationships between the numbers.

How important is it to find that key number? Consider what happened in my records storage business after I saw the decline in the new-box count. Up to that point, we'd been in constant hiring mode. It took lots of people to handle all the new boxes coming in, and we had to recruit four times as many people as we needed, since only one out of four new hires wound up staying with us. When I saw the drop in the new-box count, I was immediately concerned that our rate of growth might be slowing, which would mean we wouldn't have as much cash flow as we'd anticipated. To be sure, the drop might have been a one-week aberration, but I didn't want to take a chance. If our annual growth rate really had fallen as much as the drop indicated, we were already overstaffed by about thirty people. While we could let normal attrition take care of that problem, I didn't want to keep adding people at the planned rate. If sales didn't bounce back, we might be forced to do a layoff.

So, based on one week's numbers, I put in a temporary hold on hiring. "I want to protect everyone's job," I said. "Let's see how this plays out." We waited for sales to revive, but the slowdown continued. As one week turned into one month and then four months, it became obvious that we weren't dealing with an aberration. The market had changed. Evidently, customers had finished clearing out all the records they'd wanted to move off-site after 9/11. Although our sales were still growing, the rate had plunged from 55 percent to about 15 percent annually.

My caution was vindicated, which is the best part of having a key number. Afterward, you look like a genius. My staff was very impressed that I saw the reduction in our growth rate so early and acted so quickly. I just told them it was all in the numbers.

Paying for Growth

Let me just return to the point I made earlier about the importance of tracking things other than sales, especially cash flow. I mean, sales are nice, and profits are nicer, but businesses live or die on cash flow. Where most first-time entrepreneurs trip up is in failing to understand that more sales almost always mean less cash flow—and less cash flow means trouble.

As usual, I speak from experience. I had no concept of the relationship between sales and cash flow when I started my first company. I thought sales were everything. If someone came and offered me a million dollars of new business, my only question was, "When does it start?" I took all the business I could get, as fast as I could get it, and the company grew like crazy. Our sales went from zero to $12.8 million in five years—fast enough to put us on the 1984 Inc. 500 list. We had cash flow problems all the way, but I didn't focus on them. I was too busy selling.

Ask Norm

Dear Norm:
I've reached a stage where I need to graduate from using two
part-time accountants to having a full-time controller. As I
get ready to make the change, I'm wondering what numbers
I should be watching on a day-to-day basis.
* Gary*

Dear Gary:
Every business has its own critical numbers, and my guess is
that you already know what yours are. How do you tell whether
you're having a good week or a good month? What happens
when your sales drop? How long does it take you to collect your
receivables? Those are all simple, commonsense things. Your
financial person should be helping you figure out the numbers
you need to be looking at and then providing them to you on a
regular basis. When you're interviewing for your new controller, make sure that he or she is up to the task. If you feel as
though you're a little weak on the numbers, don't be afraid to
say so. Put your questions to the candidates themselves. If they
can't give you answers that make sense, don't hire them.
  —Norm

The whack on the head finally came in the form of a cash crunch
that forced me to go without a salary for four straight weeks. Elaine
was pretty upset. "What do you mean, you can't pay yourself?" she
said. "I thought business was fabulous. I thought sales were going
through the roof. How can you be doing so great, and yet you can't
bring home any money for four weeks? Explain that to me. It doesn't
make sense."

The truth is, I couldn't explain it to her because I didn't understand it myself—but I realized I had better figure it out. Eventually, I did. What I learned is that you have to look ahead. You have to figure out how you're going to get the cash required to increase your sales at whatever rate you have in mind. If you don't, you run the risk of selling yourself into a corner. I'm talking about losing control of your situation, about decisions being taken away from you, about being forced to do extreme and unwise things just to stay alive. Going without pay is the least of it. Many people stop paying their withholding taxes, which is not only illegal but stupid. Between interest and penalties, there is no more expensive money in the world. Meanwhile, your creditors are banging on your head because you can't pay your bills in an orderly fashion. It's a nightmare.

So how do you plan for growth? More precisely, how do you determine the amount of additional cash needed to cover new sales? To begin with, you have to ask the right questions about the new business coming in:

1. How much is it, and over what time frame?
2. What's the gross margin?
3. How much overhead will you have to add?
4. How long will you have to wait to get paid?

If you know the answers to those four questions, you can make a rough estimate of how much extra cash you'll need.

I'll give you an example. Let's suppose you're anticipating that sales will increase by $100,000 over the next year. You have a gross margin of 30 percent, and you don't expect it to change because of the new business, but you know you'll have to add $10,000 in overhead—for commissions, bookkeeping, whatever. You further expect your average turn of receivables (collection time) to hold steady at, say, sixty days.

Here's what you do:

Start by figuring out your cost of goods sold (COGS) on the new business—the amount of money you'll have to lay out to produce or acquire whatever you're selling. Since your gross margin is 30 percent of sales, your COGS is 70 percent, or $70,000. Add to that the extra overhead you're going to need—$10,000—and you get $80,000 in new spending to fill $100,000 in new orders. Divide the total by the number of days in the period covered—in this case, 365—and you find out that the new business is costing you $219.18 per day. If you then multiply that number by the number of days it takes you to collect your receivables, you get an idea of your additional cash needs. For safety's sake I always increase the collection period by 20 percent, so in this example I'd multiply by 72 days instead of 60. The result: 72 days × $219.18 per day = $15,781.

Understand, this is a rough, down-and-dirty formula. Some people might say it makes a number of dubious assumptions—for instance, that you pay all your own bills at once. But forecasting is inexact by definition. You need some simple tools to guide you. This one allows you to make a reasonable guess about your future cash needs, and it errs on the side of caution, which is always a good idea.

What do you do with the information? You obviously aren't going to turn away good, high-margin business. So you look for ways to generate the additional cash. Maybe you can reduce the collection days on your current accounts. Maybe you can extend your payables by a week or two. Maybe you can make a deal with the new customers to get paid more quickly than usual. Or maybe you go to your major vendors and say, "Listen, I have great news for both of us. I just landed a new account that's going to bring in a lot more business, but I'll have to pay you in sixty days rather than forty. Can you handle that?" There are very few vendors who would say no.

As a last resort, you can always borrow the money, if you don't mind increasing your bank debt and adding to your costs. Then again, you may decide it's better to go without a salary for a few weeks. I myself haven't had to take that route in recent years and would prefer to avoid it in the future. I'm sure my wife feels the same way. She likes it when I get paid every week. So do I, for that matter. It gives us both a sense of being in control. In business, you can't be in control if you aren't on top of your cash flow. That's a lesson worth learning as early as possible.

Ask Norm

Dear Norm:

I'm an entertainer and a tennis professional with a sports-education business, teaching tennis through on-court musical tennis shows and specialty clinics. I want to grow the company, and I have the passion and the long-term vision to do it, but I don't have a business background. Do I have time to become a businessman, or do I need to find people to grow the business for me?

David

Dear David:

My guess is that you have many more business skills than you give yourself credit for. You have customers, don't you? You must have selling ability and marketing ability, and those are two of the most important skills a businessperson can have. OK, so you may not know accounting. That doesn't mean you can't learn the numbers, and it's the numbers you need to know, not the technicalities of accounting. My advice is to go ahead. There's only way to acquire business experience: you have go out there and take your lumps. You can't succeed without trying. At worst, you'll get a great education for your next business.

—Norm

The Ultimate Prize

In the end, of course, the payoff for building a business is the reward you get when you sell it. Unfortunately, many business owners miss out on that reward—or a big part of it—because they don't understand the factors that go into calculating it and don't keep the financial records that would allow them to get full value for what they've created. But that doesn't stop them from having grossly inflated notions of what their companies are worth.

The companies on *Inc.* magazine's annual list of the 500 fastest-growing private companies are prime examples. I've looked at some of the applications they submit. I remember one that had lost money on sales of about $60 million the previous year, and yet its owners thought it was worth between $50 million and $100 million. Evidently, they hadn't heard what happened to all those profitless Internet companies of the 1990s. Another company had a net profit of less than $335,000 on sales of about $6.5 million—which doesn't explain how the owners came to believe it was worth between $100 million and $200 million. In fact, I'd say that about half of the companies I've looked at reported absurdly high valuations. The rest were just extremely high.

I can easily understand how Inc. 500 CEOs, and former Inc. 500 CEOs, get such ideas. As a group, after all, we tend to have fairly large egos, which isn't entirely bad. You need one to grow a business fast enough to make the list. But our egos can get us in trouble when putting a dollar value on our businesses. We generally take the highest valuation we've heard of for a company somewhat like ours—and multiply it.

But it's not just the fast growers who think their companies are worth much more than they are. Consider a deal that was brought to my attention by my former partners in the document destruction business, Bob and Trace Feinstein. They'd heard about a smaller company that was looking to be acquired. The owner was asking for two times annual sales, or about $1.2 million. Since other document destruction companies had been selling for three times annual sales, Bob and Trace thought we ought to buy it. In fact, they were making the most common mistake in the book.

You can't value any company simply by looking at its sales. Yes, it's true that every industry has a rough rule of thumb for doing valuations, and usually it's expressed as a multiple of sales, but that's simply a matter of habit and convenience. What most buyers are interested in is something called free cash flow, and free cash flow is a function of profit, not sales.

As it turned out, the company Bob and Trace were talking about had very little profit at all. It consisted of a father and his son who had a truck with a shredder on it. All they cared about was earning a living, which they could accomplish by doing massive amounts of shredding at an extremely low price—6¢ per pound. They probably did all right for themselves, but the business had absolutely no value to a company like ours.

To begin with, it would cost us more than 6¢ a pound just to collect the paper and make sure the shredding was done in a secure manner—forget about any contribution to overhead. Of course, the father and son *could* forget about overhead: they didn't have any. They had no significant expenses above and beyond the cost of actually providing the service. As a result, they could get by without producing gross profit. But no business that does have overhead can survive without gross profit. It's the gross profit that covers the overhead expenses and provides the net profit you need to build the company and get a return on your investment. We would never consider buying a business without gross profit. We wouldn't even buy the father and son's customer list. Once we started charging realistic prices, the chances of our holding on to the customers would have been zero to none.

So how, you might ask, did the father and son ever get the notion that their business was worth $1.2 million? The same way most people do. When you hear that a company in your industry has sold for three times sales (or whatever), you naturally figure that your company must be worth something in that range, just as you're likely to think your house is worth approximately what the one down the street just sold for—even though you know nothing about what's in that house or why the buyer wanted it.

I finally cured myself of that tendency by talking to people interested in buying my company, and I'd recommend that other business owners do the same. You need to begin by understanding what potential buyers are looking for. That, of course, depends a lot on who the potential buyers are. Some companies do acquisitions for strategic reasons, some because they want to gain market share, some because they see a potential for synergy, and some because they want to boost their bottom line. Whatever may be driving them to do a deal, however, it's a safe bet that they will look first at your earnings before interest, taxes, depreciation, and amortization, or EBITDA. When you subtract from that number the minimum amount of new capital expenditures required each year (or CAPEX), you get a pretty good measure of free cash flow. That is, you see the amount of cash a company generates in a year after paying all of its operating costs and expenses and meeting its minimum new-capital requirements but before covering what it owes in taxes and interest (which the acquirer might not have to pay) and before deducting depreciation and amortization (which are accounting mechanisms reflecting the cost and life span of certain assets).

Assuming acquirers can determine your company's EBITDA, other factors then come into play. I say "assuming" because most small companies don't have audited financials and don't keep financial records good enough to let them even make a reasonable guess at EBITDA. Without that information, you probably won't be able to sell your business to a sophisticated acquirer, and you certainly won't get top dollar for it.

Let's suppose, however, that your company has nice, solid EBITDA and you can prove it. You're still not home-free. Acquirers will want to know where that EBITDA comes from. Do you have a broad, diverse base of customers? Have they signed long-term contracts with you? Are your prices in line with the market?

I know a guy in an industry where some companies are going for three or four times sales. He'd like to sell his business and can't understand why no one wants to buy it. The trouble is, he has a couple of big customers that contribute more than half of his sales, and they're paying through the nose. That can happen. Maybe an account has grown over time, and the customer isn't getting the discounts it's entitled to. Maybe the person it has overseeing the account is incompetent, or not doing the job properly. Whatever the reason, you make out like a bandit in the short run, but in the long run you have problems. As soon as the customer wakes up, you'll lose the business. If the account represents a large percentage of your sales, the loss could be devastating.

Smart acquirers will take note of the danger and discount your business accordingly—or maybe decide it's not worth buying.

But let's assume you have a well-run company. What you can get for it will probably be somewhere between five and ten times EBITDA. (I'm excluding Internet-based "concept" companies here, or at least those with the potential for explosive growth, which get valued according to a set of rules all their own.) The exact multiple depends on various factors, such as interest rates. As they go up—and money becomes more expensive—the multiple tends to fall. If they go down, the multiple usually rises. It can also be affected by the amount of competition among potential acquirers and the number of good businesses available, as well as other factors related to your particular company. Unused capacity, for example, might boost the price. But in the end it will be somewhere between five and ten times EBITDA no matter what industry you're in.

Why? Because what acquirers buy is the potential to make money in the future. The more money they're likely to make, the more money they're willing to pay. Conversely, the greater the risk that the cash flow will be cut off prematurely, the less they're willing to pay. Yet, as obvious as that may seem, it's not how people in your industry will talk about what an acquirer has paid for your company after you sell it. In fact, it's probably not how you'll talk about the price you got. Instead, you'll convert it into a multiple of sales or some other rule of thumb that everybody is familiar with. In the records storage industry, for example, we often hear that someone has sold a business for so many dollars per box. That may literally be true if the acquirer has bought only the accounts and the boxes that go with them, but if the whole business has been sold, the rule of thumb is just a form of shorthand. Regrettably, it gives people like the father and son shredding team the wrong idea about their company's value.

So did all this mean the father and son would never be able to sell their business? Not necessarily. I doubt any rational human being would ever have paid $1.2 million for it, but it could have had value to the right type of buyer, namely, a person much like themselves. The first question was, did the business generate enough cash for someone else to earn a living from it and still have money left over to make monthly payments to the father and son for, say, five or six years? The second question was, would that be a better deal for the buyer than simply starting from scratch? I can't answer those questions, but I hope that the father and son did before they made plans to retire on the money they would get from the sale of their business.

The Bottom Line

Point One: Whenever you launch a new business, keep track of your monthly sales and gross margins by hand until you have a good feel for them.

Point Two: Find the key number that tells you how your business is doing in real time, before you get the sales report.

Point Three: More sales usually mean less cash flow. Figure out your future cash needs while you still have time to address them.

Point Four: Understand EBITDA, and use a multiple of that—not sales—as the measure of your business's value.

CHAPTER SIX

The Art of the Deal

Before we go any further, I want to take some time to talk about negotiating, which is—as I'm sure you realize—a fundamental business skill. Indeed, much of business *is* negotiating. From the day you start thinking about having your own company to the day you cash out, you're involved in one negotiation after another. You may call it something else—"raising money," "selling," "leasing space," "hiring," "buying insurance," "getting a phone system," whatever—but you're negotiating every step of the way, and you'll pay a price if you don't recognize the process for what it is. Why? Because you'll be inflexible. You'll focus too much on your own needs, and you won't hear what the other party is saying. As a result, you'll miss opportunities to get better deals.

I can give you a fairly typical example that arose at one point when we had some unexpected delays in the construction of one of our warehouses. It became clear that the warehouse wouldn't be finished in time to accommodate all the new boxes we'd be getting in. We'd have to find additional storage space immediately, and not just any space. We needed a particular type of warehouse, one with very high ceilings; it had to be located within a few blocks of my facility; and we had to be able to move in at once.

I knew there were only a handful of places that could meet the first two conditions. As a result, I would be in a pretty tough negotiating position. Anyone who could meet all three would have me over a barrel. Had I been thinking only about finding the space, I might have been tempted to throw myself on the mercy of a real estate broker. But

I was also interested in getting as good a deal as possible, which ruled out that approach. If I wanted to get the space *and* a good deal, I'd need to negotiate.

The negotiation began with my call to the broker. That's a general rule: you start negotiating when you have your first interaction with an outside party. I told the broker my specifications and said I was willing to pay the going rate—about $5.00 per square foot. He said there were very few such places available in my area at any price.

I said, "Well, I'm also looking in other areas. See what you can come up with. I'd like to stay around here, but—if the price and terms are ridiculous—I'll go somewhere else."

This was at least partially a bluff. Going somewhere else was the last thing I wanted to do. Yes, I would have considered it if the price and terms were absolutely outrageous, and I was keeping an eye out for good deals in other parts of the city just in case. But I didn't want the real estate agent to know exactly how important it was for me to find space in the area. In a negotiating situation, you have to keep the other party guessing about your real needs and priorities, or you may not get what you want. If you do get it, you'll have to settle for a less attractive deal.

The broker called back a few days later. He said he'd found a place that met my requirements. Why didn't I take a look? I did. It was perfect. "This might be OK," I said to the broker. "What's the price?"

"The owner wants $6.50 per square foot and a five-year lease."

"Ridiculous," I said. "I won't pay over $4.75."

Again, I was bluffing. I'd have paid his price if I had to. My need was that urgent. But now I had another factor to consider. Our second warehouse was going to be ready within a few months. If I signed a five-year lease, I ran the risk of being stuck with too much capacity. So why did I focus on the money rather than the terms? It was a matter of strategy. That's another one of my rules: negotiate first about a secondary matter, understanding that—at the end of the process—you'll probably let the other party get most of what it wants on the issue in question. Your concession on the first negotiating point will give you additional bargaining power when you bring your number one issue to the table.

For the next few weeks, we haggled over price, with the broker serving as the go-between. Eventually, the landlord came down to $5.80 per square foot, and the broker told me he wouldn't go lower, since he already had two other tenants paying that rate. I said, "Well, there are other issues involved here. Maybe he and I ought to sit down and talk."

A face-to-face meeting of the principals is always a crucial point in a negotiating process, and most people blow it by concentrating all of their attention on getting what they want. Negotiating is give-and-take. To get what you want, you first have to find out what the other party wants. There's only one way to do that—by listening. I make sure I listen by following two more of my negotiating rules. The first is: don't go in with any preconceived notions. By that, I mean don't make any assumptions about what the other party is thinking. Right or wrong, your assumptions will cloud your mind and keep you from hearing what's being said.

The second rule is: always assume that everyone else in the room is smarter than you. If you get the idea you can outsmart other people, you stop paying attention to them. So I bring a yellow pad with me to negotiating sessions. On the fourth or fifth page, I write the word *dummy* three times. Whenever I catch myself thinking how brilliant I am, I open the pad to that page, give myself a silent whack, and go back to listening.

The landlord didn't follow my rules. In fact, he didn't come to negotiate. He walked in and immediately started talking about the price. He said he wouldn't even consider anything less than $5.80 per square foot for the space. It was his rock-bottom offer. He had two other customers who were paying $5.80 already, and he wasn't going to budge. Period. End. In addition, he said, he wanted a five-year lease.

I listened and heard exactly what he was saying. The price was nonnegotiable—but we could discuss the five-year lease.

That was all the room I needed. I said, "Listen, I think $5.80 is too much, but let's put it aside for a second. Let's talk about the terms of the lease. I can't make a five-year commitment. There are too many uncertainties in my business right now."

I explained my situation. He said, "OK, but I want the $5.80."

I said, "Well, if that's what you have to get, I suppose I can live with it, as long as you let me have a chance to get out of this lease at some point." In the end, he agreed to give me an option to void the lease after seven months, and I agreed to pay him $5.80 per square foot. It was a fair deal. We both got what we wanted most.

But the landlord could have done better if he'd approached the meeting differently. He should have come in prepared to listen. He should have forced me to talk first. He should have opened by saying, "Nice meeting you, Mr. Brodsky. I understand you've talked to our real estate agent, who has explained the terms of the lease. Are you ready to sign?"

I'd have said I thought the price was ridiculous. He'd have insisted that he couldn't charge me less than his other tenants. Then I'd have brought up the five-year term of the lease. At that point, he could have cut the discussion off, saying, "Do we have to go through every line in this contract? First, you want to talk about price. Then you want to talk about terms. Next, you'll want to discuss the heating and air-conditioning. Either we have a deal or we don't!"

He would have put me on the defensive. He would have called my bluff. I might still have been able to get a cancellation option out of him, but I'd have had to pay for it. Instead, he gave it to me for nothing—and I walked away with what was, in effect, a short-term lease for the same price that people with long-term leases were paying.

The upside for the landlord, I suppose, was that he had a happy customer. What's more, my circumstances subsequently changed, and we wound up staying for the full five years of the lease and then some. Fifteen years later, we were still there, and we were leasing more than twice as much space as we'd had to begin with. So it turned out to be a good deal for us all.

Ask Norm

Dear Norm:

I've often heard that there's a point in every negotiation when the next person who talks loses. I'm trying to land a large account I want very badly. I've made a proposal, and my contact has passed it along to his financial people. He's supposed to come back with a counteroffer. I've called him twice, and he hasn't had the information. I know that he thinks we can provide his company with savings it can pass along to its customers. He was planning to give one of his customers the savings info at a meeting coming up shortly. Should I call him before the meeting or wait for him to make the next move?

    Daniel

Dear Daniel:

If I followed that rule about not talking first, there would be dead silence in many of my negotiations. I don't think you should worry about losing the negotiation as much as landing the customer—if not now, then later. The question is, why isn't your contact calling you back? Some people are embarrassed to deliver bad news. You need to make it easy for them, or you'll never find out what the problems were. If I were you, I'd wait until the deadline passed and then leave him a voice mail saying, "I realize the meeting was yesterday, and I just want you to know that we're still interested in working with you in the future, even if the answer on this deal is no. So please give me a call."

    —Norm

The Detective Habit

I don't mean to suggest that successful negotiating is all about strategy. After all, how do you choose the right strategy? Experience plays a role, as does instinct, but most important, I believe, are those habits of mind I mentioned in the introduction—especially the habit of questioning what you see on the surface, examining the underlying elements, digging to find out what's really going on. That habit allowed me to make the best purchase of my life.

My business, as you may know, is located on the Brooklyn side of the East River, directly across from midtown Manhattan. Our first warehouses occupied most of one block. Alongside that site were 588,000 square feet of undeveloped waterfront land. For years, I'd wanted to buy the block next to mine (172,000 square feet) and build a new warehouse on it, but it wasn't available. Then suddenly, in the fall of 1999, all 588,000 square feet came on the market just as I was getting ready to close a deal on some real estate a couple miles away. I immediately put that deal on hold and began looking into the possibility of buying the land next door.

On the face of it, I didn't have a chance. The land, though relatively cheap by Manhattan standards, was way out of my price range. What's more, there was bound to be competition. I knew that a lot of people would be interested in an opportunity to buy waterfront property zoned for commercial development and located in the heart of the city, with a panoramic view of the Manhattan skyline. If there was a bidding war, I'd lose.

But that was, as I said, on the face of it. Was a bidding war inevitable? Not necessarily. Most people assume that money is always the key factor in a sale. In fact, many other issues come into play, and some of them may be more important than money. Only the seller can tell you for certain which ones will be decisive.

Then again, sellers are often reluctant to give out that information—for the same reason I didn't want the warehouse landlord to know my priorities. It's always better to keep the other side guessing. In this case, moreover, the seller was a bank based in the Netherlands that had an office in Iowa. A real estate agent was handling the deal. I knew the agent wanted to sell the property for as much as possible, but what did the bank want? Maybe the obvious answer—a lot of money—wasn't the correct one.

Fortunately, I had on my staff two people, Ben and Sam, who had experience in these matters. (See chapter 15.) Ben tracked down the banker responsible for the property and let him know we were interested. "So is everybody else," the banker said. "Get in line."

"But our offer is real," Ben said.

"I have a lot of real offers from companies bigger than yours," the banker said. "Where's your financing? I'm getting sick and tired of not being able to close this deal."

It turned out that the bank had given a mortgage on the land to a guy who'd defaulted in the late 1980s. The bank's attorneys had tried to foreclose, but the buyer blocked them for years with various legal maneuvers. After finally taking possession of the property, the bank had signed a contract to sell it to a developer, subject to certain conditions. When the conditions weren't met, the sale fell through. "I'm not going through that again," the banker said.

Although the banker didn't name a price, it was apparent that the size of the offer wasn't the primary issue in his mind. The bank had already contracted to sell the property once for a lot of money and been burned. I thought about what the banker had said. What he really wanted, I decided, was a deal that was absolutely certain and that would close fast, preferably before December 31, when his bosses would total up his numbers for the year and see how well he'd done. My guess was that we could get the land for 20 percent less than its market value if we could communicate our willingness to satisfy what I thought were the banker's biggest concerns.

By *communicate*, I don't mean "*talk*." The banker wasn't going to believe mere words. We were going to need rock-solid financing, and we'd have to put down at least 10 percent of the bid as a deposit. To demonstrate our commitment, moreover, we'd have to make a significant portion of the deposit nonrefundable.

Sam and I contacted the investment company we knew in Washington, D.C., Allied Capital. What we wanted was a letter of commitment for the full amount of the bid. I asked the investors to come in as partners. We'd buy the land together; I'd keep the block next to mine for the new warehouse; then we'd sell off the remaining 416,000 square feet, and the investors would keep the proceeds. I'd get the land I wanted, and they'd get a substantial profit. The investors agreed, provided I met two conditions: I had to put up the nonrefundable portion of the deposit, and I had to find someone else to come in as a partner and commit to buying a portion of the remaining land.

Finding that partner proved easier than I expected. I called a friend of mine who owned a business in the neighborhood. His land had recently been rezoned for housing, which had made it much more valuable. "Yeah, sure," he said, "I'd buy some of your property in a second. I'm going to sell my land anyway, and I'd like to stay in the area."

So all the pieces were in place. We could make an offer and close the deal fast. As long as the title was valid, we didn't have to attach any more conditions. Other bidders would probably insist on doing an environmental study and an appraisal, but I knew that an environmental study had been done recently. I had a copy of it. As for the appraisal, I'd just had one done on my own land next door. Why would I need another?

In October, my partners and I submitted our bid and asked the bank to name its conditions. The next day, a purchase-and-sale agreement arrived, with a closing date in thirty days. We were instructed to sign and return the contract with a 10 percent deposit, all of it nonrefundable. Those terms weren't acceptable, but they confirmed my assessment of the bank's priorities. What's more, we were prepared. We offered to close in sixty days, instead of thirty days, and insisted that only a quarter of the 10 percent deposit be nonrefundable. After a week or so of tweaking, the agreement was signed. Sixty days later we owned the land.

I'm sure that the other bidders were surprised. At least one of them, a major utility, had offered 20 percent more than we had, and I suspect there were others that had put in even higher bids. Immediately after we closed the deal, people began coming to us wanting to buy the unsold portion of the property for twice as much as we paid for the entire site.

Even the bank's attorney was baffled by our success. "How did you get this deal?" he asked us. We just smiled.

Once the sale closed, the friend I'd brought in got his 25 percent, and we eventually built warehouses on our 25 percent. The rest we wound up selling to the Trust for Public Land, so that it could be turned into a state park.

Don't Worry, Be a Little Unhappy

In a perfect world, all negotiations would end like the ones I've mentioned—with both sides walking away happy to have achieved its most important goals. But the world isn't perfect, and not all negotiations are amicable ones. Take the dispute I got into with one of our suppliers a while back, a company that handles long-haul shipping for my delivery company. We were paying the supplier in thirty days, but—because of its billing procedures and banking arrangements—it wasn't actually getting the cash for almost fifty days. The guy we were dealing with at the shipping company told us we had to pay faster. We said it wasn't our fault that it took so long for him to get the cash. If he needed the money sooner, he should speed up his billing process and change banks. We argued back and forth for a while. Then the guy announced he was going to hold on to one of our shipments until we paid $6,700 that he said was past due.

I was furious. Understand, I'd been working with these people for a long time. I'd been a good customer. I'd sent them a lot of business. Now, instead of negotiating a reasonable settlement to our dispute, they were holding my shipment hostage, forcing me to choose between paying their ransom and jeopardizing our relationship with a customer. That wasn't fair. When I tried to complain to the shipping company's owner, he wouldn't return my phone calls. So I asked my people how much we owed the supplier altogether. It was about $13,000. I said, "OK, pay the $6,700 and get the shipment released. Then don't give them another dime. Let them sue us for it. We will never, ever do business with these people again."

Unfortunately, those kinds of disputes happen all the time in business. They go with the territory. A customer, a supplier, an employee, a competitor, a partner—every now and then someone delivers a low blow that hits you where it really hurts, and you get angry. So what do you do? Call a lawyer, of course. That's what I did for the first twenty years I was in business. I didn't think twice about suing people who'd done me wrong, or forcing them to sue me. Compromise was not in my vocabulary. Once you crossed the line, forget about it. You became the enemy. I was willing to duke it out in court no matter what the cost.

It took the experience of going through bankruptcy to knock some sense into me. After I filed for protection from creditors, there was a series of hearings to determine whether my bank would be allowed to close me down. I was in violation of my loan covenants, and the bank wanted out. My only hope lay in the bankruptcy code. Under Chapter 11, I could petition the court to order that my arrangement with the bank continue as before, in effect forcing the bank to keep lending us money. With some six hundred jobs at stake, I figured I had a strong case—so strong that I didn't even consider trying to negotiate a new deal with the bank. I was certain I would win.

The judge had a different idea. At the end of the first morning's arguments, she announced that she was leaning toward deciding in favor of the bank. I was shocked. I was panicked. I was about to lose my company. Out in the hallway, I went up to the bank's lawyers and offered to do a deal. They wouldn't even listen. "You heard the judge," they said.

That afternoon, there were more arguments—and the judge surprised us again. "At this point, I'm inclined to grant the plaintiff's motion," she said as we were getting ready to adjourn for the day. "We'll continue this hearing in the morning." On the way out, the bank's lawyers said they'd reconsidered and were ready to talk after all, but now I was in no hurry to settle.

The next day was a repeat performance. I finally realized that the judge was sending us a message: she wanted us to negotiate our own deal. During one of the breaks, my lawyer and I sat down with the bank's lawyers and hammered out an agreement that neither side liked very much, but that we both could accept. Back in the courtroom, we informed the judge of the deal. She looked at me and said, "Mr. Brodsky, you understand now, don't you?"

I said, "I understand what you were doing, but I don't know why you did it."

"Then let me explain," she said. "The best deal in the world is

Ask Norm

Dear Norm:

For eight months I've been negotiating a licensing agreement with a company to produce a toy I've invented. The process has been painfully slow. I'd send a proposal in; the company would ask for changes. I'd compromise. The company would ask for more changes; I'd compromise again. At one point, my contact insisted on taking the contract to a lawyer—who tore it apart. So we started all over again. After several more months of this, I received a fax demanding a whole new set of changes. I couldn't believe it. I'm beginning to think that my negotiating partner isn't serious. Whenever we get close to signing, he comes up with more stuff to change. At what point should I give up and move on to another manufacturer?
  John

Dear John:
You shouldn't be surprised at what's happened. Good negotiators always try to get the best deals for their company by taking as many bites of the apple as the other party will allow. Your problem is that you let the other side set the ground rules. You should have insisted up front on separating business issues from legal issues and not letting lawyers raise business issues after they've been settled. I'd advise you to tell your contact something like, "I'm sorry, but I've gone as far as I can at this time. I still think that your company is best for my product, but you're leaving me no alternative other than to look elsewhere. Maybe I'll find out I'm being unrealistic. If so, I may come back." If the guy says you can't come back, he probably wouldn't have done the deal anyway.
  —Norm

when everybody walks away a little unhappy. You're not going to get everything you want here, Mr. Brodsky, and neither is the bank. I could tell you what to do, but isn't it better if you work it out by yourselves?"

For me, it was a revelation—probably because she was talking to me at a point in my life when I was ready to listen. In any case, her words changed my entire approach to handling disputes. Prior to that day in September 1988, I must have been involved in forty lawsuits, many of which went all the way to trial. Since then, I haven't had a single dispute wind up in the courts.

Good things happen when you accept the idea of walking away from a dispute a little unhappy. You stop letting your emotions dictate your business decisions. You don't get caught up in anger, or revenge. You look for solutions instead of problems. You start to think about outcomes you can live with, rather than trying to get everything you want. In the process, you save yourself a lot of money. I'm not talking only about the legal fees, either. Even more costly is the time you spend thinking about a lawsuit, meeting about it, worrying about it—not to mention getting deposed and sitting in court. When you look at the numbers, it almost never pays to use lawyers to resolve disputes.

Which brings me back to the dispute I had with the long-distance shipping company. The supplier's people said I owed them another $6,500. I said that, by holding up a shipment, they'd violated our contract and damaged my relationship with a customer, and I shouldn't have to pay them anything. It would have cost each side at least $10,000 to go to trial. When the dust settled, even the winner would have been several thousand dollars out of pocket. Meanwhile, we would have endured months of aggravation and countless distractions from what we should have been doing, namely, building our respective businesses.

At first, the shipping company's owner didn't get it. He hired a lawyer who threatened to take me to court. I called the lawyer and made what I said was a onetime offer to settle the case for $3,500. I knew that I was in control. After all, I could always pay the full $6,500, without incurring any additional expenses. Meanwhile, the shipping company had lost a good customer and run up a legal bill. We eventually settled for the $3,500—and both walked away a little unhappy.

The Bottom Line

Point One: Listening is the most important part of any negotiation. Make sure you hear what is really being said.

Point Two: Go in with no preconceptions, and always assume that the other side is smarter than you.

Point Three: Develop the habit of questioning what you see on the surface and digging to find out what's really going on.

Point Four: In an adversarial negotiation, the best deal is one that leaves both sides a little unhappy.

CHAPTER SEVEN

It Begins with a Sale

As I mentioned in the introduction, my father had various expressions that encapsulated his business philosophy and shaped mine. They were all great, but there was one in particular that became my all-time favorite and had the biggest impact on my approach to business: "You don't ask, you don't get." Therein lies the secret to becoming a good salesperson.

Let me tell you a story. A few years ago, my wife, Elaine, and I attended a big dinner at which Al Gore—who was still vice president then—was the guest of honor. There must have been a couple thousand people in the banquet hall, most of whom had come in hopes of meeting Gore. We had, too, but we were sitting at a table way off to one side, separated from the vice president by several hundred other guests and a contingent of security guards and Secret Service agents. After we finished the main course, I stood up from the table. "Where are you going?" Elaine asked.

"I'm going to speak to the vice president," I said.

Now understand, there was no objective reason to believe I'd be able to get anywhere near the man. I had no better claim to his time than 1,999 other people, and the Secret Service wasn't letting anybody through. But I didn't think about the odds of succeeding. If I had, I probably wouldn't have tried. I was just going by my father's precept: you don't ask, you don't get.

I walked up to the vice president's table. A security guard stopped me. "You can't go there," he said.

"Al's a friend," I said. "I just want to say hello." At that moment, the vice president looked over at me. I waved, and he waved back. "See, he's waving at me," I said. The guard turned around, saw Gore waving, and let me in.

I sat down next to the vice president and began to chat with him, at which point Elaine and my friend Erwin walked up to the guard. I said, "Mr. Vice President, that's my wife and a close friend of ours. Would you mind letting them in, too?"

He called out to the security guard, "Those two people are OK." So we all talked to the vice president for a few minutes, then shook his hand and left. Meanwhile, there were dozens of other couples lining up to see him, but the guard wouldn't allow any of them through.

I do that sort of thing all the time. A lot of people think it takes nerve, but nerve doesn't enter the picture. You need nerve only when you're afraid of being rejected. I have no fears and no expectations in those situations. My attitude is, I'll give it a shot and see what happens. If I get what I want, great. If not, well, I can laugh, and smile, and walk away. The secret is an attitude, a philosophy that's summed up in that expression, "You don't ask, you don't get." It took me a long time to understand exactly what the phrase meant. Eventually, I figured out that it was all about losing your fear of asking. You realize that you'll never get anything unless you ask for it, and so you might as well try. In the process, you accept the fact that you're going to get turned down fairly often. The surprise is that you get turned down a lot less frequently than you'd ever imagine.

So I developed certain habits that proved extremely valuable when I finally went into business. Among other things, my father's principle helped me become a pretty good salesperson, since I wasn't afraid of getting *no* for an answer. You always hear that salespeople have to overcome their fear of rejection, but the concept of rejection didn't enter my mind. Even in doing cold-calling, I never felt as though I'd been rejected when I failed to make a sale. I'd just think, "That didn't work. I'll have to try something else." A *no* was nothing more than an opportunity that didn't happen. I didn't take it personally, and I didn't get upset.

That's a tremendous advantage in business. I learned that, with such a mind-set, you can get more sales and negotiate better deals because you don't stop asking. You don't restrict yourself. Yes, you're polite. You listen carefully. You try not to offend people by being overly aggressive. On the other hand, you don't back off. You're willing to keep going until the other party balks—which is the only way to be sure you've gone far enough. What's more, you're not shy about enlisting other people to help you build your business. You have no qualms about going to friends, associates, suppliers, whoever, and asking for referrals and leads. Of course, you then have a responsibility to do the same for them, so you have to be a little careful. You don't want to recommend people to a customer unless you have confidence that they'll do a good job. But I have great confidence in a lot of my colleagues, and they've always delivered for me. My three biggest customers have come from a person I exchanged leads with.

It's really my father I have to thank, however. He was the one who inculcated in me the habits and lessons that have allowed me to thrive in business.

What Business Are You *Really* In?

Of course, there's a little bit more to selling than simply asking for the sale, as important as that may be. There's also the need to figure out what exactly you have that people might want to buy. That means figuring out what business you are really in, which isn't always obvious on the surface.

My friend Mike once told me a story that illustrates the point beautifully. He grew up on the south shore of Long Island, where his father owned a fish restaurant. The fish came from a company owned by a guy named Fred, who supplied numerous restaurants in the region. One day Mike was talking to Fred about his business. "You want to know why I'm successful?" Fred asked.

"Because you sell to a lot of restaurants?" Mike replied.

"No," Fred said, "because I know what business I'm in."

"You're in the fish business," Mike said.

"Not exactly," said Fred. "I'm really in the banking business. I make loans to restaurants in the form of fish. You see, a restaurant is a seasonal business. Like any good banker, I know when my customers are short of cash, and I know when they're busy. I carry them during the slow periods and collect after they've had a big week. They pay me not only for the fish but for the credit I extend to them. I build the cost of the credit into my price."

Unconventional as Fred's perspective on his business may seem, his experience is not unique. Companies often become successful for reasons that aren't obvious at first glance, and smart entrepreneurs understand that. They know they have to think differently about the business in order to distinguish themselves from their competitors. It's part of the process you go through to define your niche. Once you've determined what business you're really in, you can use that knowledge to build a solid customer base in even the most competitive markets.

My records storage business is a case in point. When I started it back in 1991, I thought I was getting into a typical service business. As I noted earlier, my strategy was to offer competitive prices and to bring customers in by promising great service, state-of-the-art technology, and easy access to our warehouse. At the time, there were very few records storage companies that could provide all three of those benefits.

I thought we had a dynamite pitch, but it turned out to be a dud. We quickly discovered that our technology and location weren't as important to customers as I thought. They cared mainly about getting a box back when they needed it. Where we stored it and how we kept track of it were our concerns, not theirs. As for service, who doesn't promise great service? Until you've been in business for a while, moreover, you can't offer testimonials or any other proof that your service is different from anybody else's.

So we weren't able to move people with the three levers we'd been counting on. On top of that, we found that most potential customers were already signed up to long-term contracts, and those contracts included a standard provision under which the customers would be charged a so-called removal fee for every box they permanently removed from the storage company. In effect, customers agreed up front to pay a substantial bounty if they ever decided to switch suppliers. I had great confidence in our service, but those were huge obstacles. We couldn't get potential customers to pay attention to us, I realized, unless we could offer them a way out of their contracts and a significantly lower price.

Now, normally I don't like competing on price. It's a dangerous game. For openers, low price can connote poor quality. People wonder whether you can really provide the benefits you're promising and, if so, for how long. Competitors will use your pricing against you, telling customers you're fly-by-night and can't survive. In fact, you may not be able to survive if your gross margins are too thin. By the time you realize that, it may be too late. If customers have come to you only because you're cheap, they're likely to leave when you raise prices.

On the other hand, I have no qualms about offering a lower price than my competitors do if my costs are lower as well. Not that I'd ever compete strictly on price—I'd also sell the quality of my service—but I don't mind using a lower price to get my foot in the door, provided I have the kind of gross margins I need to be successful. So how could I get better gross margins than my competitors in the records storage business? I realized I had to look at the business differently. I had to ask myself, "What business am I really in?"

The answer came to me out of the blue: real estate. We weren't just storing records; we were renting space in our warehouse to boxes. And how do you get more rent out of a building? By fitting more rental spaces into it. If we could accommodate more boxes per square foot than our competitors, we could charge less per box and still have better gross margins. So we found a warehouse with very high ceilings and put up racks that allowed us to make full use of the space.

Meanwhile, I kept trying to think like a real estate person. I asked myself what I'd do if I had a brand-new office building in a cold market.

How would I attract tenants? For one thing, I might offer rent concessions. If tenants signed a five-year lease, I might give them six months
free. Or suppose a prospective tenant had a year left on its lease in
another building. I might pay off the lease or offer the tenant a year's
free rent in my place. And what if the tenant had good credit but was
short on cash? I might agree to build out the space and increase the
rent to cover the cost of the build-out.

Those were all tactics I could use in the records storage business, I realized. I could treat the removal fees like build-out costs, for
example. If a customer wanted to switch to us, I might work out a deal
whereby we'd cover the removal fees at the other storage company and
make it up later by charging higher rates per box. We started applying
those techniques, and the business grew like crazy. Our competitors
went wild. They told customers, "Brodsky's nuts. He can't survive. He
won't be around in two years."

My response was to bring the customers to my warehouse. I'd say,
"You're probably wondering how we can offer you lower prices than
anyone else." They'd nod. "Well, look at the height of our ceilings,"
I'd say. "We get more than 150,000 boxes per 10,000 square feet. Our
competitors get 40,000 or 50,000. Our warehouse holds three or four
times as much as theirs. So I'm really overcharging you."

The customers would laugh and ask for a price break. I'd laugh and
say, "No, that's what we have to charge—because we provide so many
other services. . . ." Then I'd go on from there.

Thinking differently about our business turned out to be the key
to our success. Just like Fred, the fish distributor, we thrived because
we'd figured out what business we were really in. Less than ten years
later we had one of the largest independent records storage companies in the country. Of course, success brings its own problems. Many
of our competitors eventually adopted the same approach—building
bigger warehouses, paying removal fees up front. We'd had our own
little niche, defined by the way we looked at the business, and now it
was gone. We and our competitors were all in the real estate business
together.

Ask Norm

Dear Norm:
My partner, Jon, and I have a two-year-old technology start-up.
Our problem is that neither one of us is a salesperson. Jon is
an engineer, and I'm a systems analyst. I'd rather have den-
tal surgery without Novocain than go out and sell. So we need
a salesperson, but I'm worried about hiring someone who will
give away the store. We offer a one-year, complete-satisfaction-
or-your-money-back guarantee. If we wind up buying too much
back, we'll go out of business. With our reputation at stake, we
can't afford to go the gold-chains-red-sports-car route. How
can we make sure we get the right type of salesperson?
  Eric

Dear Eric:
You need to begin by recognizing that you are, in fact, the best
salesperson for your product. You know it better than anyone
else, and you have a passion for it. You probably have trouble
making the initial contact with prospective customers. Fine.
Hire someone to do that for you. Look for a personable individual who is good at cold-calling, turning up leads, and identifying prospects—and who can deal with the hardest part of
selling, namely, rejection. Let that person bring you prospects
who are prequalified and ready to buy. You'll become the
closer. That way, you'll have control over their expectations.
  —Norm

A Niche in Time

That sort of thing is not unusual. Niches come and go, and—contrary
to popular belief—most companies don't start out in one. You generally discover the niche *after* you've launched the company, not before.

It's not uncommon, in fact, to find that the business you wind up in is not the business you thought you were going into—because you never know for sure how to make money in any business until you've actually tried it. I'm talking about rolling up your sleeves, heading into the market, and beginning to sell. Once you do that, funny things start to happen. You run into unexpected obstacles. You stumble across surprising opportunities. You may discover that your original plan was so far off, you have to come up with an entirely new approach.

That's pretty much what happened to me with my first business, Perfect Courier. When I started out in 1979, I thought I was going into the messenger service business. It was a highly competitive industry at the time, with between 300 and 400 messenger companies in New York City alone. I quickly discovered that the only way I could count on making sales was to come in at a cheap price. The problem was, we couldn't survive by competing on price, and I didn't want to be in a low-margin business anyway. I realized I had to either find another path or get out.

Then, one day, I was pitching our service to the manager of a big advertising agency called Scali McCabe Sloves, who wasn't very receptive. "We're really happy with the people we use now," he said. "What can you do for us that they can't do?"

"What problems do you have?" I asked.

"The only problem we have is in our accounting department," he said. "The billing is a nightmare."

"How's that?" I asked.

"We have a heck of a time matching up the customers with the deliveries."

Like many professional-service firms, Scali McCabe charged the cost of a pickup or a delivery back to the customer on whose behalf it was made. Whenever people from the agency called for a messenger, they were supposed to give the dispatcher an account code to note on the delivery ticket. The messenger company then bundled the tickets together and included them with the bill it sent to the agency every week. It was up to the agency's accounting department to sort out the tickets and figure out the total charges for each account.

I asked to meet with the people in the accounting department, who were delighted to tell me about the system and all the headaches it engendered. I said, "Look, we can solve this problem for you. We've got a brand-new IBM-32 computer. Give me fifty of these delivery tickets, any fifty, and I'll show you what we can do."

Those were all truthful statements. We had, in fact, acquired an IBM-32 computer. But whether we could use it to solve the charge-back problem, I had no idea. Remember, this was before the micro-computer revolution. We couldn't just go out and buy the appropriate software. When we wanted our IBM-32 to perform a specific function, we had to have programs written especially for us. The programmers I spoke to about this particular matter weren't so sure they could produce what we needed. Nevertheless, I was determined to come up with a solution. I gave the fifty tickets to the best typist in our office and told her to create a bill from them, with the individual charges grouped according to the agency's account codes. We must have done twenty versions before we got it just right. Then I took it to Scali McCabe's accounting people.

They loved it. They said, "It's fantastic, but can you change a few things?"

I said, "We can do anything you like."

The accounting people were thrilled. They went to the manager who'd turned us down and said they wanted the agency to hire us, provided that we made the changes they'd requested and, of course, that our service was good. The manager called me. "Listen," he said, "I feel an obligation to the people we've been using. I don't want to dump them without giving them an opportunity to do the same thing you're promising. Can I show them this sample bill you've put together for us?"

I said, "Sure. Absolutely."

A few days later he called me back. "They say you can't do this," he said. "They say it's impossible."

"We can do it," I said. "We just need a little time to set up."

"How much?"

"Three weeks."

"OK," he said, "you've got three weeks. Then we'll run an experiment for one week. At the end of the week, we'll decide who gets the account."

Now we had to get the computer programmed, and the programmers weren't making any promises. Our fallback position was to produce the bills on a typewriter, which would have been extremely expensive. Fortunately, we didn't have to go that route. The program worked, the test went well, and we wound up with the whole account, boosting our sales from $10,000 to $35,000 a month.

And that was just the beginning. The new billing system quickly became our mainstay—our "core competency," as it were. For a while at least, it was the one thing we had that our competitors couldn't offer, and by the time they caught up, we had a foothold in the market and were known for providing that service. Indeed, it defined us as a business. It determined who our customers were, how much we could charge, how we went about selling, what additional expenses we provided, and so on.

Technically, we were still a messenger company, but only in the sense that we delivered things and charged according to the number of deliveries we made. What we sold—what our customers bought—was our ability to solve their charge-back problems. Without even realizing it, we had moved from messenger service into information processing, and we rode that business all the way to the Inc. 500 for three successive years.

That's another example of the importance of being flexible when you're starting out. It's equally important to remain flexible after you've built your company. No niche lasts forever. If it's a profitable one, it's going to attract competitors sooner or later. Other companies will start copying what you do. The more profitable the niche is, the faster it happens. When it does, you lose the advantage that defines your niche, namely, the ability to offer something other suppliers don't have. At that point, you need to find another niche—unless your business is well-enough established by then to operate without one. How? By building a great reputation.

Ask Norm

Dear Norm:

What should I do about an unethical competitor? I recently opened a service business that has been very successful, but our success has drawn the attention of a large established company in town, which is taking aim at us with marketing materials that misrepresent our service and professionalism. These people have played dirty before. I'd like to think their practices would catch up with them, but that hasn't happened yet, and I'm afraid they have so much cash they can outlast the rest of us. Any advice?

> *Rob*

Dear Rob:

Yes. Don't lose your focus. Provide great service at competitive prices and develop a reputation as the class act in town. Give prospects the names of customers they can call to check you out. Above all, don't bad-mouth your competitor, even if it's bad-mouthing you. Customers will think less of you if you do. That's an iron rule in my company. If I'm asked about a competitor I consider unethical, I say only, "I don't think they can provide the type of service you want." People get the message. If your competitor doesn't mend its ways, it will be the loser in the long run.

> —Norm

Your Good Name

So what exactly do I mean by *reputation*? I'm talking about what people think of the way you do business, how they assess your character as a businessperson. Do you compete fairly? Do you run a nice, clean operation? Do you treat your employees well? Do you go around bad-mouthing other companies in the industry, or do you speak about them with respect? Those are all factors that help to shape your business reputation, which in turn affects your ability to hire people, attract customers, get financing, make deals, and do everything else that goes into building a successful company.

I've long believed that a good reputation is the most valuable asset you can have in business. What's odd is the role your competitors play in creating one. Their opinion, I believe, counts more than the view of any other group—because of their credibility within the industry and with potential customers. Competitors have a unique perspective of you and your company. They face the same pressures and have to make the same choices that you do. If you have the respect of your competitors, you probably deserve it. If they think you're a lowlife, you could be headed for trouble.

So it's important to act in a way that's going to earn their respect. Not that you shouldn't compete as aggressively as possible, but you need to play by the rules. Which rules? I have three:

1. Never bad-mouth a competitor. When I compete for an account, I always ask which other suppliers the prospective customer is considering. Most prospects name the same two or three records storage companies, our major competitors. "Those are all fine companies," I say, "and you're going to be happy if you choose any one of us. Of course, I think you'll be happiest with my company." Then I talk about our strong points, taking care not to say anything negative about the other companies. To be sure, the customer occasionally includes on the list a company I don't hold in such high regard. In that case, I simply say, "Well, that firm isn't really a competitor of ours, but the others we compete against all the time, and they're very good. I just think we're better, and here's why."

2. Don't be a sore loser. It's always tough when a competitor takes a customer away from you, especially if the account is a big one. You get angry. You can't help it. But you have to remind yourself that you never know what the future holds. The people you deal with at the account may not agree with the decision to switch suppliers; if they go to work somewhere else, they could bring you another customer. Even the customer you just lost could come back again someday, provided you keep your cool. In any case, you can only hurt yourself by letting your anger show. No matter how upset I may feel inside, I make sure we treat our customers as well when they leave as we do when they come in. I want them to remember us as a class act all the way, and I want our competitors to hear about it.

3. Always be accommodating. There are times when we have to deal directly with competitors—for example, when a customer is moving into or out of our warehouse. That's an opportunity for us to send our competitors a message. Even if someone is taking a big account away from us, we're as nice as can be. We acquiesce to the other company's schedule and handle the process however the competitor wants us to. We're equally accommodating when we're moving a new customer out of a competitor's facility. We tell our drivers to be patient if they're kept waiting, as they often are. They can take all day if they have to. We don't want to provoke any fights or arguments, and we don't want to rub salt in a competitor's wound.

Now, I'm sure some people will ask, "What's the payoff for following those rules?" Often, I admit, it's hard to quantify, but every now and then I get direct confirmation of the importance of having our competitors' respect. Years ago, for example, I received a call from a lawyer representing an anonymous client in the records storage business. The client had asked him to find out if I'd be interested in acquiring its accounts. "How did they get my name?" I asked.

"To tell the truth, I don't know," the lawyer replied.

I insisted on meeting with the lawyer, who even then wouldn't divulge his client's identity. He did say, however, that he'd been told there were about 200,000 boxes involved. At the time, I had about a million boxes in my warehouse, so 200,000 was an interesting number. I told the lawyer we should keep talking.

Over the next two months, the lawyer and I negotiated the terms of a possible deal—how much my company would pay per box, when we'd take over an account, and so on. Although the lawyer still wouldn't identify the seller, I could tell from the average account size and the billing method that it wasn't one of our principal competitors. Most likely, it was an older moving-and-storage company. I also learned that five potential acquirers had been contacted initially. Through the negotiating process, the seller had whittled that group down to three companies, then two. Finally, the lawyer called and told me that we'd been selected to do the deal, but the seller wanted to meet with me first.

He turned out to be a guy named Jack, whose family owned two or three moving-and-storage businesses in Manhattan. We'd taken some clients away from him in the past, and he'd liked the way we handled the transfer. He'd also checked us out with other people in the industry—our competitors. That's how we'd wound up on the first list of potential acquirers. We survived the next cut because we were more flexible than our largest competitor. Jack was very protective of his customers, many of whom had been with the company since his father had run it. He put a lot of conditions on the sale, which we had no trouble agreeing to. Our giant competitor wouldn't bend its own rules to fit Jack's, and so it was dropped from the list.

In the end, the choice came down to us and a company we constantly compete against. We won that round because of our financial strength. It turned out that the deal was much bigger than we'd been told—not 200,000 boxes, but more than a million, almost all of them in very small accounts, my favorite type. Jack felt we had deeper pockets than the other company had and went with us.

So, in one fell swoop, we doubled the size of our business, adding the best kind of customer base you can find. Financial strength played a role, as did flexibility, but we wouldn't even have been in the running if we hadn't played by the rules and earned the respect of our competitors. Sometimes it really does pay to be nice.

The Bottom Line

Point One: The secret of successful selling lies in losing your fear of asking. You don't ask, you don't get.

Point Two: You probably won't discover your company's niche until *after* you've launched the business.

Point Three: No niche lasts forever. You may have to discover new ones as you go along.

Point Four: Your reputation is your most valuable business asset, and your competitors play a critical role in shaping it.

CHAPTER EIGHT

Good Sales, Bad Sales, and the Ones That Get Away

While I completely agree with the old saying that "nothing happens without a sale," it does not follow that all sales are equal. Some sales are much better than others—a concept that salespeople often have a hard time dealing with. That's partly because they have a sales mentality. They've been conditioned to think that any sale is a good sale, and the larger the volume, the better. In fact, the size of the sale is a lot less important than the amount of gross profit you're going to earn on it. Too many low-margin sales can drive you out of business.

By the same token, many entrepreneurs think that they should focus on signing up big customers. I remember an e-mail message I received from a young man who was launching his first company, an advertising and marketing firm. He said that he had everything he needed to get started—money, contacts, experience in the business, a well-equipped office, and so on. There was just one problem: he wasn't sure what kinds of customers to target. "I don't want to bore myself with small clients," he wrote, "but bigger clients seem out of my reach. Any thoughts?" My advice was to forget about boredom. Growing a business from scratch is never boring. Instead of shunning small accounts, he should sign up as many as he could handle and charge premium rates. In the long run, he'd be much better off with a lot of small customers than with one or two big ones.

Small customers are the backbone of a solid, stable, profitable business—especially a service business. I'd like nothing more than to own a service company with 10,000 small customers, each good for about $5,000 per year in sales. That's my ideal. Not that there's anything wrong with having big customers. Sooner or later, most of us need them to grow. But you should never look down on your small customers or take them for granted. The more you have, the happier you'll be. Why? I can give you three reasons.

First, you get better gross margins with small customers because they pay more for your services. They have no choice. They simply don't have the negotiating power of large customers. As a result, you can charge small customers the top price. I'm not talking about gouging anyone. In my industry, the records storage business, for example, most companies have a book rate. That's the price per box they charge any customer who's storing up to, say, 500 boxes. A customer with 10,000 boxes usually will pay a much lower rate. I would never let the price go so low as to undermine our gross margins, but I have to offer some kind of discount because we're competing with other suppliers for the business. With small customers, I can afford to insist on the book rate, which helps strengthen our margins.

Second, small customers bring stability to a business. If you treat small customers right, they'll stay with you forever. That's partly because they're loyal, and partly because—like most of us—they tend to resist change. It's also true, however, that they're much less likely than big customers to be lured away by competitors, if only because most companies don't seek out small customers. When I was in the messenger business, for example, everyone knew where to find the big accounts—the law firms, advertising agencies, and so on—and everyone went after them. It took almost as much time, effort, and money to land one of those customers as it took to locate and sign up the guy who'd have five messenger calls a week. What's more, you'd need two hundred of the small customers to provide you with the same volume of business as one large customer. So our competitors' salespeople generally ignored the small accounts. When we got one, it rarely left.

Third, a broad base of small customers makes your business less vulnerable to the loss of any single customer. That's why—when you apply for a loan—a bank will ask you to list all of your customers that account for more than 10 percent of your sales, as well as the percentage of sales that each one represents. If you do more than 30 percent of sales with any single customer, you're in trouble. For openers, you have to be at that customer's beck and call. If you're on vacation and the customer wants to have a meeting, you have to drop everything and come back. If you have a contract with the customer, you sweat bullets when it comes up for renewal. The truth is, you're not in control of your own business. The large customer can pretty much dictate prices and terms, and you can't afford to put up too much resistance. It's a lot like having a boss, which probably isn't what you had in mind when you decided to go into business in the first place.

Of course, you may not have the luxury of starting out with a base of small customers. A lot of people launch businesses on the cash flow from sales to one or two big customers, and there's nothing inherently wrong with that. But you need to start immediately to expand and diversify your customer base with small customers, or you'll quickly become a slave to the big ones.

What's the goal? I don't think any company can be considered secure until its biggest customer represents no more than 10 percent of its sales—and I wouldn't stop there. As much as I love my large customers, I still feel vulnerable to them, and so I continue to add as many new customers as I can get, especially small ones. That's not easy. For the same reason that small customers give your business stability, they are hard—and expensive—to find. You can't ask salespeople to devote all of their time to looking for them. Instead, I used to instruct our salespeople to drop by three or four potential small accounts whenever they made their cold calls on large accounts. If all the accounts were in the same building, the additional visits usually took another hour or so, and the results added up over time.

Sometimes you get lucky. That's what happened with the acquisition I wrote about at the end of the last chapter. Almost all of the accounts were small ones—literally thousands and thousands of them. I asked Jack, the owner, how he'd managed to sign up so many small customers without having large customers to provide cash flow. "Well, we used to have large customers," he told me, "but we lost them to guys like you. All that was left was our base of small customers. Of course, it took us sixty years to build that base, so it's substantial."

To be honest, I thought Jack's customer base was better than mine. When I lost a 40,000-box account, it really hurt. He would have had to lose about 200 accounts to experience the same level of pain. Fortunately, I didn't have to spend the next sixty years trying to match his situation. In about twenty-four months, we'd finished moving all of his accounts—about 400,000 of them—to our facility.

When the Price Isn't Right

Unfortunately, most accounts don't fall into your lap as easily as those fell into mine. Indeed, making a sale at a good gross margin is almost never easy, and at times it can seem almost impossible. We went through a period in the late 1990s when selling was the toughest I can remember. It wasn't enough to come in with a low price, because everybody's prices were low. Sure, there were some pockets of overpricing, but by and large the fat had been squeezed out of the system, and customers knew it. They knew they weren't going to save much by buying strictly on price. So, to get their business, you had to offer something worth more to them than a discount. You also had to overcome customer loyalty, which was unusually strong. Customers would say up front—when you first went in to solicit their business—that they liked their current supplier and probably wouldn't switch. When that happens, it's not enough to tell them why your product or service is better. You have to show them.

At one point, for example, I got a chance to pitch our records storage service to a large accounting firm in New York City. A friend of mine had helped me arrange a meeting with the partner who handled purchasing for the firm. I knew going in that this firm would be a tough sell. The partner had a close relationship with his current storage company, and he didn't try to hide it. He said, "I have to be honest with you. I've been doing business with these people for a very long time, and I like them." He also told me he planned to show them any proposal we made. My guess was that they wouldn't have to match our bid to keep the business. They'd just have to come close. In effect, he was using us to negotiate a better deal with them. That's all he really wanted.

What I wanted, of course, was the contract. To have a shot at winning it, I had to show the partner how we could help the firm save money. I suggested that I spend some time in the firm's records room, studying how its files were managed. "Records management is my business," I said. "It's not yours. I think I know more about it than you do, and I can give you some suggestions on how to improve your system." He thought that was a great idea and had his office manager take me down to the records room.

What was I looking for? Two things: internal savings and external savings. I wanted to find ways that the firm could save money, not only by changing how it operated internally, but also by reducing the charges it incurred for external services. As it turned out, I had no trouble spotting opportunities to do both. The firm had what was essentially a manual system for keeping track of its files. There wasn't enough space in the records room for someone to enter the contents of files directly into a computer. So, instead, the records people would write the information down in a log, send the boxes out for storage, and do the computer work later. They were a year behind, however, and used the computer mainly as a backup.

The system was extremely inefficient. It required too many people, wasted tons of time, and resulted in costly errors. It also led the firm to spend more money than necessary on archive retrieval services. Because there were too many boxes on the premises, for example, the firm was constantly having to send some back to make room for new ones coming in. As a result, it wound up ordering—and paying for—five deliveries a week, when it should have needed only one.

I spent about two hours in the records room. Later I called the partner. We agreed to have a follow-up meeting, including three people from my company and seven from his. The meeting began at 5 p.m. and ran for almost five hours. I told the people from the firm everything I'd found and gave them numerous suggestions for cutting costs, many of which they could implement immediately. I also offered to help them find the software they needed to upgrade their computer-based tracking system, using contacts we'd developed in our work with other businesses.

Understand what I was doing here. First, I was educating the partner and his people about my business. I was teaching them how to save money by being smart consumers of records storage services. The more I told them, the more questions they asked. It was as if they'd never really understood what they were paying for.

Second, I was letting them see what they *weren't* getting from their current supplier—without saying a negative word. As I noted earlier, I never bad-mouth my competitors to customers. I believe that when you do, you wind up looking bad. Still, you have to show how you're better and why the customer is going to benefit from using you rather than them. So I took care to point out a number of potential external savings that I knew the accounting firm couldn't get from its current supplier. Our competitor didn't have the right technology. We did.

Third, and most important, I was building trust. How? By giving away our ideas and our expertise. By going forward without any guarantees. By investing a significant amount of time and effort in helping the firm save money, with no promise of a return. In effect, I was making the case that the partner should give us the account because he could depend on us to watch out for the firm's best interests. I was showing him not only that we could help him save money but that we *cared* about saving him money, that we were trustworthy. I was giving him the best reason in the world for switching suppliers: peace of mind.

That's exactly what you have to do if you're going to compete successfully in an environment of extreme customer loyalty. You have to prove that you deserve a customer's loyalty more than your competitors do. Believe me, it's a long, difficult, and expensive process, and you don't always walk away with the sale. Fortunately, in that particular case we did, but it took another eight months. During that time, we continued to offer our advice to the firm and spent hours upon hours working on the specific terms of a possible deal. Meanwhile, the firm was also negotiating with our competitor. In the end our patience was rewarded, and we landed the account, much to my relief.

Of course, we probably wouldn't have pulled it off if I hadn't been so involved in making the sale. I'm not bragging here. The fact is, you need to know your business extremely well to be able to sell this way, and who knows it better than the person who built it from scratch? In other words, an entrepreneur's knowledge is a significant competitive advantage. I use mine whenever I can.

Ask Norm

Dear Norm:

I have a three-year-old company that produces job fairs, and we're riding a roller coaster. Business is great for three or four months in the spring and again for two or three months in the fall. In between, there's nothing. Our cash flow falls to zero. Meanwhile, we still have to pay our employees. We've tried attracting customers by offering off-season discounts—to no avail. The cash crunch gets so bad that we spend most of the good months just recovering. This problem is crippling the business and my emotional stability.

   Kent

Dear Kent:

First of all, off-season discounts usually don't work and may undermine the profitable part of your business. Instead, you should look for ways to diversify. Are there other types of shows you could produce in the down months? Could you do consulting during those times? You have to be creative, but diversification is generally the best solution to seasonal fluctuations. Meanwhile, deal with the cash-flow problems directly. Can you negotiate to pay your leases during the months when you have more money in the bank? Can you speed up your collections when cash is tight? Also try explaining the problem to your employees and asking for their suggestions. They may well come up with ideas you'd never think of.

   —Norm

Listen and Earn

Oddly enough, one of the best ways to increase sales is also the most obvious, although you'd be amazed how few people actually use it. I'm talking about listening to customers. It happens so rarely these days that you can actually gain a competitive advantage just by doing it.

I'll give you an example. One day, I was showing two people from a large New York law firm through our records storage facility, hoping they would give us their business. We hadn't gone too far before one of them, the office manager, said, "By the way, we want to keep all of our boxes in numerical order. If you take one out, we want it put back in exactly the same spot."

Now, normally, we don't file boxes in a particular order. Our bar-coding system allows us to find boxes instantaneously no matter where they've been stored. But I always try to give customers what they want, and this potential customer had just told me what she wanted. I said, "Fine, no problem."

She looked at the other person, then back at me. "Aren't you going to tell me I'm crazy?" she asked.

"You didn't ask my opinion," I said. "You told me what you wanted, and I'm sure you have your reasons."

She started to laugh. "Well, everywhere else we've gone, they've tried to talk us out of it. You're the first person who just said, 'Yes.'" We got the account.

In telling this story, I don't mean to imply that listening to customers is easy. On the contrary, it's the most difficult part of the selling process. All kinds of extraneous issues get in the way. For one thing, you often believe you know what's best for the customer, and sometimes you may even be right. I can readily understand, for example, why my competitors tried to discourage the law firm from keeping the boxes in order. From a storage company's point of view, it's an inefficient practice. You get nothing but hassles with no apparent benefit, and the customer winds up paying more for the service. The other companies may well have thought they were offering the law firm a better alternative. There was just one problem: it wasn't what the customer wanted.

And, when you're selling, your entire focus should be on figuring out what your customers want and then, if possible, giving it to them. You don't really know what's best for them, after all. How could you? In any situation, there are numerous factors of which you are completely unaware. I'm not arguing against helping customers find better ways to deal with their needs, but you have to be careful. It's too easy to confuse your needs with their needs, particularly when you're trying to make a sale.

Pride also gets in the way of listening to customers. As a salesperson, you naturally want to emphasize the best things about your company, and why shouldn't you? You're proud of them, and justifiably so. You want people to know about the special services you offer, or the hot, new product line, or the state-of-the-art computer system in which you've just made a six-figure investment. So what happens? You oversell. You don't hear the customers when they say the computer system isn't important to them. You think it *should* be important to them. You know that, if they knew more, it *would* be important to them. So you keep on touting its benefits, and you don't notice that their eyes have glazed over. You've lost them.

Then, of course, there's ego. I give tours to prospective customers, and some of them will look around at all the boxes in my warehouses and say, "Gee, are you afraid of having a fire in this place?" In fact, I'm not afraid of a fire, and I might well respond, "No, we're protected. It's not a concern." But that would be my ego talking. When a customer asks such a question, it's because *she* is worried about a fire. Why she's worried is none of my business. The point is that I need to respect her fear, not minimize it. So my answer is, "Yes, certainly, I've thought about the danger of fire, and let me show you what we've done about it." Some people might say I am being disingenuous. I prefer to think I am being unselfish. I'm putting my ego aside and responding to the concerns of the customer.

And that is my goal as a salesperson. I don't worry about closing sales. I worry about making customers feel as though they've been heard, understood, and responded to. I want them to leave with a warm and fuzzy feeling. If they do, the sales will follow.

You can't make customers feel warm and fuzzy if you don't listen, if you don't shut out all your preconceptions and prejudices, your agendas and opinions, and hear what they're really saying. Doing that doesn't come naturally. It requires discipline and practice. You have to develop routines to block out the distractions. I myself sit quietly for a couple minutes before taking customers on a tour of our facility, and I try to make my mind a blank slate. I repeat over and over, "No preconceptions. No preconceptions." I wipe out any thoughts I might have that would keep me from hearing or observing the customers. Yes, I'm going to talk about our product, emphasizing what I consider to be the important features and benefits, but I'm not going to push anything on people. I'm going to find out what they want. I'm going to look for the clues, verbal and nonverbal. I'm going to listen to what they say and what they don't say, and I'm going to respond accordingly.

And it works. I watch, I listen, I hear, and I find out unexpected things. Sometimes a comment will be made about an issue on which I have a strong opinion, and I'll have to remind myself, "Don't take sides. Don't take sides." It does require some effort to avoid being distracted. The selling part, on the other hand, becomes much easier when you listen carefully to what people are saying. You just turn around and tell people what they want to hear. Not that you should mislead anyone. The information has to be true and accurate, but you can emphasize the parts they're most interested in. You don't have to create a sales pitch. Your customers tell you what to say.

The Capacity Trap

I hope you understand that I'm *not* suggesting you give customers whatever they ask for. Sometimes they ask for things you can't, or shouldn't, provide, such as a price substantially below what you need to charge in order to earn a reasonable profit. Most businesspeople are smart enough to realize they can't do much discounting of that sort without getting into serious trouble. There is one form of price cutting, however, that even experienced businesspeople fall victim to. I've seen it wreck entire industries and bring down established companies, not to mention countless start-ups.

Ask Norm

Dear Norm:

I am a fledgling neckwear designer, and I've finally gotten all my ducks in a row. I contacted a local menswear chain and persuaded the buyer to take a look. I sent him tie samples, fabric swatches, photos, everything. Two months ago he assured me he was going to place an order. Since then I've called him repeatedly, and he always tells me he's about to fax the order, but he never does. I'm having second thoughts about doing business with someone whose word doesn't mean anything. Should I keep pestering him?

    Pam

Dear Pam:

I'd bill him for the ties with a tongue-in-cheek note. Say something like, "I'm sure you loved my ties so much, you're probably wearing them, but as a small-business person, I have to get paid for my services. If you are not satisfied with the ties for any reason, you can always return them. Otherwise please send me a check."

    —Norm

I'm referring to the practice of selling unused capacity at a discount in order to make sure it doesn't go to waste. The extra capacity might take the form of an empty warehouse, or machinery that's used only sporadically, or even the time of, say, a consultant. When an opportunity comes along to sell that capacity at a reduced rate, most people find it hard to refuse. They think only about the money they're going to make on something that would otherwise go to waste. They ignore the problems they'll create if they charge significantly less for their service than it's worth.

I call this the capacity trap. Why a trap? Because, at first glance, it looks as though you're making a sound business decision. In fact, you're putting yourself on the road to bankruptcy.

Let's take the classic example of a guy who leases a truck, hires a couple of workers, and goes into the freight-hauling business. He charges the standard rate—say, $45 per hour—and manages to book three days a week of business. Then he hits a dry spell. He can't find anyone else who wants to buy his service at that price. Finally, a customer shows up and offers to rent the truck for the other two days at $25 per hour. The guy thinks, "Why not? I have to pay for leasing the truck anyway. I might as well get some income out of it. I sure don't want it to just sit here." He accepts the offer, which brings in an additional $400 per week in sales. The guy is satisfied. He is getting full use of his truck. He's not letting any capacity go to waste. What could be wrong?

Plenty. For openers, he is no doubt making less money on the sale than he imagines. That's because he's focusing on one factor: capacity—what it costs to lease the truck. Meanwhile, he's ignoring all the costs he incurs only when he uses the capacity—gas, wear-and-tear, maybe labor. He might actually do better by letting the truck stand idle those two days, but he wouldn't know it because he's looking only at sales, not profit. It's a common failing, especially among people starting out in business. Unfortunately, it's sometimes a fatal one.

But let's assume this guy has taken his operating costs into account and figured out he can make a profit on the sale. It's still a bad idea for him to rent the truck at a lower price. I'd argue that it's almost always a bad idea to cut prices simply to avoid having unused capacity—for four reasons.

First, there's the cost of capital. Whenever you make a sale, you are, in effect, loaning money to a customer, at least until the bill gets paid. It's like making an investment in the form of credit. You need to make sure that you're getting a good return on your investment—that you're using your capital to generate enough profit to keep you going. It's a mistake for any business to waste capital on low-margin sales. It can be suicide for a new business, which has limited capital by definition and will never get beyond the start-up phase if its capital runs out.

Second, there's the opportunity cost. When you fill capacity with low-margin sales, you leave no room for high-margin sales. What will the freight hauler do if he finds another customer who's willing to pay the full price? Will he even bother looking for another full-price customer?

Meanwhile, by cutting his prices, he has just brought a new competitor into his market: himself. This is the third reason not to go after low-margin sales, and it's based on a general rule of business—namely, that prices always seek their lowest level. When you charge two prices for exactly the same service, you are competing against yourself, and it's only a matter of time before the competitor with the lower price wins. Customers are not stupid. Sooner or later, they'll figure out that you're willing to sell for less. When they do, you'll have a very hard time getting any of them to pay more.

By then, moreover, you will probably have lost your current full-price customers—which is the fourth, and most important, argument against discounting to fill capacity. The practice alienates precisely those customers you must have to be successful, maybe even to survive. They'll be furious when they find out you're charging other people less for exactly the same service. They'll think you've been ripping them off all along. From then on, forget it. I don't care what price you offer them. Those customers are gone.

The truck example is a clear case of the capacity trap, but you also have to beware of it in bidding situations. I remember a large city contract that came up for auction. I really wanted it, but I lost it to a new records storage company that had offered a monthly rental fee of 13¢ per box, about 40 percent below my bid. I just laughed. At that price, I didn't want the business. Frankly, I couldn't see why anyone else would want it, either. A couple of weeks later, the guy who won the contract—we'll call him Jerry—came to see me. The owner of his company is a friend of mine and had asked me to give the kid some pointers. I quickly realized that Jerry was perplexed at how the bidding had gone. "I was surprised you didn't come in lower," he said.

"I'd never bid what you did," I said. "There's no way you can justify 13¢ a box. You're losing money on the deal."

"That's not true," he said.

"Oh, no?" I replied. "Let me show you something."

We sat down, and I took out a pen and paper. I asked Jerry how high his building was and then calculated the number of boxes he could fit from floor to ceiling. Since we knew the total number of boxes involved and the size of each box, we could figure out how much floor space the stored boxes would take up. We also knew the total monthly revenue from those boxes. Dividing the revenue by the floor space, we determined that Jerry would be getting monthly rental income of $6.60 per square foot for storing the boxes. "You could rent that warehouse to another guy for $8 or $9 a square foot, and he would pay the taxes, the heat, and the lighting. With this deal, not only do you get less revenue, but you have to cover all those expenses yourself."

"Omigod," said Jerry. "I never thought of it that way."

Now I know some people would argue that Jerry did the right thing. After all, his warehouse was empty at the time. He was already paying the taxes, heat, and lighting, as well as numerous other expenses. Even at 13¢ a box, the city contract would help him cover those expenses. So why shouldn't he have taken what he could get? Something is always better than nothing, right?

The answer is no. I mean, what sense does it make for Jerry to go to all the trouble and expense of having a records storage business when he could do better being a landlord? In fact, it should always raise questions if you find that you could earn more money by using your capital another way. Unless you have a clear plan for improving your returns in a specific time frame, you're probably doing something wrong.

To be sure, there are exceptions to every rule, and this one is no different. I have to admit that selling capacity at a discount does make sense occasionally, as long as two conditions are met. First, you and the customer must agree up front on the duration of the discount and what will happen when it expires. Second, you must be able to explain the deal to other customers who raise questions about it. They need to feel that you've been fair. At one point, for example, I used some of my excess capacity to take a 200,000-box account away from my largest competitor. The customer had discovered that it was paying above-market rates, thanks to a series of automatic price increases, and had begun looking for another vendor. We proposed a ten-year contract with the first two years heavily discounted. We could make that offer because we temporarily had a lot of extra space in one of our warehouses. In the third year of the contract—when the customer started paying normal rates—we finished building a new warehouse. We then replaced our construction loan with a mortgage, and the increase in revenue from that one account covered the monthly mortgage payments.

So the customer knew in advance exactly what the deal was. And if other customers asked me about it, I could point out that we gave all of them discounts in the beginning as well. I could even offer them the same deal we'd given our new customer—provided they were willing to sign a new ten-year contract for 200,000 boxes.

That's an unusual situation, however. In general, it's a bad idea to discount excess capacity, which is not the same as saying you should never offer customers a discount. There just has to be a reason for it other than excess capacity. Volume, for example, is a reason that everyone understands. Or you might offer a discount to a customer who agrees to certain special terms. Better yet, maintain your price but offer something extra, a value-added service. What it is will vary from customer to customer, depending on their needs. Even if it costs you something to provide the service, at least you're putting your money to good use. You're getting a full-price customer. You're not undercutting your normal prices. And you've done nothing to alienate your existing customers. The worst that can happen is that they'll want the service, too. That's a positive, not a negative. If you get known for this value-added service, customers will start coming to you for it, and you may find that you can charge more to provide it.

Then again, you may not be so lucky. You may be sitting there with an empty, idle truck, and a customer will come along who is not interested in a value-added service, or a volume discount, or whatever. He just wants to rent the truck for $25, instead of the usual $45. In that case, you go back to the first lesson of business, the very first lesson: you can't do business with everybody. There are people in this world who want more for their money than you can provide, and no amount of negotiating will change their minds. There is only one word you can use to deal with them, and you have to learn it, hard as it may be to say when the customer is standing in front of you and the sale is on the line. That word is *no*.

The Bottom Line

Point One: You're better off with a base of many small customers than with a few large ones.

Point Two: Showing is more effective than telling when it comes to signing up new customers. Let them experience what you have to offer.

Point Three: Listening is a lost art. You can gain a competitive advantage just by listening carefully to what your prospects and customers are saying.

Point Four: It is almost always a bad idea to reduce your prices just to fill unused capacity. You will just undermine the more profitable part of your business.

CHAPTER NINE

Customers for Keeps

There is a basic rule of business that's easy to forget, especially when you're competing with other companies for the same customers: Winning is not just about closing the sale. You win when you close the sale and at the same time lay the foundation for a good relationship that allows you to keep the customer for a long, long time.

The name of the game is customer retention. Growing a business is much harder if you are constantly having to replace customers you've lost. Which would you prefer, after all—making fifty sales in a year and having a 100 percent customer retention rate, or making a hundred sales a year and having a 50 percent retention rate? I'll take the former any day of the week. Yes, you'll have more sales during the year, and you'll wind up with the same number of customers at the end, but, if you lose one account for every two you land, you'll spend twice as much time, energy, and money to get them as you would if you made half as many sales but were able to hold on to all the customers you signed up.

I went through that with my messenger business, Perfect Courier. We regularly lost 25 percent of our customers every year, mainly because we were operating in an intensely competitive industry with no barriers to entry and almost nothing to stop customers from switching from one supplier to another if they could save a few dollars. I'd wake up every morning and ask myself, "Which customer am I going to lose today?" People would switch suppliers for pennies. We'd sometimes lose accounts to competitors who we knew wouldn't survive six months at the prices they were offering. The customer would say, "We'll come back when they go out of business."

And yet we managed to make the Inc. 500 list for three consecutive years. We did it partly by coming up with mechanisms that would tie customers into our service—for example, the invoices that showed them the amount of money they could charge back to each of their customers. Because we were one of the very few messenger companies with a computer back then, we were alone in our ability to produce the invoices. Even with such tie-in devices, however, we still began each year having to replace a quarter of our sales just to stay even, let alone make the Inc. 500.

So how can you make sure that you hold on to most of *your* customers? Clearly, it helps to be in an industry with high barriers to entry and numerous obstacles to switching suppliers, as is the case with my records storage business. But mainly it's a matter of building strong relationships. No customer enjoys the process of switching suppliers. It's a pain. It takes time and money that could otherwise be spent elsewhere. The people responsible for the function in question have to get the rest of the company to buy into the change. They have to meet with new suppliers. They have to negotiate new agreements. Why would they go through all that? Usually it's because they're really upset with the current supplier.

That said, it's also true that customers do not treat all suppliers alike. Everyone makes mistakes from time to time, but not everyone loses accounts as a result of its mistakes. In some cases, the customer's people say, "They're a good company. Let's give them another chance." In other cases, they say, "These people can't do anything right. Let's find someone who can." What's the difference? It almost always has to do with the relationship that the supplier has cultivated with the customer.

That relationship starts, not when the customer signs on, but rather when the initial contact occurs, long before any deal is closed. You need to find out in advance what it will take to keep the customer happy after you've closed the sale. For instance, I want to know how long the customer waits to pay its bills. If you don't ask about that, you could be headed for trouble. You may assume the customer will pay in thirty days, as is your policy. Its accounting people may assume they can pay in ninety days, as they do with their other suppliers. When you call up after forty-five days and discover that you're not getting paid for another forty-five days, you're not happy. You pressure the customer's people, and then they're not happy. The relationship goes downhill from there.

And whose fault is that? I say it's your fault for not inquiring beforehand about the customer's bill-paying policy. If you'd known what it was, you could have built the carrying costs into your proposal, accepted the payment terms, or simply decided not to take the business. Whichever option you chose, you would not have had the bad feelings engendered by a misunderstanding that could easily have been avoided.

But beyond learning what you need to know to keep from inadvertently souring a future relationship, it's also important to use the period before the sale to start building the trust that will let you hold on to the customer for the long term. That means going out of your way to show your intention to do whatever is necessary to ensure that the customer will be happy after the sale.

There was the time, for example, when we found ourselves competing for the business of a medium-size law firm and—as usual—invited its representatives to come visit us, see our warehouse, meet our people, and assess our capabilities. We gave them the standard tour. Afterward, we told the firm's records manager that we'd like to visit his offices in Manhattan. He was surprised. Nobody else had made that request. "Why?" he asked.

"For one thing," I said, "I want to see how long it takes to get up and down on the elevators. I also want to see what the building looks like. And I want to see how you do things. Maybe we can give you some suggestions."

"What if we don't select you?" he asked.

"So we'll have spent a day with a couple of nice people," I said.

As it turned out, we were the only contender who bothered to visit the law firm. When the bidding began, most of the other records storage companies were quickly eliminated. Of the three finalists, we were the most expensive. The records manager contacted our salesperson and said, "We want you, but there are certain things in your package we can't live with. You can have the account if you're willing to make some changes."

"Why do you want us?" our salesperson asked.

"Nobody else came to our place," the records manager said. "Nobody else asked us the questions you asked. You're the only one who understands how we operate."

We had to make certain concessions, but we did get the account, and we had the opportunity to get it for one reason: we'd built a relationship.

Ask Norm

Dear Norm:
I am the owner of a small handbag company that is facing a tremendous amount of competition. My business was doing very well until about a year ago, when sales started to slip. I have received wonderful editorial credits in the top fashion publications and have had placement in the finest stores in the country with good sell-through. Last year I decided to take sales in-house, because I thought I could be the best spokesperson for my product. My primary goal is to build a solid brand. How can I get to the next level?
*   Nancy*

Dear Nancy:
Handling your own sales is not how you build a brand. You need to develop a certain mystique as the person whose name is on the product. You can't do that if you're spending your time qualifying leads, making sales calls, getting doors slammed in your face. To build a brand, increase your sales, and grow the company, you need to turn responsibilities over to other people. That can be hard, I admit, particularly when you believe you can do the job better than anyone else. I was the first dispatcher in my delivery business, and I always thought I was the best at it. But if I were still dispatching, I'd have a very small company today.
    —Norm

Building Loyalty

To be sure, you can't stop working on the relationship after you've made the sale. Customer relationships—like other relationships—atrophy unless they are constantly nurtured. There are many ways to do that. One of them is to teach your customers your business. They want to cut costs, and you're in a unique position to show them where they can find savings. After all, you know your business better than they do. You know where they lose—or waste—money. You know how they can cut costs by operating a little differently. In short, you can help them to be smart buyers and smart consumers.

In the records storage industry, for example, one of the first things you discover is that most people keep their records forever. Customers give a company their boxes and forget about them. There's often no reason to hold on to the records after a certain number of years, but nobody checks to see which ones can be destroyed. Meanwhile, storage fees pile up.

We saw a chance to help our customers by developing a system whereby we enter a destroy date in our computer for every box we receive. When the time arrives, we notify the customer, who then tells us whether to destroy the records or continue holding the box. In the process we've saved some customers as much as 40 percent of their storage costs.

Understand, we wind up with fewer boxes as a result. So our sales are somewhat lower than they might otherwise be. But we do get compensated for showing customers how to save money. They pay us by staying with us even when they might get a slightly cheaper price somewhere else. Over the long run, that loyalty is worth much more to the business than the extra boxes.

Another way to build the relationship is to make a point of treating established customers like new prospects. That's a bigger challenge than you might suppose. There's a natural tendency to treat customers differently after they've been around for a while. You'll do anything for them when you're trying to win their business, but once you've landed the account, your attitude starts to change. By the time you go back to renegotiate the contract, you've developed a whole new set of expectations. You're not focused on making the sale anymore. Now you're thinking about getting a better deal. It's an easy way to lose business. You leave yourself wide open to competitors who are looking at the customer the way you did when you were starting out.

So I do everything I can to make sure we treat our established customers with the same care that we showed them the first time they walked through our door. It's a promise I make to them when I'm closing the sale, and it's a way of thinking I try to instill in my staff. I want all of us to ask ourselves constantly how we can improve our service, what we can do to make our customers' lives easier. For example, we developed a new computerized service at one point that allowed customers to dial in and look up anything they want to know about their account, the records they have in storage, the status of their boxes, whatever. When we did it for them, it took longer, and we had to charge them $1.50 a lookup. I preferred that we didn't do any lookups. We had many more profitable ways to use our resources. By using the online service, customers saved themselves time, money, and aggravation, and they helped us reduce our costs, which makes it easier for us to maintain our prices.

The Customer Touch

In all this, it's important to remember the critical role that you—as the entrepreneur in the business—have in building and maintaining the customer relationships. Unfortunately, the more successful your company is and the bigger it gets, the harder it is to play that role. You have fewer and fewer opportunities to interact with customers. You just can't spend as much time with them as you did in the early days. There are always more pressing matters to attend to—problems to solve, financing to arrange, people to hire, deals to make, and on and on. You increasingly count on employees to handle the day-to-day relationships with customers, while you yourself become more and more removed from them. It's a process that can undermine even the most promising young company—unless somebody makes a conscious effort to ensure that doesn't happen.

Let me tell you about an experience I once had on a flight from New York to California. As usual, I was flying JetBlue. I boarded the plane with the other passengers, and the door closed. As we sat there, buckling our seat belts and checking out the televisions in front of us, a middle-aged man with slightly graying hair stood up in the front of the plane. He had on the long apron that all JetBlue flight attendants wear, with his name stitched onto it. "Hi," he said, "my name is Dave Neeleman, and I'm the CEO of JetBlue. I'm here to serve you this evening, and I'm looking forward to meeting each of you before we land."

Sure enough, as soon as we reached our cruising altitude, he and the other attendants started coming down the aisle with the baskets of snacks that JetBlue offers passengers to stave off their hunger pangs en route to their destination. Of course, if the passengers in the rear had had to wait for Neeleman to serve them, they would have starved. Beginning in the first row, he slowly made his way through the plane, stopping to chat with anyone who cared to talk to him, answering every question people asked. I was sitting in the eleventh row, and it took him more than an hour to reach me. "Nice airline you have here," I said. "Where do you come up with all these great ideas—like the televisions?"

"I get most of my ideas on flights like this one," Neeleman said. "The customers tell me what they want."

"Oh, listening to your customers," I said. "What a novel idea!" He laughed.

After talking to me and the other people in my row for about twenty minutes, Neeleman excused himself and moved on to the next row. I went back to watching television. The other flight attendants continued making their rounds. When they came by my row, I asked them if they'd ever worked with their CEO before. "Oh, yeah," one of them said. "We bump into him all the time."

"So what do you think of him?" I asked.

"He's very nice," she said. "What you see is what you get."

Sitting there, I couldn't help reflecting on Neeleman's business acumen, not to mention his devotion to his company. After all, he didn't have to spend five and a half hours doing customer service. I'm sure he'd put in a full day's work before ever setting foot on the plane. I'm also sure he could have used the time productively in other ways.

Then again, look what he got out of his conversations with customers—all those wonderful ideas, to begin with. He told the guy across the aisle from me that JetBlue would soon be implementing one of them, Wi-Fi in its airport lounges, and that it was working on providing another, high-speed Internet connections on flights.

Second, by keeping in touch, he had a real-time sense of the market. He knew firsthand what was going on out there, and he could see trends before his competitors. That's one of the biggest advantages of having direct contact with customers. Markets change. Technologies change. Customer wants and needs change. If you have your finger on the pulse of the market, you're a step ahead of the competition. If you don't, you run the risk of getting blindsided.

Meanwhile, Neeleman was also shaping the company culture. Employees saw him working the crowd, going out of his way to help a customer, and they did the same. They heard him talking about the plans to introduce new services, and they spread the word. Above all, they knew that Neeleman wasn't sitting behind a desk somewhere, counting his stock options. He was putting in overtime, and he was doing it with them. They could rest assured that he understood what was happening on the front lines because he'd been there. He was on their team—and vice versa—not just in words but in deeds. And the result? An unusual level of trust, respect, and goodwill all around.

The whole experience had an interesting effect on me as a businessperson. I've long believed in the type of leadership and service that Neeleman exemplifies, but I don't always demand it from my own suppliers. I've tended to make excuses for them. After flying with Neeleman, those excuses seemed pretty thin. I mean, there I was, get-

Ask Norm

Dear Norm:
One of my salespeople recently resigned and started his own company competing with mine. I subsequently learned that he had been conducting his new business on the side while he was still working for me. What should I do?
  Vennie

Dear Vennie:
You should do nothing. Keep building your company and forget about the guy. Don't let this incident cause you to lose focus on what's really important to your business. People waste a lot of time and energy worrying about ex-employees who become competitors. When employees leave to go into competition, I wish them well and send them a plant. It's a cactus. This guy should be history as far as you're concerned. If he's an unethical person, he'll eventually get his comeuppance.
  —Norm

ting first-class, in-person customer service from the CEO of an airline that had sold me a ticket for $154. Shouldn't I expect the same from suppliers to whom I was paying tens of thousands of dollars? I wound up firing our insurance broker, our accounting firm, and our bank. When they didn't understand why, I suggested they take a trip on JetBlue.

The Bottom Line

Point One: Customer retention is the key to growth, and you retain customers by building strong relationships with them.

Point Two: One way to build relationships with customers is to help them become smarter buyers by teaching them your business.

Point Three: Make a point of treating old customers like new prospects. Otherwise, it's easy to start taking them for granted.

Point Four: You will lose contact with your customers as your company grows unless you build customer face-time into your schedule.

CHAPTER TEN

How to Lose Customers

I have a little game I like to play. I keep track of the number of episodes of bad customer service I hear about, or experience, over a six-month period and use that as a rough gauge of the general level of customer service in my part of the world. It's gone up and down over the years, but—no matter where it stands—I'm always struck by the number of service providers who seem to believe that a customer exists only to help them maintain a comfortable lifestyle.

Take the dentist I went to when I needed to have my teeth capped. His office—on Park Avenue in Manhattan—was one of the most spectacular I've ever seen. The bathroom was all shiny black marble and chrome. On my initial visit, I was given my own "personal hygiene space," where I could keep my special toothbrush in a little locker with a key. The doctor did a thorough examination and took X-rays of my mouth from every conceivable angle. He then had me return a few weeks later to hear how he intended to proceed.

He had an elaborate presentation planned. As I sat in his office, he started to explain to me in great detail what he was going to do, and why, and how. I interrupted him. "OK," I said. "I believe you. What's this going to cost?"

"The total?" he said. "About $45,000."

I was floored. "Well, Doc," I said, "I was given a list of the four best dentists in the city, and you were right at the top, but that price is unbelievable."

"Do you mind showing me the list?" he asked. I gave it to him. He smiled as he looked it over. "This one was my student," he said. "And this one used to work for me. I trained him myself."

"Is he any good?" I asked.

"Yes, he's very good, but he's in Rockville Centre, on Long Island," he said. "You could probably get your teeth done there for less, but you wouldn't get all this." He motioned around the office.

I got out of my chair and said, "Thanks a lot, Doc."

"Where are you going?" he asked.

"I'm going out to the guy on Long Island and see what he charges," I said. "But I've got to say one thing. This is a bad sales pitch you have, telling me I'm paying for your Park Avenue office." I walked out and made an appointment with the dentist in Rockville Centre, who charged half of the Park Avenue dentist's fee. I said I'd come at the latter's suggestion. He didn't believe it. I told him the whole story. He laughed and asked how much the Park Avenue guy had wanted. "I'll tell you," I said, "but only after you finish the job."

"Why?" he asked.

"Well," I said, "you're probably going to raise your prices, and I don't want you to do it now." He laughed and laughed—but he didn't deny it.

Raising Prices

To be sure, price always plays a role in the customer relationship, and there's no easier way to lose customers than to hit them with a sudden, and big, price increase. No one wants to do that, but—if you don't raise your prices gradually over time—you could wake up one day and discover you have no choice.

My wife, Elaine, came across a good example. For years, she was getting her hair done at a salon near our home. She started going there partly because the location was convenient, partly because she was tired of the fancier places in the area. Price was not an important factor, although it didn't hurt that the owner, Judy, charged substantially less than other salons for the same services. Elaine took advantage of the lower rates by going twice a week instead of once.

Ask Norm

Dear Norm:

We are a $40 million manufacturer, and we distribute our products through 250 independent dealers in North America and Europe. How can we use the Internet to sell products to the end user without upsetting our loyal dealers?
   Chris

Dear Chris:

I doubt your dealers will be upset as long as you sell at the same price they charge and give them a commission on any sales in their area. In fact, they'll probably encourage you. It's trickier if you're planning to sell your products for less. You're going to need the dealers' permission to do that, and you may have to agree to pay them their normal commission on the sales in their area. In any case, the key here is communication. I'd start by sending out a questionnaire to the dealers. Tell them you want to give them an opportunity to make a lot more money by earning commissions on sales over the Internet. Explain how the system would work, and ask them what they think. As long as you communicate properly, you should be all right. If you don't, you'll have a problem no matter what you do.
   —Norm

Then one day Judy suddenly announced a set of huge price increases, effective immediately. A basic cut went up 25 percent, as did the cost of a blow-dry. The price of a coloring jumped 85 percent. The increases came as a shock to the customers. Some of them were angry enough to talk about leaving. Even Elaine was upset. She asked Judy why she'd done it. Why such big increases? Why do them all at once?

"I don't have a choice," Judy said. "We haven't had a price increase in ten years. I've been giving the staff raises every year, and I haven't been getting any additional income. Now I'm at a point where I can't go on without a significant increase. I won't be able to pay my bills. The place won't survive."

She had my sympathy. It's never easy to raise prices. As for big increases, you make them at your peril. There's simply no way to do it without antagonizing customers and thereby putting your most important relationships at risk. Faced with resistance, a lot of businesspeople are tempted to forgo price increases altogether, or at least to put them off for as long as possible. If you do either one, however, you're making a big mistake. Granted, you may not feel the pain for a while. If your sales are going up, you'll probably be able to take home the same amount of money from one year to the next. As a result, you may not see the risks you're taking. In the short term, you'll think you're doing fine.

But, in fact, two things are happening. First, your profit margins are shrinking—because your costs are going up. Certain costs always rise. It's what I call "creeping expenses." Some types of expenses have a life of their own. If you don't watch them like a hawk, they go up all by themselves. They may even go up if you do keep an eye on them. In most small businesses, for example, you can count on payroll increases every year. You can expect regular hikes in insurance rates as well, and I'm not just talking about health insurance. The costs of utilities and supplies also have a tendency to rise over time. OK, some things have grown cheaper over time—basic phone service, for example— and faster computers let people work ever more efficiently than before. Nevertheless, your average costs per dollar of sales are going to rise from year to year. They may rise only 2 percent annually, but compound the increases over five or ten years, and eventually you won't be earning a profit anymore—unless, of course, you raise prices.

Even if you don't let the problem go that far, however, you're damaging your business in other ways by not raising prices on a regular basis. For one thing, you're gradually undermining the perceived value of your services or products. Like it or not, there's a natural tendency to link quality and price. I'm not saying you always have to charge as much as the most expensive suppliers, but—if the gap between your prices and theirs gets too large—customers will start to regard you as the cheap alternative in the market.

At the same time, you'll be undermining the *real* value of your business as a whole. That's a point most small-business owners miss. They look at the company only as a source of income. They forget that it's also a major asset, probably their most valuable one, and—like any asset—it needs to be maintained. That means, among other things, making sure the company has strong profit margins—as good as or better than the rest of the industry. If you let your margins erode, you're going to have trouble when you try to sell the business. Indeed, you may not be able to sell it at all.

It's sort of like selling a house. If the place needs a new roof, buyers will discount the price accordingly, or they'll look for a house that doesn't need one. By the same token, business buyers are going to shy away from a company with weak margins, especially if they're weak because prices are too low. Who wants to buy a business and immediately start raising prices? Even under the best of circumstances, it's tricky to maintain a customer base through a change of ownership. It's almost impossible when you have to begin by doing something that will antagonize every customer you have.

That's why I believe that, as a matter of sound business practice, companies should raise prices on a regular basis. The increases don't have to be big ones. Sometimes they can't be. I've often had to fight for one, but I always insist on raising the price at least a little. Had Judy raised her prices a dollar or two per year over the course of the decade, she'd have had competitive rates at the end of it, and no one would have complained. Instead, she was forced to take the kind of action that was certain to drive her customers crazy.

Rules for Rules

If all else fails, you can always lose customers by providing really poor customer service. The use of that technique seems to have increased over the past thirty years. Some people blame the trend on changes in the workforce. That may be a factor, but I think the major fault lies elsewhere. In most cases, it's not the employee who creates the problem. It's the employer. How? Usually by establishing a bad rule.

Ask Norm

Dear Norm:

I have a small business that tutors people in writing. I've been running it out of my home as a sole proprietor, using independent contractors. One woman who has been editing for me wants to come on as a full-time employee doing marketing and sales. I need someone to do that. Still, taking her on full-time would be a big financial commitment. She might also generate more business than I could handle. So am I crazy to consider hiring her?
   Sharon

Dear Sharon:

It's never crazy to hire an employee, provided you have the need and understand the financial consequences. That involves determining the additional sales you'll have to generate in order to cover the new expenses. To do that, add up those expenses over a period of time and divide by your average gross margin. Suppose, for example, that in the first year it will cost you $39,000 to bring on this employee and make other changes, and your gross margin is 30 percent. You would then need to increase your annual sales by $130,000 at the same gross margin to cover the new expenses and maintain your current profitability. To reduce the risk, try an experiment. Have her work part-time in sales and continue doing her editing until you both have a better sense of the new arrangement.

—Norm

Here's an example from my wife's uncle Arnold, who lived in upstate New York until he passed away. He was a great businessman himself. Once he told me about an experience he'd had when he took his car to be repaired at a dealership in town. This was the second time he'd brought it in for the same problem. When he returned to get the car, he was told the bill came to a couple hundred dollars. "Fine," he said, "but I want to take it for a test-drive, just to make sure the problem is really fixed."

"OK, but you have to pay first," said the guy at the service desk. "We aren't allowed to let any car leave here until the bill has been paid."

Now, Arnold was not a stranger to these people. He'd been doing business with them for forty years. He used to be the head of administration at the local hospital. In that capacity, he'd purchased five or six cars a year from the dealership, which had even assigned a salesman to his account. In addition, Arnold had bought a new car for himself every four or five years. So he was a million-dollar customer.

And the guy at the service desk knew exactly who he was. Arnold was incredulous. "Wait a minute," he said. "Are you really telling me that I can't drive my car out of here because you don't trust me to pay a minor repair bill?"

"I'm sorry, sir," the guy said. "Those are the rules, and we can't change them."

Arnold went home and called the owner of the dealership. He said, "Jim, what's going on here? This is ridiculous." The owner apologized and told him not to worry. He'd take care of it. He'd personally bring the car over. Arnold could drive it for a day or two and pay the bill when he was satisfied.

So what had the owner accomplished with his rule? He'd aggravated one of his best customers. He'd made an employee look like a fool. And he'd caused himself embarrassment and inconvenience.

I can sympathize. I've done it myself.

I understand why companies have rules. You get to a certain size, and you suddenly realize that you need them. Employees have to know where the boundaries lie—how they're supposed to conduct themselves, what's going to get them into trouble and what isn't. Some rules you establish for survival's sake, to avoid mistakes that might put you out of business. Others you have because you want to maintain certain standards. Still others you decide you need after you get whacked on the head. Then there are those you institute because you think you've discovered a terrific new way to boost your sales or streamline your management system or cut your costs—whatever.

Behind every rule there's almost always a good reason, or at least a good intention. At the time you establish them, the rules appear to make all the sense in the world. And yet, if you're not careful, you run a high risk of creating rules that will hurt your business. What happens is that you take away your employees' ability to use common sense in responding to the reasonable requests of customers.

In my business, for example, customers often ask to have boxes delivered to their offices. We charge a regular fee for the delivery and an additional fee when the boxes have to be delivered in a rush. As in any business, customers sometimes call up afterward to dispute the charges. A couple of our customer service representatives were giving in too easily, and so I established a rule: no credits could be issued without the approval of someone in management.

The rule came back to haunt us whenever a dispute arose in which we were truly at fault. Say a customer placed a rush order and, for some reason, the box didn't arrive on time. The customer would call up, irate, refusing to pay for the delivery. The customer service rep would say, "I'm sorry. We made the delivery, and you have to pay for it."

"But it came too late to do us any good," the customer would say. "We're not paying."

"Well, you'll have to speak to a manager," the rep would say.

The manager, of course, would waive the charge after hearing the story, but the customer would still be angry. First, because the delivery was late. Second, because we would have charged for it anyway if no one had complained. Third, because it took a call to a manager to get the charge waived. So the customer went away thinking, "That damn service stinks." And the next thing we knew, the account was in jeopardy because the person responsible for the contract had heard that we charged even when we didn't deliver on time.

By the time I realized what was happening, my rule had already done some damage. Needless to say, I got rid of it. Subsequently, our customer service reps were allowed to decide for themselves whether or not to issue a credit. At times when we were at fault, I hoped they did. Did some reps make bad decisions? Yes, but then we just had to train them to do better. In retrospect, it was obvious I'd made a mistake by establishing a rule just because a couple of employees were loose with credit. The right response would have been to put in the time and effort required to get them up to speed.

And that's really the point. We tend to make bad rules not when we're attacking problems but when we're avoiding them. We fall into the trap of looking for shortcuts and easy answers. So one bad customer drives off without paying his bill, and we put restrictions on all our good customers. Or one employee uses poor judgment in issuing credit, and we tie the hands of all those whose judgment is perfectly sound.

The result is bad customer service. Our employees take the rap, but we're the ones to blame. If you're lucky, you find out about the problem and eliminate the rule before too much harm has been done. You may get upset with yourself when that happens, but at least you can minimize the damage. What should worry you are the bad rules you've set and haven't yet found out about.

The Bottom Line

Point One: Customers don't like feeling that they're supporting your lavish lifestyle. Don't give them reasons to think they are.

Point Two: Make a habit of having small price increases on a regular basis so that you aren't forced to have a big increase later on.

Point Three: Your company is probably your most valuable personal asset. Don't undermine its value by letting your margins erode.

Point Four: Beware of the rules you make. They may inadvertently force your employees to provide poor service to customers.

CHAPTER ELEVEN

The Decision to Grow

Most company owners have a regular routine they go through every year, usually in December or January. They sit down with a calculator and try to figure out where their business is going over the next few years and how it can get there. It's an important exercise, and yet it gets an awful lot of people into trouble. They make the mistake of focusing on their business plan before they've figured out their life plan, and the life plan must come first.

Many of us, unfortunately, come to this realization fairly late in the game, after we've already taken our lumps. If you'd asked me in the 1980s what I wanted to do, I would have answered without hesitation, "Take my business to $100 million." What else I might do with my life, and why I wanted a $100 million company, I never even thought about. I was simply determined to have one, no matter what. And, as you know, I got my wish. Granted, my life was crazy. I had no time for my family. I never took a vacation. I wasn't doing a lot of the things I most enjoy. Still, I did have my $100 million business for a while, thanks to the disastrous acquisition I wrote about in the second chapter. Then the company started hemorrhaging cash, and the next thing I knew, I was in Chapter 11.

It took three years, but I eventually brought the company out of Chapter 11. The experience was one I'll never forget and hope never to repeat. Like most such experiences, however, it was incredibly educational. Among other things, it forced me to go back and ask myself why I was in business in the first place. These days, that is usually the first question I ask people who come to me looking for advice.

Consider Mike Baicher, who contacted me in the mid-1990s for advice about growing his business. He said he had to hire some salespeople, but he didn't know if he could afford the expense. Would I help him come up with a plan? I agreed to meet with him. It turned out that Mike had a family-owned trucking business, hauling containers to and from the ports around New York. The company had been in operation for thirty-two years and was doing about $1.7 million per year in sales. Mike said he wanted to take it to $10 million or $15 million in five years. My question was, "Why?"

He gave me a funny look and said, "What do you mean?"

I said, "Listen, let's forget about business. Business is just a means to an end. The question is, what's the end? Where do you want to go in your life? Where do you want to be in five years from a family standpoint? What do you want to earn? How much time do you want to take off?"

Mike didn't have answers to these questions. He hadn't given them much thought. People seldom do. He had to discuss them with his wife. He had to talk with other members of his family, several of whom were in the business. In the end, he decided that what he really wanted was to double his modest salary. He and his wife had two kids, and their house was too small. He said he'd like to earn enough to afford a bigger one. He added that he'd also like to take some time off now and then. Nothing much—maybe two or three weeks a year. As it was, he worked every day and took few, if any, vacations.

I said, "Well, then, you don't want to grow your business to $10 million in five years. You probably don't have the money to do it in any case, but—if you did—you'd wind up working eighteen hours a day, seven days a week, and you'd never see your family."

Understand, if Mike had given me a different set of personal goals, I'd have given him a different response. Some people, after all, really *are* driven to grow their companies as fast as possible, and they're willing to sacrifice plenty of things in the process—including their families. I don't try to argue with people like that. They won't listen. I know. I used to be one of them.

Mike wasn't one of them, however, and so we were able to come up with a new business plan that would allow him to get what he wanted. He would aim to grow the business to about $3 million in sales in five years, rather than $15 million, and he wouldn't hire any new salespeople just yet. Mike himself would be making sales calls. He enjoyed selling, and he was good at it. He just hadn't been able to do much of it because he'd been needed in the office. But he had a brother who'd been driving a truck full-time while getting paid a family member's wage. With a little training, the brother could take over some of the office duties, freeing Mike to go out and sell. So instead of spending $50,000 per year on a new salesperson, the company would be spending $10,000 per year on a part-time truck driver to fill in for the brother, and Mike would be focusing on the areas where he could have the biggest impact. I also suggested that he look for other services he could offer his current customers, on the principle that the easiest customer to get is the one you already have. When we finally got around to doing sales projections, we figured that the company could reasonably be expected to do $3.2 million in the fifth year of the plan. Mike thanked me for my help—and disappeared for five and a half years.

Then, one day, he called me out of the blue to ask if he could drop by. I was eager to see him and find out what had happened. When he walked in, I could see at once that Mike was a different man. He'd lost forty pounds and was far more relaxed than I remembered him. He laughed as he told me how his life and his business had changed.

To begin with, he'd fulfilled all his goals. He was making more money. He had a larger house. He took vacations and spent lots of time with his kids and his wife. Since hiring a dispatcher, he'd been able to shut off his phone and leave work most days at 5:00 or 5:30 p.m. On the business side, he'd begun selling storage services to his trucking customers and now had several warehouses that provided an additional revenue stream. Business was great, he said. With obvious pride, he told me that the company had finished the fifth year with $3.6 million in sales, beating our projections by $400,000. He expected to do $5 million the following year.

"That's terrific, Mike," I said. "Congratulations."

"Yeah, I'm happy," he said. "I'm ready to go to the next step."

"What's that?" I asked.

"Buying other trucking businesses," he said.

An alarm went off in my head. "That can be awfully tricky," I said. "You can really hurt yourself with acquisitions."

"What do you mean?" he asked.

I explained to Mike the inherent risk in every business acquisition. For openers, you never know exactly what you're getting until you own the company and it's too late to go back. Buying other trucking businesses would be especially risky because most of the contracts are at will. Mike could acquire a company and discover that a lot of customers were leaving, or that the salespeople controlled the accounts and were threatening to take them away, or a million other things. Since he'd have to borrow money to do acquisitions, he could get into major cash flow problems. In the worst case, a bad acquisition could bring the company down, as I'd learned to my chagrin in the 1980s.

Understand, I'm not saying that people should never buy businesses. Sometimes it's the best way to grow. Moreover, there are steps you can take to protect yourself—for example, by persuading the sellers to let you pay them out of sales and over time. But Mike had another issue to consider. He'd just spent five years creating a good life for himself. Did he really want to take a chance on throwing it away?

"Well, I have a concern," he said. "I do almost all of my business with two large customers. I'm really in good with them, but it would be tough if one of them dropped us, or cut way back."

That, I had to agree, was a pretty serious concern, but there were better ways to address it than by doing acquisitions. Mike could, for example, spend more time on sales. He was good at it, he enjoyed it, and he'd have a much better chance of keeping the customers he got by doing it. Instead of borrowing to buy companies, he could leverage his relationships with his two main customers—one in cosmetics, the other in apparel. They were fabulous references, and they gave him great entrée to their respective industries. Even if he signed up just two or three more customers of equal size, he'd be in much better shape than before. You can sleep a lot more soundly when your largest customer accounts for 20 percent of your business than you can when it represents 50 percent or more.

Mike wasn't completely convinced. "Getting more customers that way takes a long time," he said.

"Yes, it does," I said. "But you know something? There are no real shortcuts in business, and when you look for them, you usually get in trouble. It took me a long time to realize that. People like me want instant gratification. One of the hardest lessons I had to learn is that you can't expect good things—like more customers and better sales— to happen overnight."

Mike still had reservations. He said he wanted to think it over. I said I thought that was a good idea. I made it clear that—if he was dead set on buying companies—I'd help him lay down some ground rules to minimize the risks he'd be taking. But when we got back together, he told me he had decided against going the acquisition route. I have to say I was relieved. It would have been a shame for him to jeopardize the good life he'd created for himself when there were other ways to accomplish what he needed to. But the urge to grow often leads people to make those kinds of mistakes—which is why the life plan has to come before the business plan.

The Mystery of Success

Now, I'm not saying there's anything wrong with wanting to grow your business. On the contrary, if you have a successful business, it's only natural to want to expand it. Just don't fall into the trap of growing for growth's sake. Bigger isn't always better, and the reasons for your success may be difficult to pinpoint.

That's the problem with success. When you fail in business, you can look back, see what you did wrong, and learn the appropriate lessons, but it's often difficult, if not impossible, to figure out why a particular business concept clicks. While you may be able to list a number of important factors, you still won't necessarily know exactly what combination of them came together at the right moment and in the right proportions to make the business take off. You should bear that in mind when you're deciding how you're going to take your business to the next level in sales. If you don't really know what's driving your success, you have to be careful about the strategy you adopt. There's a risk, after all, that you may accidentally undermine whatever made your company successful in the first place.

Ask Norm

Dear Norm:

Five years ago, my father brought me into his company so that he could spend more time doing outside sales. Lately, he seems to be working less and taking more cash out. Once I was told I'd be given the company; now it turns out I'll have to buy it. I'm thirty years old. I want to grow the business, but I can't unless we start reinvesting our profits. So it's time to make an offer. I don't want to pay too much, but I also don't want to insult my father with a low offer. Any advice?

    Robert

Dear Robert:

Before you offer anything, you need to do some soul-searching and life planning. Where do you want to be in ten years? What kind of life do you want? Then design an offer that will allow you to attain your life goals. Do some research into the value of comparable businesses, and figure out what you can afford. Your proposal should specify how much you'd pay, when you'd start paying, over what period of time, how much salary your father could continue to draw, and so on. You can't fault your father for wanting to sell you the company. He built it. He has a right to get something for it. But you don't necessarily have to buy it. In fact, you may eventually decide it's better to leave. Just make sure you can leave on good terms. Tell your father, "Here's my plan. I think I can do it if I buy the company from you under these conditions. I love you. I love the company. I'd like to stay. But I need a plan that's going to let me achieve my goals."

    —Norm

Take, for example, a friend of mine whom we'll call Seymour. Back in 2000, he owned one of the hottest little clothing stores in the New York metropolitan area. Let's call it Hot Pants. It was a tiny shop—about 1,250 square feet—located in a suburban strip mall, and it specialized in jeans and casual clothing, mainly for young women and teenage girls. From that one location, Seymour racked up several million dollars a year in sales, giving him one of the highest sales-per-square-foot figures in his segment of the retail clothing industry.

For Seymour, the shop was a dream come true. A self-taught businessman and dyed-in-the-wool entrepreneur, he'd had several previous ventures that did well enough, but none of them took off the way Hot Pants did following its launch in 1994. His plan, he said, was to grow the business and sell it in five years or so. Toward that end, he opened a second Hot Pants in another town about sixty miles away from the first store. He also had a discount outlet, where he sold his old and discontinued inventory.

One day, I got a call from Seymour, who said he had to see me. A big opportunity had come along, and he wanted my advice. It turned out that the space next to the original Hot Pants was becoming vacant. Seymour wanted to lease it, knock down the wall, and double the size of his store. He figured he could generate between $1 million and $2 million in additional sales pretty much overnight. What did I think?

Now, you have to understand that Hot Pants was a very crowded place. On most days there were lines at the cash registers and the dressing rooms. Somehow Seymour had managed to generate tremendous buzz among middle-class girls of a certain age—say, thirteen to eighteen years old—and large numbers of them showed up on a regular basis, not only to shop but to socialize with their friends.

That was good for the buzz, but Seymour thought he was losing a significant amount of business from customers who didn't want to wait in line or deal with the crowds. He figured he could solve the problem by expanding. I was skeptical. For one thing, I wasn't sure he could make enough additional profit to justify the investment. "What does the landlord want?" I asked. Seymour said the landlord wanted him to give up his old lease and sign a new one for the combined space at the current market rate. Because rates had increased since he'd signed his original lease, he would wind up paying about 25 percent more on his old space, in addition to the rent for the new space. He'd also have to put up "key money"—a sort of signing bonus for the landlord. Then there was the cost of fixing up the new space, carrying additional inventory, and hiring more staff.

"You have to look at the effect on your margins," I said. Seymour agreed. So we sat down and went through the numbers. It quickly became clear that he'd need more than $1 million in additional sales just to break even on his investment.

And could he, in fact, count on getting those sales? I had my doubts. A specialty-clothing store is not a restaurant. When a would-be diner walks out of a restaurant because the wait is too long, that sale is probably lost. Why? Because it almost always goes to a competitor. I wasn't convinced, however, that the same thing happened when Seymour's customers decided against waiting to pay for—or try on—a pair of jeans. When you have a hot store, people come partly because they want to say they bought from you. They're looking for prestige as well as merchandise. My guess was that most Hot Pants customers who left because of the crowds would simply return when the store was less busy.

In that case, I pointed out, Seymour was losing few, if any, sales because of overcrowding. He'd saturated his marketplace. Everybody who wanted to shop at Hot Pants already did. "Well, then, maybe I'll bring in new lines," Seymour said, "like for young guys."

That's what I was afraid of. To justify his investment, Seymour might be tempted to change his concept. "You're talking about a whole new business," I said. "You could be jeopardizing what you already have. Maybe the girls want to be there alone." The truth is, Seymour didn't know why his business was so successful, and neither did I. It could have been the music he played or the quality of his staff or the store's name or his own personality. Most likely, it was some combination of those things and a dozen other factors—perhaps even the lack of space. The kids may have liked being jammed together. They may not have minded waiting in line to use a dressing room.

All Seymour knew for sure was that he was blowing away all the standard projections for a business of his type, size, and location. His sales were two and half times the amount anyone would have predicted for a jeans store in a strip mall with limited foot traffic. You can't explain that kind of success. You can only recognize it, respect it, and handle it with care. Seymour's most valuable asset was the brand he'd created. By doubling the size of his store, he would be taking a chance that he'd inadvertently devalue the brand. It was a risk that, in my view at least, was way out of proportion to the potential reward.

I wasn't saying that Seymour shouldn't grow his business. He already had a second Hot Pants up and running. It hadn't yet matched the performance of the first store, but then it hadn't been around very long. I urged Seymour to think about starting a third Hot Pants. I suggested he choose a location near enough to the original store that the local kids would have heard the buzz but far enough away that they wouldn't already be regular customers. If the new store did well, Seymour would have a proven concept that he could sell in five years to someone interested in taking it national. If the spin-off failed, well, at least he wouldn't have damaged his core business.

But Seymour wasn't looking for that type of advice. He mainly wanted to know whether I thought he was crazy to double the size of the original Hot Pants. "Do you think I'll go out of business?" he asked.

"No," I said, "but I think you'll hurt yourself."

I guess Seymour disagreed, because he went ahead with his expansion plans anyway. That may, in fact, have been the right decision for him personally, even if it was wrong for the business. It's much easier to expand an existing store than to start a new one. It's also less expensive. Seymour was already working six or seven days a week, putting in long hours every day, and he was a guy who likes to have direct control of operations. So he may have decided he'd be happier with a larger main store than with a third smaller one. That was a perfectly good reason for him to make the decision he did. (Remember, life plan before business plan.) I was just afraid he would lose some of the value he'd worked so hard to build.

In the end, I don't think the expansion did undermine the value of Seymour's business—but he didn't get much benefit from it, either. He had to borrow money to do it, and he struggled to pay back the loan. The increase in sales scarcely made up for the time, energy, and aggravation it cost him. That often happens when you grow just for the sake of growing.

Ask Norm

Dear Norm:
My sisters and I started a bath-and-body company on a shoe-string three years ago. This year we're on target to hit $4 million in sales. We have great distribution, sell to every major department store in the country, and have been approached by Disney, Warner Bros., and others to create private-label products. We'll soon be entering the mass market under a different name. The problem is that our opportunities are outstripping our resources. What do you advise?
  Sara

Dear Sara:
I'll give you the advice I wish someone had given me before I took my first company to $120 million—and wound up in Chapter 11. Your core business must always come first. No opportunity is worth going after if it jeopardizes your core business even one iota. It's not just about money. You also have limited time. Ask yourself two questions about each new opportunity: Will it keep me from putting in the time required to build or maintain my core business? And, if the opportunity turns into a financial disaster, will my core business be crippled? If the answer to either question is yes, you probably should rethink whether or not this is a good opportunity.
  —Norm

Size Matters

My point is that growth is a matter of choice. You don't have to grow at all if you don't want to. You certainly don't have to strive to get as big as possible as fast as possible. If that's what you want, more power to you, but there's no rule of business that says you must. I can think of many situations in which smaller companies actually have a distinct advantage over larger ones. In fact, I've often found that it's easier to compete against a big company than against a well-run small company. That's certainly the case in my records storage business. We beat the giants on service. We beat them on flexibility. We beat them on location and price. I can count on the fingers of one hand the number of customers (other than national accounts) that we've ever lost to the giants of records storage.

I don't mean any disrespect toward our large competitors. I consider Iron Mountain, the giant of our industry, to be a great company with first-class operations and people, but it can't offer what we have: a highly focused, tightly knit, family-oriented small business with owners who are on the scene and actively involved. We play that advantage for all it's worth. All prospective customers visit our main warehouse and meet with me personally. I tell them, "Anytime you have a problem, you can just call me." Sometimes the prospect will say that the big companies offer the same thing. I say, "Oh, really? Why don't you try calling their CEOs? See how long it takes to get them on the line. I wear a digital phone wherever I go. If I'm in the country, you can reach me."

The message is one of accessibility and personal service, and we constantly look for ways to reinforce it. Every new customer receives a thank-you note from me and my wife, Elaine, who owns the company with me and plays a key role on our management team. I myself visit as many customers as time will allow in the course of a year. We invite all of them to our company parties. We name warehouse aisles after the ones who place a certain number of boxes with us. We do all kinds of little things.

Beyond the symbolic gestures, we offer customers a degree of flexibility that the big companies simply can't match. Our salespeople, for example, have much more leeway than theirs do in negotiating prices and add-on services with customers. Suppose a small customer—one with fewer than 2,000 boxes—wants to use its own forms instead of ours to keep track of what it sends us. We say, "Fine." A big company can't afford to accommodate such requests from small customers. It would have chaos in its operations if it tried. And, besides, why bother? If you have 40 million boxes in your warehouses—as the big companies do—you don't even notice when you lose a 2,000-box account.

So our size has been an advantage, especially in going after the small to medium accounts, which are the bread and butter of our industry. Our primary competition for them used to come not from the giants but from the other regional specialists, whose owners ran their businesses much as I ran mine. And that entrepreneurial edge is precisely what two of them lost when they were acquired by large companies. I just hope we don't share their fate as CitiStorage grows from a regional to a national business.

The Bottom Line

Point One: Business is a means to an end. Do a life plan before you make your business plans.

Point Two: When trying to move to the next level of sales, don't assume you know all the factors that led to your initial success.

Point Three: Growing a business is a matter of choice. Before deciding to grow, make sure you know why you're doing it.

Point Four: Bigger is not always better. Small companies have some advantages that large companies can't match.

CHAPTER TWELVE

Becoming the Boss

We all face a major challenge as our companies grow. It's a challenge, moreover, that most of us neither understand nor want. I'm talking about the necessity of becoming the boss. I myself hated the idea of becoming the boss when I started my first company. I didn't even like to admit that I had employees. I'd talk about them as people who worked *with* me, rather than *for* me. It was as though we were all equal in the business—we just had different roles. That wasn't true, of course. It never is. Someone always has to be the boss, even in a start-up. If you don't accept that reality, you're headed for trouble.

There are actually two types of mistakes that people typically make when they're new to the boss's role. The first involves their relationship with employees. The second has to do with their assumptions about their own job.

To be a good boss, I've learned, you need to maintain a certain distance from your employees. You have different responsibilities from theirs. As the boss, you always have to be thinking about what's best for the business as a whole, and you can't let emotional attachments interfere with your decisions. Not that you shouldn't care deeply about your employees and their families, but I believe it's a mistake to develop personal relationships with them outside the business. Employees should not be your social friends, and your social friends should not be your employees. Yes, you should treat employees with respect. You can laugh with them, cry with them, be happy and sad with them, but neither you nor they should ever forget that it's a business relationship. If you do, you're going to create problems for you, for them, and for the company.

Now, that's advice I wish someone had given me before I launched my first company. I'm not sure, however, that I would have listened. The problem is, it runs counter to all our human instincts, and it seems to defy the spirit of the start-up. When you start your first business, you can't help but get close to your employees. After all, you're working sixty to seventy hours a week together in an incredibly intense environment, struggling to survive. It's a thrilling adventure, and you're depending on one another to succeed. There's a wonderful feeling of camaraderie, of all-for-one-and-one-for-all. The last thing you want to do is create barriers. Your employees are among the most important people in your life. Why shouldn't they be your friends outside the business as well?

That's what I thought when I started my first business. I had seven employees, and all but one became personal friends of mine. They came to my home, and I went to theirs. Our families spent time together. We went on joint vacations. And I learned the hard way that I'd made a big mistake.

To begin with, I tended to promote people to positions for which they were completely unqualified. We had a driver I liked, and I brought him into the office to answer telephones. Four weeks later, I made him our head of customer service. Why not? We needed someone to do the job, and he was my friend. He just happened to have none of the skills required to succeed in that position. Later I got angry when I realized how much I was overpaying him, but the fault was mine, not his.

I was also inclined to hold on to people longer than I should have. When we needed a sales manager, I gave the job to one of our salespeople, another friend. It was a disaster. He was a hotshot. He took over all the best accounts and claimed for himself every sale that closed in the office. And yet I kept making excuses for him—until I discovered one day that he'd been lying to me and inflating his commissions on one of our biggest accounts. I fired him.

But there was one episode in particular that convinced me I'd gone too far. It involved my head dispatcher, who'd been with me from the start and had become a close friend. Our families had gone away together. We'd shared many good times. I considered myself part of his family, and him part of mine. Then I caught him stealing from me. He had access to our petty cash, and it turned out he'd been using it as his own personal piggy bank. He'd gotten away with it because I'd trusted him as a friend, and so I didn't check on him the way I should have. That hurt. It really hurt. Not that the amount was enough to jeopardize the company, but the emotions were just too much to deal with—I mean, much too much. Before I even confronted him, I went home and cried.

Unfortunately, it often takes an experience like that to make you aware of the perils of getting too close to your employees. I've watched countless entrepreneurs go through it. Anisa Telwar, whom I wrote about in chapter 5, is a case in point. She came to me one day and said she felt lost. She'd been having problems with two longtime employees, both of them salespeople who'd helped her start the business. One of them she'd had to let go, which she said was an agonizing experience because she regarded the person as a friend. I could feel her pain.

Meanwhile, she was making the second common mistake of first-time entrepreneurs who suddenly find themselves in the boss's chair. She felt that, to be a good boss, she had to become a manager. Accordingly, she was spending more and more time in the office, attending to various administrative chores, taking care of a thousand little details that allow a company to run smoothly. It was the kind of work she hated, but she thought it was her responsibility to do it. I made that mistake, too, and I nearly wrecked my company in the process.

"What do you like to do?" I asked her.

"I like the excitement of solving problems and building a business."

"Well, I'm the same way," I said. "And I've learned that not only am I not a good manager but I don't want to be one. I want to do what I like. So what do I do? I surround myself with anal people." Anisa laughed. "It's true," I said. "They love the detail, love the follow-up process, love writing letters and memos, love doing all the things that you and I hate."

"You're right," she said. "I hate that stuff."

"Yes, and there's no reason you should do it," I said. "You don't have to sit in an office to be in charge of a business. Management is just another job. You wouldn't think twice about hiring an accountant to handle the books. Why should you assume that you have to be the manager? You're the best salesperson you've got. There's nothing wrong with focusing on sales. You can still give the company direction. You can still set the standards. But first you need to extricate yourself from management and turn it over to people who are good at it. Then you can go back to doing the work you enjoy."

Finding the right person is another matter. I was lucky in that regard. Remember, there was one guy from the start-up whom I didn't socialize with outside the business. He was thirteen years younger than me, he lived far away, and he had a style that was very different from mine. He was ana——, well, maybe I should say he was detail oriented. In any event, he became the president of my company and my partner in the business. I love him and depend on him. Thank goodness we never became social friends.

When Employees Steal

I want to come back to the issue of employee theft, because I think it's one of the toughest ones we all have to deal with, and the first time it happens is always the hardest. The sense of betrayal is often devastating. But if you're not careful, you may respond in a way that undermines you and your business.

I'll give you the example of a person I know who owns a couple of successful bed-and-breakfast places. We'll call her Naomi. After working in the business for nine years, putting in fifty-five-hour weeks, she decided she needed a break from day-to-day management. Both B&Bs were doing well and had general managers she trusted completely. The time seemed right to let go.

So she did. For the next two years, Naomi had a wonderful life. She traveled. She got married. She devoted a lot of time to recreation, hobbies, and charity work. Once a month, she would sit down with the general managers to talk over business issues, and occasionally she'd drop by her establishments to have lunch with the staff, but by and large she left the company alone. Everything seemed fine, and she was happier than ever. Why mess with success?

Ask Norm

Dear Norm:
After my mother died, I took over her business. I hired a girl,
who brought along a friend, and I reluctantly hired her, too.
I've been living a nightmare ever since. These women drive me
crazy. They abuse my kindness, abuse my phones, misfile, can't
type, mess up my computers, complain constantly, spend all
their time talking to one another, and never complete assign-
ments. Yet I'm scared to say anything for fear I won't be able
to replace them. The people I've interviewed want benefits, and
my business is too small to provide them. What should I do?
    Renee

Dear Renee:
Fire them both as soon as possible, and do it on your own
terms. What kind of life do you have with those people around?
You deserve better, and you'll feel better as soon as you make
the decision to let them go. Believe me, you can replace them,
even if you can't afford benefits. Maybe you can offer something else—a flexible work schedule, for example. Find new
people, train them over the weekend, and have them start on
Monday. When your two current employees come to work, tell
them they're no longer needed. You may have to put in extra
hours for a few weeks, but your life will be easier in the long
run, and you'll be happier.
    —Norm

Then she began to pick up murmurs of problems at the larger
B&B. One of her most loyal employees, the head housekeeper, told
Naomi that she'd heard disturbing things from close friends of hers
who worked part-time at the front desk. A couple of the people there

weren't honest, they'd said. Naomi spoke to the B&B's general manager, Janice, who dismissed the report, noting that the housekeeper
often exaggerated. That was true, Naomi agreed.

But there were other signs. Guests would sometimes check out
and call back a couple of weeks later, asking for a receipt, and the
B&B would have no record of their stay. What seemed like exces-
sive charges for room furnishings and entertainment appeared on the
company credit card. When Naomi checked the petty cash drawer
one day, she was shocked to find almost $1,000 there, instead of the
usual $100. Janice said that some people were asking to be paid in
cash. "We don't do that," Naomi said and took the extra cash to the
bank.

The truth is, Naomi didn't want to know what all the signs were
pointing to. She was enjoying the life she had and had no interest in
going back to fifty-five-hour workweeks. Besides, she trusted Janice, who
was not only one of her general managers but also a personal friend—
or so she thought. But the signs kept mounting, and the housekeeper
kept insisting. She noted that she had detailed records of the rooms
her staff had cleaned. They could be checked against the records of
the rooms guests had paid for. Finally, Naomi gave in and did an audit,
which took her more than two months to complete. The result: about
thirty rooms per month were unaccounted for. That translated into the
disappearance of more than $50,000 a year.

Naomi could no longer ignore the evidence. She insisted on implementing new procedures. When Janice resisted, Naomi fired her and
began working full-time again at the B&B. It soon became clear that
the situation was even worse that she'd imagined. Another employee,
caught red-handed, confessed to stealing $30,000 over two years. He
said Janice had coached him—and walked away with far more money
than he had taken.

I know just what Naomi felt at that point. She was mortified. She
was angry. She felt betrayed and violated. How could people do that?
She blamed herself for allowing it to happen and swore that, in the
future, she'd watch the business like a hawk. No one could be trusted
to run it in her absence. From now on, she'd be there full-time. That

was my reaction when I learned about my head dispatcher stealing from the company. The loss of the money was the least of it. Far worse was the sense of betrayal. I felt completely alone. I didn't know whom I could trust anymore. I decided to trust no one—which was exactly the wrong response.

The biggest problem with employee theft is that it often leads you to make bad decisions about your business and your life. The emotions are so overwhelming that you tend to overreact. You can't get back to making good business decisions until you take the emotions out of the process. The first step is to understand that theft is a business issue and needs to be addressed as such. In most cases, it happens because there's a problem with the procedures in your business. Maybe you've neglected to establish a certain check or balance. Maybe people weren't following the procedures you already have in place. Maybe you just weren't paying attention. In any case, something went wrong. You need to find out what it was and fix it.

You shouldn't stop trusting people, however. Yes, a small number of individuals are thieves. No matter what you do, they're going to look for ways to beat the system, and sometimes they'll succeed. But the vast majority of people are honest. You'll be doing yourself and them a tremendous disservice if you start running your company as if you believe that nobody can be trusted.

That's why you need to have the right procedures. They allow the business to run smoothly and let people relate to one another on the basis of trust, while simultaneously making theft more difficult and helping you to nip it in the bud when it happens. Accordingly, one of your major responsibilities as the owner is to check your procedures from time to time, making sure those you have are being followed and looking for new ones you may need. And when you come across something that doesn't make sense, it's important to ask questions.

In my company, for example, there were always three people who signed the weekly paychecks. At one point, they weren't around, so I decided to sign the checks myself—which I hadn't done in a long time—simply to see how our procedures were working. As I was going through the checks, I came to one for $1,100 made out to a driver who has a two-hour run each day. At ten hours a week, he would be making $110 an hour. That couldn't be right, I thought, and put the check aside. I continued to sign until I came to another check that looked wrong to me: $600 for one day's driving. That would be $3,000 a week, $150,000 a year. Nice work if you can find it. I put that one aside as well. Out of about three hundred checks, I found four that I thought required further investigation.

So I went downstairs and examined the drivers' backup logs and tickets. Three of the four checks turned out to be correct; the fourth was not. One guy had figured out how to beat our system by putting in duplicate tickets. The scam was costing us $300 a week. How long had it been going on? I didn't ask or care. I never look back. It only gets you aggravated. Instead, I had a meeting with the check signers and reminded them that their job wasn't just to sign checks. I could buy a machine to do that. They were supposed to think about what they were signing and notice if the amounts didn't make sense. In that case, at any rate, we didn't need a new procedure. We just had to do a better job of following the one we already had.

Clearly, Naomi didn't have the right procedures in place before she decided to step back from her business. If she'd had a simple system for comparing, say, the number of rooms cleaned each week with the number of rooms paid for, she would have caught the problems much sooner than she did. Then again, she really didn't want to know about them, as she herself admitted.

Naomi's response was to make the opposite mistake. She believed she couldn't spend any significant time away from the business without running the risk of having it stolen from under her. Her only way out was to sell it, she said. Those were her emotions talking. Granted, it wouldn't have been wise to become an absentee owner again, but—with the right procedures and regular monitoring—there was no reason she couldn't hold on to the business and still lead a full and balanced life. Fortunately, she came to her senses before she made another mistake she would have lived to regret.

Ask Norm

Dear Norm:

About two and a half years ago, I hired someone to be the oper-ations manager of my company. He was the perfect fit for my business at the time. Now, however, the company has outgrown his ability to handle the job. He is still an asset to the team but not in his current position. I would like to keep him on the bus and move him to a different seat. It's a tough situation. He is thirty-three years old and has a family. But I feel I must do something. Any suggestions?

    Eric

Dear Eric:

We all wind up in your situation sooner or later, and I agree—it's tough. You feel guilty because it's your fault for putting him there in the first place. I used to try doing what you're suggesting, but things seldom worked out well. The issue was compensation. If I cut a guy's salary, he would be resentful. If I didn't cut his salary, I would become resentful. You need to think clearly and unemo-tionally about this situation. If you have another job on the same pay level that the guy is suited for, by all means, move him over. But don't do it if his new responsibilities won't justify paying him what he's been getting up to now. It's better to let him go. If your conscience bothers you, give him a big severance package.

—Norm

Necessary Losses

Bear in mind that becoming the boss is a journey, not a destination. You go through stages of understanding your role, but you never stop having to learn something new, because the job is constantly evolving. Some stages are harder than others.

For me, the most difficult stage came when I realized that it was time for me to get out of management and let my managers run Citi-Storage. The truth is, I'd put off delegating authority to my management team for as long as I could. Who wants to give up being the chief cook and bottle washer in his own company? Sure, the managers told me that our problems were serious, and that I was creating a lot of them, but I didn't listen. So what if we lost a few people? So what if morale wasn't the greatest? So what if the managers spent a lot of time putting out fires? They were getting paid, weren't they?

I'm not sure what finally convinced me to do it. Maybe it was my own frustration with certain aspects of our performance. Maybe it was the nagging memory of what had happened with my messenger business as it grew to $100 million. Maybe my managers just wore me down. Whatever it was, I finally gave in and agreed that we had to change. The business needed things I couldn't provide, and it couldn't acquire them as long as I was always around, making the key decisions and running the show. So I took myself out of the chain of command and put my management team in charge.

In retrospect, I can see that company was ready for the change long before I was. People were desperate for order and structure. Me? I prefer chaos. Deep down, I like having problems. I enjoy the excitement of working in a crisis atmosphere. That's one of the reasons I get so much pleasure out of starting businesses. You have nothing but problems when you're starting out. You're always on the firing line. You're juggling a dozen balls, and you can't afford to let any of them drop. Everybody is counting on you. No one questions your decision-making process. You're almost like a god in that situation, and you run on pure adrenaline. It's exciting, stimulating, and challenging, and I love every minute of it.

That stage doesn't last, however. If your business is successful, it eventually moves beyond the start-up phase and starts to grow. You can hang on for a while, but sooner or later the company develops a set of needs that entrepreneurs like me aren't good at dealing with. You can't ignore those needs. I did once and lived to regret it. When I looked back on my experience with the messenger business, I realized that—among the many things I did wrong—I'd made the crucial mistake of keeping the company from getting the management, stability, and structure it needed. I just wouldn't back off. I made all the final decisions and didn't let the managers do their jobs. In the end, I paid a steep price.

I decided I was not going to make that mistake again, but delegating authority doesn't come easy to someone like me. In fact, I can't think of anything more difficult in business than changing the way your company is run—going from one-person rule to shared leadership. What's more, it was not an area in which I had any expertise, and I knew that when I began the process of turning day-to-day operations over to my managers. There were, in fact, three challenges I faced.

The first challenge was to find someone else to manage the transition for me. That didn't mean hiring a new CEO. Whenever a founder decides to step back, people always start searching for a replacement, and it's rarely the right solution. I knew we didn't need a new boss, and we didn't need new managers. What we needed was a new management system—and someone to help us set it up. There was simply no way that I was going to be able to oversee my own company's transition to team-based management. All my instincts led me to resist the change. People like me not only thrive in unstable environments but we breed instability, and management is all about creating stability through planning, organization, and commitment.

So I realized that someone else had to lead this process—a professional manager, a person who found building companies as exciting as I found starting them. There are consultants who specialize in these transitions, but I can't think of one I'd feel comfortable turning my business over to. Nor was I about to bring in a big company executive who knew nothing about operating in a small-business environment. I needed someone whom I knew extremely well and trusted completely, whose thought process I both understood and respected. A major part of this person's job, after all, was going to involve dealing with me. I was very anxious about the whole process. My company is my baby. Other people helped raise it, but it began as a sparkle in my eye. So I had to have complete confidence in whomever I hired to take it to the next level. Fortunately, my future partner Sam Kaplan, whom I'd known for twenty-three years at that point, was available. He was someone whose judgment I trusted even when I disagreed with him, which was essential. Giving up control was scary. There were moments when it was hard for me to go forward because I was afraid for my company, just as I'd be afraid if someone took my baby away. You need to have blind faith in the person who's guiding you, or you won't make it. I have that kind of faith in Sam.

You also need to find something else that you can do in the company—which was the second challenge I faced. I mean, if I wasn't going to be running the business anymore, how was I going to spend my time? I have many outside interests, but I couldn't just walk away from the company. I still loved it. I loved the concept. I found the business exciting. I wanted to be close to it. And yet I realized as well that I had to get out of the way. I knew I wasn't going to enjoy my reduced role. I've always had a hard time not having the final say. I want to be included in every decision, and I knew I'd have trouble accepting that people could make decisions without me. I'd have even more trouble going along with decisions that weren't the same as the ones I would have made.

So what was I going to do? Sit alone in my office with the door closed, biting my tongue and grinding my teeth? Or fall back on old habits and undermine the entire process? I'd learned over the years that the best way to break a bad habit is to replace it with a good habit. I'd also learned that CEOs are responsible for putting people in positions where they can make the greatest contribution to the company— and I would still be the CEO.

What were the best jobs for me? One of them was sales, no question. I enjoyed it, I was good at it, and I had a lifetime of contacts to draw on. I was also pretty good at negotiating deals and overseeing projects—and we were going to be building new warehouses for years to come. So I decided to divide my time between making sales calls and supervising the construction of the new buildings. Those two jobs, I figured, would keep me involved with the business and out of everybody else's hair. I'd stay away from the office as much as possible.

I wouldn't attend staff meetings. I'd let my managers make their own decisions and do my best to abide by them.

That was the plan, at any rate, but old habits die hard. The third challenge turned out to be sticking with the process. There were moments when I wondered how long I could keep it up, and how far I could let it go. My goal was to turn 100 percent of my authority over to my management team, but it took me almost a decade to achieve it. Occasionally, the managers would ask me what I wanted to do about something. I sometimes couldn't help giving them an answer, even though I knew they should be making the decision themselves.

Sam kept telling me that I shouldn't make any decisions at all. As long as the managers stayed within the budget and met the financial goals, he said, I shouldn't care how they did it. In theory, he was right, but I had a lot of growing to do before I could practice what he was preaching. Not that the improvements weren't visible. I could see a tremendous difference in the company as time went by. Our employee turnover went way down, partly—I'm sure—because we began doing much better hiring. Under the new procedures, two people had to interview every job candidate. To me, that rule was a luxury. But what can I say? It worked.

Meanwhile, my accounting department did a complete turnaround. Before, I could never get enough information when I wanted it. Afterward, I would get more than I needed—from the same people. I'd always blamed the head of the department for the problem, but it turned out that I was the real culprit. She reported to me. All she needed was more structure and a new boss, and she became a star.

Indeed, most of our employees thrived under the new regime. Morale was higher than ever. The reason was obvious: People wanted structure. They wanted to know what the rules are, and they wanted the same rules applied evenhandedly across the board. They didn't want us to deal with each case individually, as I used to do it. They actually worked better when they believed everybody was getting equal treatment. If you'd told me that before we started the process, I'd have said you were crazy, but I couldn't deny what I saw with my own eyes.

Granted, there were some exceptions. We lost our head dispatcher, for example, a guy who'd been with us for thirteen years. I felt sure he'd make it, but he couldn't handle the changes. He just walked out one day with no warning. I was shocked. To my managers, I'm sure, the biggest surprise was that I stayed committed. They made it easier for me by keeping me well informed. I could see they were making intelligent decisions—maybe not the ones I'd have made, but intelligent ones nevertheless.

And in the end, there was a big payoff. As time went along and I gained confidence, I had the satisfaction of knowing that my business was in good hands and would continue to grow without my direct involvement. As a result, I had the freedom to do the things I loved and to live the kind of life I wanted. I can't imagine a better reward.

The Bottom Line

Point One: As close as you may be to your employees, neither you nor they should forget that it's a business relationship and needs to be treated as such.

Point Two: If you, like most entrepreneurs, prefer selling to managing, remember that you can hire other people to do management. You don't have to do it yourself.

Point Three: The way to deal with employee theft is to improve your systems, not to stop trusting people.

Point Four: When the time comes for you to step aside and turn day-to-day operations over to your managers, get someone you trust to help you with the transition, and find other ways that you can contribute to the business.

CHAPTER THIRTEEN

The One Thing
You Can't Delegate

It goes without saying that great employees are a blessing to any boss and any company, and I feel as though I've been more blessed than most in that regard. I certainly wouldn't have had the business success I've enjoyed, or the wonderful life I've led, without the extraordinary people who work for our companies. It took me quite a while to put the team together. When I started my first business, I knew I wanted to have a great team, and I thought that assembling one was a fairly straightforward process. You just had to hire the best people and then take care of them—pay them well, provide good benefits, offer various perks, whatever.

But like many ideas I had back then, that one proved to be an illusion. For openers, I discovered it's very hard to tell in advance who the best people really are. After making more hiring mistakes than I can count, I came to realize that no matter how sharp your instincts are, no matter how many people you have interview each candidate, no matter how diligently you follow up with reference calls, you simply never know how an individual will do on the job until he or she is actually working for you. Some of the most promising candidates we hired turned out to be duds. Then again, the president of CitiStorage is a guy who nobody thought would last when he first started working for me.

That's the rule, not the exception. More often than not, I've learned, first-rate employees turn up unexpectedly. All you can do is to make your best guess in hiring people and then give them a chance to perform. Some will disappoint you, and some will exceed your expectations. Either way, it will be months or even years before you know exactly whom you have. But I've also learned that assembling a great team isn't all a matter of luck. The most powerful recruitment tool you have is your company's culture, over which you have a substantial amount of control. Every day you have opportunities to shape that culture, and it's important not to let them slip by.

Let me tell you about Elsa the cat, who lived in one of our warehouses. Our people took care of her, and in return she helped with pest control. She also liked to hang out with the cat in the warehouse across the street, as we discovered one day when she showed up with a whole litter of kittens. Only then did we realize she'd been pregnant.

Our employees loved the kittens—who doesn't love kittens?—and many expressed interest in adopting one. We decided that, when the kittens were old enough, we'd hold a raffle to see which people would get them. In the meantime, Elsa kept the litter firmly under her control. She tolerated no interference from humans, hiding the kittens in spots around the warehouse the employees couldn't find.

Then one morning Elsa showed up in the warehouse office clearly distraught. She was crying the way cats do and would not be consoled. Obviously, something had happened to the kittens. That afternoon we received a phone call from the records manager of a law firm that uses our services. One of our drivers had left off some boxes containing records that the firm needed. "You've just delivered us a box of kittens," the records manager said.

The word spread like wildfire through the company. Everybody wanted to know where the kittens were and what we planned to do about them. I would have sent the driver back to pick them up, but we had no way of contacting him. He was already headed home, and he didn't have a phone in his van. From a financial standpoint, it made the most sense to leave the kittens where they were until we made our next delivery. But we've worked hard to build a culture based on the needs and concerns of our people, and at that moment their greatest concern was for the welfare of the kittens. So I decided to send another driver to pick the kittens up.

The round-trip took about two and a half hours. By the time the driver returned, there were more than one hundred employees—plus one cat—gathered around the loading dock. As the box with the kittens was placed in front of their mother, everyone cheered. It was a small event in the life of the business, but it wasn't an insignificant one. If nothing else, it reinforced the people-oriented culture that distinguishes our company from most of our competitors.

That culture has been by far the most important factor in our ability to build a great team over the years. To be sure, money plays a role, as do benefits, but you can't hold on to the best people with financial incentives alone. For one thing, it's too easy for other companies to come along and offer something better. Nobody is loyal to a compensation package. People are extremely loyal, however, to a company that they're proud of—that competes fairly; that does right by its customers and suppliers; that gives back to its community; and that cares, really cares, about being a great place to work. Not only will such a culture bind your current employees to your business, but other people will notice, and the quality of your job applicants will rise.

So how do you create that kind of culture? I believe there are three essential ingredients. The first is mutual trust, which requires clarity about the rules. People need to know what is expected of them and what they can expect in return. My principal rule is simple: I want my employees to give me an honest day's work. Period. As long as they do so, it's up to me to make sure they have jobs. That, I believe, is an employer's primary responsibility. If people do everything you ask of them, they should be able to have confidence that you're going to keep them employed. Without that assurance you can't have mutual trust, and without mutual trust you can't have a healthy culture.

The second ingredient is appreciation for the contributions that employees make. You have to recognize that all the good things you get from the business come as a result of the efforts of others, and you need to show your gratitude. We do that in as many ways as we can. For example, there's our box game that provides each employee with a cash bonus whenever we hit a new milestone in the growth of the business. We also buy movie tickets in bulk and make them available at a deep discount to our employees, most of whom come from the inner city and couldn't afford to offer their families such treats without our assistance. In addition, we have season tickets to local sports franchises—the Yankees, the Mets, and the Knicks—but instead of giving them to customers, we use them to reward employees for outstanding work.

We have dozens of ways of showing our appreciation, and many of them are unplanned. When New York City raised subway fares from $1.50 to $2, we immediately gave everyone an additional $5 per week. And then, of course, there was the case of the missing kittens.

The purpose of all this is to remind our employees constantly that they are valued members of a community—which is the third ingredient of a strong culture. I want people to feel that they are part of something bigger than themselves, that their work has a higher purpose. To be sure, part of that purpose is to provide excellent service to our customers, but I don't think that's enough. I also want people to believe that they belong to a community, and that their community is doing good in the world.

A few years ago, for example, we asked our employees to vote on what they wanted to do with the money we had traditionally spent on a big holiday party in December. By an overwhelming majority, they said they'd prefer to use the money to help a local charity. We set up a committee, which contacted a nearby school for autistic and mentally challenged children about the possibility of our providing them with Christmas presents. The school officials were thrilled. Like most of our employees, the children came from poor areas of Brooklyn. Any gifts we gave them would, in many cases, be the only ones they'd receive.

The teachers put together a list of the gifts that the children wanted—everything from bicycles to computers to giant toy animals. My wife, Elaine, recruited a group of employees to do the shopping. Then we set aside space in our corporate offices where our people could assemble and gift-wrap the various presents. On the appointed day, we headed off to the school with a contingent of employees from all parts and all levels of the company. There we split up to distribute the gifts and play with the children.

What happened next was amazing. The atmosphere in the room was electric. You could see the excitement in the eyes of the children, and the pride in the faces of our employees. It dawned on me that most of our people are not in a financial position to do much charity work, and they relished the opportunity to bring some happiness into the lives of the children at the school. I did, too, but I enjoyed equally the happiness of the employees. It was a wonderful bonding experience all around.

Thereafter, we went back to the school every year, and the experience was always repeated. It never failed to give me a tremendous sense of fulfillment and satisfaction. It also reminded me of the most important benefit we get from our culture: the opportunity to work with some of the finest people I've ever known.

Ask Norm

Dear Norm:
My wife and I have been married eight years, and I love her to death. A couple of years ago, we started a consulting company, which is doing well, but the challenge of living, working, eating, playing, raising children, and sleeping together is taking a toll on both of us. It's hard to keep business and personal considerations separate. How can spouses run a company and still maintain a great relationship?
Rich

Dear Rich:
I also work with my wife, Elaine, who is our vice president of human resources. We tried working together shortly after we were married. She quit after one day. Twenty years later, she decided to give it another shot, and things have gone extremely well. "You have to establish guidelines," she says. "There has to be a clear division between work life and married life. You have to figure out what you can talk about and when; how you're going to function in each role; what's acceptable behavior and what isn't. But that type of arrangement won't work for everyone. I'm not sure you've been married long enough to pull it off. Eight years into our marriage, we would never have been able to do it. If you can't set down clear guidelines both at work and at home and stick with them, maybe you should think about having separate businesses."
—Norm

The Evolution of a Culture

That's the culture we have now. The culture of Perfect Courier, my first business, was very different. In the beginning, I didn't even recognize that we were creating a culture. Entrepreneurs seldom do. The one you wind up with isn't planned; it just happens. While everybody is focusing on something else—making sales, providing service, paying bills, sending out invoices, and so on—a little community springs up, and it has its own unspoken customs, traditions, modes of dress and speech, and rules of behavior. By the time you become aware of it, the culture is often well established. You can only hope that you'll like it, because it will probably be a reflection of your personality.

I would describe Perfect Courier's culture as tough but fair. Back then, I was a hard-driving entrepreneur, in a big hurry to build a $100 million business, and I yelled a lot. I yelled when people did things I considered stupid, or careless, or misguided. I yelled when they didn't anticipate problems I thought they should have foreseen. I yelled when we lost an opportunity because we didn't move quickly enough. Whenever we made a mistake that could have been avoided, I'd blow my top. Not that I was intentionally trying to make people feel bad. I was simply frustrated. I was impatient. I wanted the thing done right and done fast. Fortunately, I usually calmed down before I did any serious damage, and I didn't carry grudges. The storm would pass, and I'd let it go.

People in the company, or at least those who stayed, came to accept these episodes as a fact of life. Maybe I'm naïve, but I don't believe they held my temper against me. They realized that I almost always had cause to be upset. They also knew that it wasn't personal. I might generate a lot of noise, but I paid them well, treated them fairly, and didn't make unreasonable demands. As long as they held up their end of the bargain, they knew I would hold up mine.

And the culture at Perfect Courier reflected all that. It was hard-driving and intense, and it involved quite a bit of yelling. People were brusque with one another. Nobody put much energy into figuring out what anybody else was feeling. The general attitude was, "We're here to do the job, so just do it, get it right, and shut up." Some employees thrived in that environment. They liked the intensity. They found it exhilarating. To be sure, it was important that they also shared our values. As tough as we were on ourselves and on people who crossed us, we insisted on absolute honesty, and we tried to be fair to everybody we did business with. For employees who felt comfortable in that kind of culture, Perfect Courier was a great place to work. Those who felt uncomfortable didn't last.

I should emphasize that none of this happened consciously. At the time, I was oblivious to the relationship between my personality and my company's culture. I was much too focused on getting Perfect Courier as big as possible, as fast as possible, to think about such things. It was not until my wife, Elaine, joined the company in 1994—after Perfect Courier had emerged from Chapter 11, and we'd started the records storage business—that I began thinking seriously about culture, mainly because her style was so different from mine. It was, in fact, the opposite of mine. Where I was brusque, she was understanding. Where I tended to focus on the employees' obligations to the company, she focused on the company's obligations to the employees. Where I just cared about getting the work done, she wanted people to be learning and having fun as they worked.

But I'm a pretty open-minded guy, and I always attempt to do what my wife wants, so I let her try things, even when I was skeptical that they would have an effect. It turned out that they did have an effect— a huge effect. The whole atmosphere of the place began to change, and customers noticed the difference. They told us that our employees seemed happier than our competitors' employees, that our people smiled more and went out of their way to be helpful. It didn't take me long to conclude that CitiStorage would be better off with Elaine's culture than with mine.

That realization had important implications. To begin with, I had to modify my own behavior. I couldn't change who I was, but I could make sure I didn't undermine what Elaine was doing, first, by staying out of the way of the managers and letting them run the company on a day-to-day basis. In addition, I needed to look for opportunities to show everybody that Elaine had my full support. For example, she introduced a bunch of games in which people would guess when we'd hit the next level of boxes stored, or they'd compete to lose weight, or they'd try to grow the most beautiful Amaryllis. I almost always took part either as a participant (weight, Amaryllis) or as an awarder of prizes (box game).

Beyond that, it was my job as the top banana to enforce the culture, a particularly important responsibility if you have a warm, nurturing, people-friendly company. There will always be a few doubters and malcontents who will take every positive thing you do and turn it into a negative. They'll refuse to attend meetings. If you insist that they come, they'll act bored and distracted. Behind your back, they'll bad-mouth the company and accuse you of hypocrisy. In the worst case, they will actively undermine you. We had a few people who were like that. We talked to them, heard them out, explained what we were doing, and urged them to get with the program. If their behavior didn't change, I would eventually call them into my office and tell them I had great news: henceforward they wouldn't have to feel so angry and miserable because they wouldn't be working for us anymore. They were free to find a place where they'd be happier. Not only did we thereby get rid of some negative energy, but we also showed the other employees that we meant what we said.

You might ask, why is it so important to enforce the culture? Why can't different managers be allowed to have different management styles? The answer is, they can as long as they all operate within the same cultural boundaries. You should never have more than one culture in a company. If you let managers create their own subcultures, you're inviting chaos and corporate politics. The inevitable conflicts will create communications problems, morale problems, coordination problems, and ultimately turnover problems. Employees will try to switch to the department whose culture they like best. You'll wind up with competing cultures, and you may lose some good people. In any case, a huge amount of time and energy will be wasted internally that should be focused externally, on making sales and serving the customer.

As the person in charge, it's your responsibility to make sure that different departments don't have different cultures. In some circumstances, it may be your most important responsibility. It's also one you can't delegate. You can let another person play a critical role in defining the culture, as I did with Elaine, but someone has to enforce it, and you're the only one who can. It doesn't matter what kind of culture you want. It just has to be consistent throughout the company. Although there can be nuances in different departments, everybody needs to have the same understanding about how people can, or should, behave.

That's not to say all cultures are equal. I've come to appreciate that certain types of cultures are more efficient and effective than others. Specifically, I can see that Elaine's type of culture is better than the kind we had at Perfect Courier. Besides, who am I to disagree with my wife?

Ask Norm

Dear Norm:
How enforceable are noncompete agreements, and what's your opinion of them? I'm an engineer for a converting company and have thought many times about going out on my own.
    Victor

Dear Victor:
I don't believe in noncompetes, and I don't have them. They're difficult and expensive to enforce, and I don't think you need them if you run your business properly. That said, I think people should live by the contracts they sign if the contracts are legal. In the case of noncompetes, that's a fairly big "if." Courts tend to interpret these contracts in favor of the employee because they don't want to prevent a person from earning a living. Obviously, you should get an opinion about your own noncompete from a lawyer.
    —Norm

Pennies from Heaven

Some people, I know, disagree with me about the importance of culture. They question how much it can actually affect the bottom line. I believe it has an enormous impact. Indeed, I'd argue that culture plays a huge role in the success or failure of any company. How? By shaping the attitudes of employees toward the place where they work. Those attitudes, in turn, guide their behavior, and their behavior has a direct impact on the financial health of the business.

Consider, for example, the phenomenon of creeping expenses—that is, the tendency of all expenses to rise over time. That phenomenon goes hand in hand with another one: the conversion of luxuries into necessities. By *luxuries*, I mean the expenses that aren't essential to the company's well-being. You don't find many luxuries in start-ups— at least not the successful ones. New companies that waste money on nonessential things don't get very far. Smart entrepreneurs know that they have to make their start-up capital last as long as possible. So they lease used furniture instead of buying new. They fly Southwest or JetBlue and stay at Motel 6. They watch their telephone, postal, and office expenses like a hawk. They do all that reflexively because they realize that every dollar they save will help them meet the next payroll and give them the breathing room they need to get the business up and running.

That habit of frugality tends to erode, however, as time goes along. People begin to spend more freely. They start investing in some things (computers, telephone systems, advertising) that will help them maximize their potential to grow. At the same time, they let down their guard in other areas. They have the leeway to spend money on stuff they don't really need, and so they do. Along the way, often without anyone noticing it, luxuries become necessities, and the organization becomes a little sloppy. Salespeople start thinking they *have* to use cabs to get around town, rather than take the subway. Office clerks think they *have* to send packages by courier or Federal Express instead of by regular mail. Executives think they *have* to fly business class and stay in the best hotels. Expenses creep, and overhead balloons.

The danger, of course, is that something unexpected will happen—it always does—and the company will suddenly find itself desperately short of cash. At that point, many companies are forced to do first what should only be a last resort: they lay people off. Layoffs are the costliest way of dealing with cash flow problems. Although the employees who lose their jobs are the most visible victims, the whole organization suffers as the people who are left worry that they'll be next and start making contingency plans.

By the time you're in a cash crisis, however, it's often too late to start thinking about alternatives like cutting back on the luxuries that have become necessities. The damage has already been done. The cash has already been spent. There simply aren't enough cuts available for the company to get by without a layoff. That's why the fight against creeping expenses has to be an ongoing struggle. Otherwise, everybody could lose.

I believe there are two aspects to that struggle. They're equally important, and they both have to do with culture. The first involves creating an environment in which people care about the company's welfare and go out of their way to help keep costs under control. It's not enough to set budgets and hold top executives accountable for them. That's part of the equation, but you can't overlook employees down the ladder. Money can be wasted in more ways than you can count, and savings can come from places you'd never dream of looking. If you really want to attack creeping expenses, you need to get everyone involved, which won't happen unless people care enough about the company to lend a hand. And that won't happen unless they know the company cares about them.

Let me tell you about Patty Lightfoot, who was our executive assistant for several years. She'd been on the job for about three months when Elaine mentioned to me that Patty had a second job cleaning offices. "She earns $75 a week," Elaine said. "She says she's saving to go back to school."

By then, Patty had already impressed us with her reliability, resourcefulness, and intelligence. We knew we wanted to keep her. Normally, she wouldn't come up for a raise until she'd been with us for six months, but I saw an opportunity to send her a message. "Listen," I said to the other executives, "if we give her a raise three months from now, it will be nice. If we give it to her now, she'll never forget it." They agreed.

The next day, I called Patty into my office. I told her to have a seat. "I understand that you have a second job you do at night," I said.

"Yes, that's right," she replied tentatively.

"Well, I'm afraid we can't allow that," I said. "We need you to be fresh and well-rested when you come here in the morning." She slumped in her chair. "I also understand that this other job pays you $75 a week. We're going to raise your salary by that amount so you won't lose any income."

Her face lit up like a flashbulb going off. "Oh, thank you," she said.

"And one other thing," I said. "You should know about a policy we have. Anybody who works here for a year can go to school, and we'll pay for it as long as you earn a B or better." Patty was beaming as she left my office. I had no doubt she knew we cared about her.

But that is, as I noted, only half the battle. The other half has to do with another aspect of the culture. People have to understand that saving money is a priority, and the message has to come straight from the top. You can't just talk about it, either. How you act will convey your concerns far more effectively than anything you say.

I'll give you an example from the early years of Perfect Courier. As our growth accelerated, I began to see more and more signs of sloppiness and waste around the company, and it bothered me. My concern reached the boiling point one day when I found out how much we were spending on new pens. We had forty employees, and we were buying pens at a rate of forty per week. That was nuts, I said to my staff. They gave me strange looks. "Is it really such a big deal?" someone asked.

"Forty pens at $1 a pen is $40 a week," I said. "That's $2,000 a year. For pens! What else are we wasting money on?"

Now I have to confess that I was probably one of the worst offenders as far as pens go. If I borrow your pen, it almost always winds up in my pocket. I don't even realize I'm taking it. I just slip it in and forget about it. At the end of the day, I'll have six or seven pens and no idea where they came from.

That said, I was genuinely concerned about creeping expenses and determined to do something about them. So I decreed that henceforth no one could get a new pen from the office without turning in an old one. Guess what. The policy flopped. People would show up in need of a pen and have all kinds of excuses as to why they didn't have an old one to turn in. They'd left it at home and would bring it in tomorrow. It was in their car; they'd get it later. Norm took it. Whatever. Two months later, we were still buying forty pens a week.

I was fed up. "That's it," I said. "Everyone has a pen, right? From this day forward, we will never buy another pen. We'll take the money we save and put it in a special fund for employees. At the end of the year, we'll figure out what to do with it."

My staff went crazy. "You can't do that," they said. "We won't get any work done. People will spend all their time looking for pens."

"Don't worry," I said. "There will be pens."

And there were. As it turned out, we got along just fine without buying pens. People quickly acclimated themselves to the new policy. I don't know where the pens came from. I suppose some people bought their own, while others managed to find the ones we'd purchased in the past. Meanwhile, the pen policy became part of our culture, a perennial joke, especially whenever I showed up for a meeting without a pen. "Are you kidding?" people would say. "You came to work without a pen?" I'd have to go back to my office to get one.

The company didn't buy another pen for twenty years, until we moved from Manhattan to Brooklyn. Although the policy didn't completely solve the problem of creeping expenses, it certainly helped. By going cold turkey on pens, we eliminated a little waste and sent a big message. The mere mention of pens became a reminder that we really cared about controlling costs. I gave people other reminders at every chance I got, but I'm not sure any of them were as effective as the pen policy.

It wouldn't have worked, however, without the first half of the formula—the part about letting employees know the company cares about them. If they have the desire to help the company and know how you feel about creeping expenses, they will not only cut down on the waste but come up with savings that will knock your socks off.

Which brings me back to Patty. I happened to notice one day that our Nextel sales representative was in the office talking to Louis, our company president. After he left, Louis came to see me. "Wow, we just got a great deal from Nextel," he said. "We got $24 off our monthly rate." That was impressive. We have about 125 two-way radios, and we'd been paying a monthly fee of $49 per phone. But apparently Nextel had a special going on whereby we could pay $25 per month and get 10,000 minutes collectively. "That's more minutes than we use," Louis said. "We'd have to go up to more than 30,000 minutes before we'd pay what we do now."

So we'd be saving $3,000 a month, or $36,000 a year. "Great job," I said.

"It wasn't me," Louis said. "It was Patty." One of her responsibilities was to check our Nextel usage. In the course of doing that, she'd found out about the special and brought it to Louis's attention. I don't mean to suggest that Patty found the savings because we'd given her a raise. She'd been a conscientious employee from the day she started. She might well have figured out how we could save money on our Nextel bill even if we'd done nothing more than pay her salary.

But by showing how much we cared about her, we may have given her a little extra incentive to do something good for the company. And who knows? If we hadn't made it possible for her to quit her other job, she might have been so tired that she would have missed the Nextel special. In any case, it all goes to show how culture can have a direct impact on your company's financial well-being.

The Bottom Line

Point One: Your company's culture can be your most powerful tool for finding and keeping great employees. Don't miss the opportunities to shape it that arise every day.

Point Two: The one thing you can't delegate is the responsibility for making sure the company has a single culture, not several competing ones.

Point Three: Expenses have a natural tendency to creep up over time. If you want to control them, you need to get everyone involved in the effort.

Point Four: Look for opportunities to send the message to employees that you really care about them, and that you want them to care about keeping costs down.

CHAPTER FOURTEEN

Selling Is a Team Sport

Hiring is, of course, one of any company builder's major responsibilities, and everybody makes mistakes in that area, especially when it comes to hiring salespeople. I figure I've hired more than three hundred salespeople in my career and made just about every mistake in the book. What I've learned is that, for me at least, there are no shortcuts. It takes time to find the right people, time to train them, time to get them acclimated to our culture. Sure, I used to think I could accelerate the process. All I had to do was hire hotshots who could start producing as soon as they walked through the door. But every time I tried it, I lived to regret it. Effective selling, I learned, requires a team effort, and—to build a great team—you need the right players. By that, I mean players who understand their roles and can work together to achieve the best results. Those salespeople, I found, were seldom the ones who could deliver the most sales in the shortest amount of time.

Eventually, I came up with four rules for choosing new salespeople. The first rule has to do with the candidates' aspirations. There are, I believe, two categories of salespeople in this world. One type will eventually go into business for themselves. The other will always work for somebody else. I like both types, but it's the salespeople in the second category that I want to hire for my company.

Don't get me wrong. I have no problem with employees leaving to start their own businesses. I don't even care much if they compete against us. I'd rather they leave than be unhappy around me. What I don't like is turnover in my sales force. I want salespeople who will stay with me forever. Other kinds of employees are different. If they don't keep moving up in the organization, sooner or later they're going to be overpaid. That creates problems for both you and them. You don't have those problems with salespeople. What they get paid is generally based on what they produce. The good ones, moreover, can go on producing year after year. Those who do are invaluable to a business. Once I find them and train them, I never want to lose them. So I try to screen out the candidates who dream of having their own businesses. They may be great salespeople, but I know they won't stick around. I wish them every success—somewhere else.

That's the first rule: hire salespeople, not entrepreneurs. The second rule grew out of some bad experiences I had with my first start-up. Like many young entrepreneurs, I was in a big hurry, and I thought I could save time and money by hiring my competitors' salespeople. Since they were already familiar with the market and the business, I wouldn't have to train them. They could hit the ground running. They might even bring some customers with them. At the time, they looked like a shortcut to growth. I found out, however, that they were just a shortcut to trouble.

For openers, most of them came with bad habits, which I could never get them to change. They'd learned every trick common to the industry and were constantly going for the quick sale. I wanted them to take a longer view, but they wouldn't listen. They thought they knew more than I did. It turned out, moreover, that they weren't such great salespeople. I had consistently better results with the salespeople I'd brought in from outside the industry and trained myself. So I got to thinking, maybe my competitors had good reasons for letting these salespeople go. Maybe I shouldn't have been so quick to believe them when they told me what a terrific job they'd done for other companies.

Did I wind up taking some market share away from my competitors? Yes, but it wasn't worth the price. Buying market share by hiring your competitors' salespeople does nothing good for your reputation in the industry. Maybe you don't care when you're young and brash, but eventually you learn that reputation is a crucial business asset, worth much more over the long run than a few extra sales. So we established a new policy in the company: no hiring of salespeople from our industry.

My third rule will strike some people as narrow-minded, but it's based on years of experience. The rule is that if you want to apply for one of our sales positions, you must have held at least two prior jobs in different companies, and one of those jobs has to have been in sales. In other words, we don't hire salespeople straight out of school. Why? Because nobody is satisfied with his or her first job. Well, almost nobody. There are always exceptions. But the vast majority of people find something wrong with the first real job they hold, no matter how good it is or how well they're treated. It's human nature. You simply can't appreciate what you've got if you don't have anything to compare it with. So what do you do? You look for greener pastures. Virtually every person I've ever hired straight out of school has moved on within two years.

There's not much point in hiring salespeople whom I know I'm going to lose right after they've been trained. Nor is there much point in training salespeople only to discover that they don't like selling or aren't comfortable in our environment. That's why we insist that candidates have experience in sales and have worked in at least two other corporate cultures. In your first job, you assume every company works the same way. In your second job, you learn that different companies have different styles, different benefits, different procedures and rules. By the third job, you realize you're choosing a company as well as a career.

My fourth rule is probably the most controversial one. I have an absolutely firm policy that we will never hire a hotshot. By that, I mean a superstar salesperson. A selling machine. If a good salesperson can make one hundred sales calls and close ten accounts, and if a great salesperson can close twenty, then a hotshot can close thirty-five. I'm talking about people who are tops at what they do. They have the gift. They have the hunger. They have the drive. They can sell anything to anyone. They are the best salespeople in the world. And I don't want them in my company—because they think about only one thing: closing sales. They'll say anything, do anything, promise anything to bag a customer.

I'll give you the example of Bert, a hotshot salesman I had in the early days of my messenger business. He talked fast and thought fast. He also produced a tremendous volume of sales, which made me very happy. I didn't have time to check up on him and didn't know I had to. All I cared about were the sales, and he was delivering.

Then the problems began. First, we started having trouble collecting from his customers. Some of them said that the prices we were charging were different from what they'd been promised. Others complained that they weren't getting the level of service we'd told them they'd receive. Then there were the low-volume customers to whom Bert had given high-volume discounts, assuring us that the additional sales would come later. When we checked, we discovered that the future sales were a figment of his imagination. In most cases, there had never been any possibility that the customer could deliver them.

Unfortunately, Bert was just the first of several hotshots I hired. They all got me into trouble. I couldn't train them or control them. They were always forty steps ahead of me. Every system I put in place they found a way to beat. I kept thinking I could overcome the problems. I told myself that the hotshots would bring in the new accounts, and I'd patch things up afterward. It never happened. The customers felt they'd been misled and held me responsible—as well they should have.

So I learned an important lesson: your salespeople represent you in the marketplace. I decided that I couldn't afford to have hotshots representing me. They operate on a philosophy that's different from mine. They believe in making sales at any cost. I don't want sales at any cost. I want sales that provide me with enough gross profit to grow my business and that will keep coming back, year after year. I want to build long-term relationships with customers, and I want salespeople who will help me do it.

And that's really my point here. I'm not arguing that every company should have the same rules as mine. What's important is to have rules of some sort—to think through these issues as your company grows and to develop your own practices. Because, when you hire salespeople, you're not just choosing employees. You're also choosing customers. Like it or not, your salespeople are going to play a major role in determining the types of customers you have and the kinds of relationships you have with them. It's worth taking the time to make sure you get those relationships right.

Ask Norm

Dear Norm:
I know that you pay salespeople by salary, rather than commis-
sion. My question is, how do you decide on raises? I suspect you
must use subjective criteria. If you based raises only on objective
sales results, it seems as though you'd undermine the team con-
cept you're striving for.
  Robert

Dear Robert:
You're right. Part of it is subjective. I look at overall company
results and at individual performance, but most important
to me is the way they work as members of a team. I want to
see people helping each other, not competing. I'll give you an
example. One of our salespeople, Patti, had to go out of town
and asked another salesperson, David, to attend a meeting
with a big account she'd been trying to land for months. When
David showed up, there were six people waiting who said they
were making the final decision that day. He closed the account,
and I give him full credit for that, but I also give three stars to
Patti for being able to say, "Okay, I trust the people I work with
to cover for me."
  —Norm

The Trouble with Sales Commissions

Getting the right salespeople is only the first step. You also need to have
a compensation system that rewards them properly and yet doesn't create problems in your company. I've developed my own system for paying
salespeople. In the process, I've become convinced that the way most
companies do it is a recipe for trouble. I'm referring, of course, to the
practice of paying sales commissions. Unless you're very careful about

how you use them, they almost always have the effect of undermining any sense of unity and common purpose in a business. How? By putting the salespeople in a separate category, by making them stand aloof and apart. Granted, sales commissions aren't the only culprit. It doesn't help that most companies put the salespeople in separate offices, hold separate meetings for them off-site, and treat them far more gingerly than other employees at performance review time.

But commissions play the largest role in distancing salespeople from other employees. The result is a lot of animosity and resentment, leading to inevitable conflicts. The accounting people complain that the salespeople make special deals with customers and then don't inform the people who do the billing. The operations people complain that the salespeople make unreasonable demands. As the owner, you're constantly having to mediate between departments while simultaneously resolving disputes among the salespeople themselves over who has which territory, who handles which customers, who gets the leads coming into the office, and on and on. It's a nightmare, and a highly unproductive nightmare at that.

Now, I realize that my position on sales commissions is controversial. I also realize that many times you don't have a choice—at least at first. Most salespeople have been indoctrinated in the cult of the sales commission. They believe it's the only fair way to handle sales compensation, and they like the idea of being paid for the sales they make. For that matter, a lot of owners share that philosophy and are convinced they'll get more sales—and better salespeople—if the latter get a piece of whatever they bring in. I used to believe that myself.

But I've learned it's an illusion. After many bad experiences, I decided to scrap my commission-based sales compensation system and move to paying salespeople a salary plus an annual bonus, with raises based half on their individual performance and half on the performance of the company as a whole. The result: My team of three salespeople and one support person has consistently outperformed all of our competitors, closing five or six times more sales per person than the salespeople at other companies in our industry. What's more, our people do it together, because they really work as members of a team.

While none of them is a superstar salesperson, they each have differ-ent strengths that complement the strengths—and make up for the weaknesses—of the others.

We have one salesman, for example, who is terrific at bringing pros-pects in the door but has a hard time closing big accounts. It doesn't matter because he can get all the help he needs doing the close. There are no territories and no territoriality. The salespeople readily cover for one another when necessary. They also work closely with our oper-ations people, often bringing them on sales calls, giving customers the opportunity to get to know the people who are actually providing the service. The salespeople themselves know all about operations. As part of their training, they've spent time working in the nonsales depart-ments, where they've formed personal bonds with the other employees and developed a keen appreciation of their contributions to the suc-cess of the business. Building on those relationships, the salespeople are able to turn in numbers that put superstars to shame.

I admit it took years for our system to evolve, and there were certain leaps of faith I had to make along the way. I had a hard time accepting that I didn't want hotshot salespeople because I'm a hotshot myself in some ways. I had an even harder time deciding to move all of our sales-people from commission to salary. Frankly, if I were doing sales for someone else's company, I'd be hell-bent to get commissions, because I think I'm a great salesperson, and I'd want to get paid accordingly. I wouldn't care about the rest of the company. I'd be furious if other employees didn't do what I wanted them to do for "my" customers. In other words, I'd be exactly the kind of salesperson I don't want to have working for me.

Once I'd made the switch, moreover, I got a bonus. Gone was the great fear that all owners have to one degree or another—the fear that salespeople will leave and take your customers with them. Although it's been many years since a salesperson left my company, it would have absolutely no impact on our sales if we were to lose one of them. On a personal level we'd be sorry to see the person go, but the thought of losing customers or sales as a result wouldn't even cross my mind.

In fact, I'd say you're much more likely to have salespeople leave and take customers if they're on commission, rather than on salary and bonus. For commissioned salespeople, the customer represents security. As long as they have that connection, they think they have a means of earning a living. Consequently, they have a strong interest in making sure the customer belongs to them, rather than to the company. So they resist letting anyone else in the company have a relationship with the customer. They're better off if the customer sees only them.

To protect themselves, owners come up with all kinds of mechanisms aimed at preventing the salespeople from getting too cozy with customers. One approach is to transfer every new account from a salesperson to a customer service representative, who handles the relationship from then on. Another technique is to reduce the commission over time. Thus, when a salesperson closes an account, he or she receives, say, a 10 percent commission on the first year's sales, 5 percent on the second year's sales, and 2 percent thereafter. In theory, salespeople won't spend much time with a customer if they're getting only 2 percent from the account. Such systems may or may not weaken a salesperson's hold on a customer, but they don't address the underlying problem. The salespeople are still not members of the team. Their focus isn't on making the company successful. It's on looking out for number one.

I want everybody in my company to be on the same team, including my salespeople. That won't happen unless everybody is paid the same way. Notice that I didn't say everybody should be paid the same amount. Because of the role they play and the difficulty of the work they do, salespeople will always earn more than most other people. That's natural. A surgeon earns more than a lab technician. But I want all of my employees to be part of the same compensation system. That is, I want them to receive a salary that is reviewed and adjusted annually, based on the performance of the company and the contributions of the individual.

If you're like most owners, you're probably shaking your head and thinking, "Yeah, great, but I could never implement that kind of compensation system even if I wanted to." You believe you have no choice but to pay sales commissions. It's how the industry works, or it's what salespeople want, or it's the only way to motivate them. I agree that commissions are the norm in most industries, and salespeople feel comfortable with the norm. I also agree that commissions are the only way to motivate *some* salespeople. But they're the hotshots and would-be entrepreneurs whom I don't want in my company. I want salespeople who do sales for a living simply because they like the work and they're good at it. They have no hidden agenda. They are motivated by the same things that motivate other employees. They just happen to sell.

Those salespeople don't need to be on commission. Yes, they want to be compensated fairly—like anyone else. But they also want what most other people look for in a place to work. They want to be part of something. They want to belong somewhere. They want to spend their lives working for a business that treats them as valued members of a team.

And yet, by definition, you're not a member of a team if you're selling on commission. The way you get paid pretty much forces you to be in business for yourself. Unfortunately, most salespeople don't recognize the problem. They're accustomed to being on commission. They've bought into the conventional way of doing things. When they interview for a sales position, the first question they ask is, "What's the commission and what's the draw?" If you offer them a salary up front, they give you a funny look. You can't fight that, and I don't. I won't risk losing good sales candidates by trying to force them into my system before they're ready. It's my job to sell them on the program, and that takes time.

So we start new salespeople with what they're used to: salary and commission. After two years, we know whom we want to keep. I'll then go to the person and say, "Listen, you've been here two years. We want you to be here forever. We'll buy out your commission and raise your salary, so you won't lose any income. In return, you'll get stability. Do you think you're going to have a good year? I'm willing to guarantee that you'll have a good year. And if you really do have a good year, I'll guarantee that next year will be even better. Then again, if the economy goes bad and you have some down years, you don't have to worry about a big drop in your income. You'll continue to earn your salary. We want to give you that security because we want you to be here for the long haul."

I also explain our annual salary review process, which most people don't understand. It begins with an assessment of how well the company did in the past year and how well we expect it to do in the coming year. We then set a range for salary increases based on the assessment. Everybody's raise falls within that range, but whether people are on the high end or the low end depends on their individual performance.

So salespeople, like other employees, are rewarded both for the company's success and for their own contributions to it. The logic is simple: We want to change their mind-set. We want them to focus on doing what's best for the company whether that means selling, or working with other employees to solve a customer's problem, or helping with collections, or spending time on important projects that don't necessarily result in immediate sales.

By doing all that, by becoming full-fledged members of the team in our company, salespeople will earn as much money over the long run as they would if they stayed on commission, and so I tell them. I also point out that they'll be able to take longer vacations in the future, because they won't have to worry about leaving their customers unattended; someone else on the team will be available to handle any problems. Above all, they'll have the satisfaction of being part of a thriving company and the security of knowing they won't be left to fend for themselves when the going gets tough.

Although it's all absolutely true, some people are more difficult to convince than others. I had one terrific salesperson, Patti Kanner Post, hold out for years. But she eventually came around and switched from commission to salary.

After almost twenty years with a largely salaried sales force, I can assure you that the system we've come up with really does work. What's more, it's good for everybody, though I have no doubt who gets the most out of it. I do. I get a cohesive company. I get people working together and pulling in the same direction. And while I've always tried not to waste time worrying about salespeople leaving and taking customers, the thought doesn't even occur to me these days. It's almost impossible to imagine. And that may be the greatest benefit of all: peace of mind.

Ask Norm

Dear Norm:
I've heard you say that—if you run your business right—departing employees shouldn't be able to take your customers with them. So what am I doing wrong? I give our project managers and salespeople a lot of freedom to serve customers. After a year or two, the employees walk off with the account. Each time, I get the same feeling as when I receive a letter from the IRS.
    Charles

Dear Charles:
Start by looking at your hiring practices. It sounds as though you could do a better job of spotting salespeople who want to be around for the long term. You also need to be proactive. You're asking for trouble if you and your operations people don't have regular contact with customers. That's the only way to make sure a customer belongs to the company, not to the salesperson. I'm careful not to step on the toes of our salespeople, and they're happy I'm so visible. My presence gives them a competitive advantage. They'd have only one reason to object: if they didn't really have the company's interests at heart.
    —Norm

Everybody Sells

My point is that selling should be a team effort, and when I talk about a team, I'm not just referring to the sales team. I've long believed that, in any company, everybody sells. By that, I mean that everybody plays a role in the sales process. Whether people work in operations, customer service, or even accounting, they have an impact on customers, and that impact—good or bad—will influence the sales force's ability to close deals and retain accounts. For a long time, however, I assumed the effect had to be indirect. I couldn't imagine how people outside sales could be *directly* responsible for landing new accounts. But then one day my employees taught me a lesson that changed the way I look at selling.

It was actually my wife, Elaine, who got the ball rolling. We'd been hearing some complaints from customers about the response they'd received when they phoned in, and Elaine—who, among other things, was our head of human resources—was determined to do something about the problem. She found a company that specialized in training phone representatives and arranged to have a trainer fly in for three days of workshops with our staff. The company claimed that everyone could benefit from the training, and so Elaine decided to include all sixty of our full-time salaried employees, about half of our on-site workforce.

The investment wasn't peanuts—$10,000 for the trainer, plus the paid time of all those people—and I was skeptical that we'd get much out of it. It's extremely difficult, I've learned, to foster long-term changes in behavior. I figured the effects would last about three weeks. Still, I don't like to discourage people from trying new things, and Elaine was adamant, so I went along.

I have to admit I was curious to see the employees' reaction to the training program since we'd never done anything like it before. Most of our people come from inner-city neighborhoods, where they've had limited educational opportunities. Nevertheless, they took to the workshops like ducks to water. They clearly loved having a chance to learn new work skills. As the trainer took them through lessons on subjects like telephone-answering techniques, they listened attentively and soaked it all up.

Afterward, Elaine looked for ways to keep the momentum going. She made up forms for people to fill out reporting what they'd learned, what they're enjoyed most, and what additional help they needed. In addition, she bought a set of sixteen short videotapes from the training company with the idea of using them to stimulate further discussion. The question was, how? Although she'd once been a teacher, Elaine had no experience in workforce training. As a result, she pretty much had to make it up as she went along. Her plan was to hold five hour-long sessions every two weeks, with twelve people in each session. There she would show a videotape and ask participants to talk about the issues it addressed. She also made what turned out to be a critical stipulation: each session had to have people from every department, and the composition of the groups would keep changing. The idea was simply to let participants interact with other employees they would never meet in the normal course of business. Elaine thought something interesting might come out of it.

I didn't attend the sessions myself, but Elaine and I talked in the evening about how things had gone. She couldn't get over the enthusiasm people brought to the program or the camaraderie it engendered. The participants loved to be called on, she said, and they loved to tell stories—about their own experiences as customers, about ways they could apply the techniques they were learning outside the business, about things that had happened in the company. At one meeting, for example, a customer service rep named Denise had singled out a warehouse worker, Chris, for praise. The week before, she said, he'd gone out of his way to make sure the right boxes were delivered to the right customer on time. The customer was relieved to get them and praised the company's performance. Denise wanted to pass along the compliment, which neither Chris nor the rest of the group would have heard about otherwise.

Making those connections between members of different departments turned out to be a major benefit of the program. Despite our best efforts to build team spirit, people didn't really get it until they sat in a room talking to employees from other parts of the company. Suddenly they had names and faces to relate to. They had a sense of the problems other people had to deal with, and they saw how work flowed through the business. It became crystal clear how the drivers depended on the customer service reps, and how the reps depended on the warehouse guys. In the process, people began to think in terms of the company as a whole, rather than focusing on their own little pieces of it.

Elaine, for her part, used the sessions to reinforce the customer service message. "I'm not paying your salary," she would say. "The customers are. They just funnel it through me." She reminded people about the bonuses they earned when we hit a new level in our box count and our policy of doing a 110 percent match of contributions employees made to their 401(k)s. "It's the customers who make all that possible," she said. "When you see Norman or someone else giving people a tour, those are usually prospective customers. We want to make them feel welcome. That means smiling and saying hello."

It didn't take long for us to see the results. The number of complaints dropped almost at once. People who called me began asking if we'd hired new operators. Meanwhile, we started getting more and more compliments on our service. Elaine had been giving $25 to anyone who received a compliment, but we were getting so many that we couldn't afford to keep paying out cash, so we switched to gift certificates and tickets to ballgames. It didn't matter. The compliments kept rolling in. In the six months following the start of the program, we received more comments, calls, and letters of praise than we'd had in the previous fourteen years.

I was amazed. I told Elaine I couldn't believe the change in our people. Not only were they nicer to our customers, but they were nicer to one another. She mentioned that they'd discussed the concept of internal, as opposed to external, customers and the importance of serving both. Evidently, the discussion had made an impression. I could see the difference in our ability to handle special requests. Say a customer needed to get a large number of files in a short period of time. In the past, I or one of the other executives would have gotten involved, invariably disrupting the normal system and screwing things up. With the new level of teamwork in the company, our employees were able to coordinate among themselves, ensuring that such requests were handled smoothly, without creating unnecessary problems.

But the most compelling evidence of change came from prospects who were deciding whether or not to give us their business. For years, we had made a point of talking to customers about our work environment. As part of our tour, we would take visitors to the area of the warehouse where we've put up charts and graphs showing how we're doing in our box game, which rewards employees for increases in the total number of boxes we store. The visitors would often ask, "Gee, can I get an application to work here?" One new customer even sent us a letter saying he was giving us his 5,000 boxes in hopes that they would get us to the next level and our employees could receive their bonus checks. So I was aware that employees played a role in some customers' decisions to sign with us, but I didn't realize how big a role it could be until we began to see the effects of Elaine's training program.

The revelation came one afternoon when Louis, the company president, returned to our executive offices with a prospective customer he had just shown around our facility. We had arranged to meet at the end of the tour. As we were sitting in my office, I asked the guy if he was considering other vendors. "Yes, two," he said and gave me their names. They were our major competitors.

My standard response is to praise the other companies, say that the customer would be happy with either one, and suggest how he or she might be happier with us. But for some reason I followed another script this time. "Did you see any differences between their places and mine?" I asked.

"Yes, I did," he said. "Every one of your employees was smiling, and they all said hello. I've never seen anything quite like it. They must really be happy."

"I hope so," I said. "Thank you for noticing."

"Because of that, in fact, I've decided to give you the business," he said.

I was completely taken aback. We almost never close an account on the spot. "That's great," I said. "I think you've made the right choice."

Afterward, I reflected on what had happened and realized that, for a long time, I've been making a mistake. I've assumed that owners and CEOs make the buying decisions on records storage. In fact, the key players are usually employees themselves. Even if they don't actually have the final say, they provide all the information on which the decision is based. As employees, they tend to identify with other employees, which is one reason they respond so warmly to our culture.

That's also why it may sometimes be possible for our line employees to close a sale. Thereafter, I gave them as many chances to do that as I could arrange.

The Bottom Line

Point One: Salespeople are your representatives in the marketplace. Make sure you choose salespeople who will represent you well.

Point Two: Beware of hotshots and would-be entrepreneurs, and don't hire salespeople from within your industry.

Point Three: Sales commissions cause divisions in a company and get in the way of building a team. Don't pay on commission unless you have to, and switch to salary plus bonus as soon as you can.

Point Four: All your employees have an impact on sales, at least indirectly. With the right training, you can teach them how to have a direct impact.

CHAPTER FIFTEEN

Help! I Need Somebody

We've covered a range of activities, practices, and disciplines involved in starting and growing a business, but there's one challenge you face regardless of the stage of the business process you happen to be in: getting good advice. Each of us has moments when we desperately need someone to talk to, someone to listen to us, someone to offer, if not advice, then a different perspective, unclouded by all the factors that keep us from seeing clearly what we have to do. Usually that person is not in the company.

Even if you're not desperate, it still helps to get an outside perspective, especially when you have a problem that's driving you crazy. After all, the problem you think you have may not be your real problem, and so the solution you come up with may not be the right solution. That happens partly because you get so close to the problem that you lose perspective on it. You see something wrong in one area and fail to connect it to what's happening in other areas, and so you miss a solution lying elsewhere. Beyond that, I think we all have a tendency to look for the type of solution we feel most comfortable with, given our personality and our skills. Thus, engineers tend to look for technical solutions. Accountants tend to look for financial solutions. And salespeople will go for the sales solution—even when the problem has nothing to do with sales.

A case in point is Mike Baicher, whom I wrote about in chapter 11. When I first met him, his family-owned trucking business was doing about $1.7 million a year in sales. Ten years later, it was a trucking and warehouse business with annual sales of $11 million. His drivers, some of whom are independent contractors, pick up giant shipping containers from the New Jersey ports and deliver them to warehouses in the area, where they are unpacked. Several of the warehouses belong to Mike himself, whose company provides storage services to some of its customers. Other customers have storage facilities of their own. The latter were on his mind when he came to see me.

He said he was thinking about hiring a salesperson. When I asked why, he said it had to do with the hassles of dealing with customers who used him only for pickup and delivery, not warehousing. For one thing, they often didn't unpack the containers in time to avoid the late fees charged by the shipping companies—which owned the containers—when an empty one was returned to the port in more than five days. Those fees ranged from $65 to $125 a day, depending on the shipper. The problem didn't arise when the container came to one of Mike's warehouses, because his people would unload it right away. But customers with their own warehouses waited until the last minute of the fifth day. By the time Mike's drivers brought the empty container back to the port, the shipping company's office would be closed, and Mike would get charged for an extra day.

"Can't you pass that along to the customer?" I asked.

"I try to, but it's tough," he said. "They say, 'What are you talking about? We emptied it in five days like we're supposed to. If you didn't get it back in time, that's not our problem.' There isn't much I can do. This is a competitive business. If I insisted they cover the late fee, we'd lose the account."

"What about calling them in advance and reminding them to unload the container before it becomes a problem?"

"Yeah, I suppose," he said, "but there's another issue with that part of the business. I can't bill the customer until I receive the paperwork from the driver, and the drivers don't turn it in on time. I'm constantly chasing after them to get it. I have some leverage with the independents, because they won't get paid if I don't have their paperwork, but with my own drivers I just have to keep nagging. I hate it."

I knew what he was talking about. I've had that problem with my drivers as well. "So what does this have to do with hiring a salesperson?" I asked.

"I want to sell more of our warehousing," Mike said. "Not just the storage, but also the value-added services, like pick-and-pack." He explained that some customers would pay him to deal with the contents of the containers. Suppose that a clothing chain was receiving a shipment of shirts and dresses from China. The customer might hire Mike's company to upgrade the hangers, add price tags, put the clothes in poly-bags, and then ship different types and sizes to different stores. That's what he meant by value-added service. He figured that if he could build up that side of the business, he could phase out the part that was giving him all the headaches.

Now, it helps to know some of the background here. When Mike's father ran the company, it was strictly a trucking business. He and Mike had a small warehouse out of necessity. There was always a wait when they picked up a container at the port, and—if they didn't retrieve it before the customer closed up shop for the day—they needed a place to keep it overnight. In addition, some customers demanded that the company provide storage, or they would take their business somewhere else.

When Mike took over the company, he changed course, expanding the warehouse business because he wanted to, not because he had to. He saw it as a profitable adjunct to the trucking business. He told customers he could handle their warehouse needs more efficiently than other vendors and, in some cases, even more efficiently than the customers themselves. Over time, the warehouse business had grown. When he came to see me, he had four buildings and hoped to add another before long.

That was a different service, however, from the one he was talking about making his primary focus. Under his new plan, he would be putting his whole emphasis on the value-added services, as opposed to the storage. Accordingly, he'd be looking for a different type of customer. "How have you been getting your warehouse customers up to now?" I asked.

"I get them from picking up their containers at the port," he said. "Maybe they don't have room in their warehouse temporarily. Or maybe they don't want to have their own warehouse. I become their warehousing department."

"Well, if that's been your source of new business, you don't want to stop doing it, do you? I mean, why give up on a proven method of getting customers and making sales? Are you the biggest guy doing this?"

"Oh, no," he said, "I'm one of the smallest around."

"So why would you stop when you still have a lot of potential customers you've never even spoken to?" He didn't have an answer. "Tell me," I said, "who does the selling now?"

"I do," Mike said, "but I hardly have time for it because of all these other problems I'm dealing with."

"What do you like to do best?" I asked.

"I like to sell!" he answered without hesitating. "I *love* to sell. I wish I could do more of it."

So here was a guy who loved to sell, but instead he was going to hire someone else to do it. And understand, in most businesses there's a significant lag time between the hiring of a salesperson and the production of sales, especially when you're selling a service. On top of that, Mike would be using a sales approach he'd never tried before. Selling value-added services is different from selling warehouse space to customers whose containers you're hauling. It's almost like going into a new business, which is fine under the right circumstances. I would have reacted differently if Mike had said, "I want to open up a new line of business because the old one is getting tougher to sell. I have a nice share of the market, and I'll keep selling as much as I can, but I think it's time to try something new." I would also have reacted differently if he'd told me that his customers were asking for this new service, that it had good gross margins, and that he could provide it without investing too much time and money. What didn't make sense was to go into a new line of business because of hassles in an old line of business that he'd had success with and that still offered plenty of opportunities to grow.

I said, "Listen, Mike, I think there's another approach you're not considering. I'm a salesman like you, and I hate dealing with those kinds of problems as well. So I surround myself with detail-oriented people. They're people who *enjoy* taking care of things like reminding customers to empty their containers and getting drivers to turn in their paperwork. They're good at it. They also start out with a lower salary base than salespeople, and they can get up to speed in a matter of days, not the three or four months that a salesperson needs."

The truth is, Mike probably didn't even need a full-time person. He could have found a college student who would do the work after school. Instead of paying someone $700 or $800 a week, he would be able to drastically reduce, if not eliminate, the major aggravations in his life for $300 or $400 a week. Meanwhile, he'd be freed up to sell.

It was a simple solution, and yet Mike hadn't seen it, which wasn't surprising to me. Like most entrepreneurs, he was a salesperson, and when salespeople run into a business problem, they instinctively look for ways to get more sales—because "good sales wash away most problems," as the saying goes. They also tend to regard administrators, accountants, and clerks as "nonproductive" employees. But what those people do is almost as important as getting the sale in the first place. They make it possible for you to keep the customers you already have. Customers aren't happy when you bill them late because you can't get the paperwork done in time. They aren't happy when they receive a bill for a fine that they may or may not have been responsible for incurring, and that you never warned them about, or told them how to avoid. And we all know what happens to unhappy customers.

No doubt the time would come when Mike would really need to hire a salesperson, but the impetus would come from opportunities that he saw and wanted to go after, not from the normal aggravations of running a business.

No Accounting for Bad Advice

As important as an outside perspective often is, there are some types of professionals you should be very wary about turning to for business advice. I'd put accountants at the top of the list. Please understand that I have nothing against accountants. I was trained as one myself, and I know they serve an important function. But it's almost always a bad idea to go to an accountant for advice about business decisions. Accountants are basically historians. That's how they've been educated, and that's how they think. They can do a great job of explaining what has happened in the past. But making things happen in the future? Forget about it. They don't even know the right questions to ask, let alone how to get the results you're looking for.

Ask Norm

Dear Norm:
My husband and I own a consulting business that we've run
successfully for fifteen years. Now we're planning to start a
retail wine business, and we think we need a board of advisers.
What do you think?
    Leslie

Dear Leslie:
If you're talking about an official group that meets regularly, I
doubt you need one. A board is useful when you want to take
an established business to the next level and you don't have a
management team with the experience to guide you. You might
also need a board at some point to enhance your credibility
with investors or important customers. For the majority of start-
ups, however, a formal board of advisers just gets in the way.
On the other hand, it's always smart to get advice from experienced businesspeople. I'd talk to as many people as I could
find with experience in wine retailing and similar businesses.
You don't need a board to do that.
    —Norm

Consider the case of a young entrepreneur named Ken, who contacted me for help in dealing with a cash flow problem. He owed a
printer $25,000 for some books he'd produced in connection with
a business he was starting. The book was an annual trade directory
for people who operated restaurants in New York City. It provided
information about getting permits, buying kitchen supplies, finding
contractors—that type of thing. Ken made money partly by selling
advertising space to vendors, but mainly by selling the books to chefs
and restaurateurs. The problem was, he hadn't sold nearly enough of

them. Of the 10,000 copies he'd had printed up, he had some 8,500 left over, and they were about to become out-of-date.

So he was in rough shape. He had no cash, a warehouse full of books he couldn't sell, and an irate printer who was threatening legal action if his bill wasn't paid. Meanwhile, Ken had to start work immediately on the next edition of the directory, or he'd be out of business. But how would he get it printed? And what if the first printer took him to court? He had no idea what the consequences might be. Understand, this is an honest, hardworking kid in his early twenties. He'd never been sued. He'd never dreamed it could happen. To be facing litigation was a total shock. He wasn't panicking—not yet, at any rate—but he was very, very upset. I calmed him down and told him I'd help him find a solution.

Now, to anyone with business experience, it's obvious how Ken wound up in this mess. He was a victim of overoptimism. The numbers can save you from overoptimism by bringing you back to reality, but only if you ask the right questions—and to do that, you usually need help from someone who is not emotionally involved and who knows the right questions to ask. Ken had gotten the idea that he could sell 10,000 of these directories. I asked him how long the selling season was in this business. "About four months," he said. In other words, he had 120 days to make all his sales, assuming he worked seven days a week. That comes to an average of eighty-three per day. How could he do it? OK, he thought he could sell some by direct mail. There are 12,000 restaurants in New York City. If he got a terrific response rate—say, 5 percent—it would still amount to only 600 directories. So he'd have to make the vast majority of sales in person. We're talking about one hundred sales calls a day and a success rate of something like 78 percent. Working ten-hour days, he'd have to average ten sales calls per hour, or one every six minutes. Impossible. Superman couldn't pull it off.

So why hadn't somebody pointed this out to him? I asked him if he'd gone to anyone for advice before starting the business. "Just my accountant," he said. "I gave him all the information, and he put together a cash flow statement showing it would all work out." To be fair, the accountant was not entirely at fault here. He'd done what accountants do. You give them information, and they feed it back to you in a different form. Unless you're basing your projections on past performance, they aren't likely to question your assumptions. After all, they're used to dealing with historical data. When you tell them you're planning to sell 10,000 directories in four months, they treat it as fact.

If you want business advice, you need to go to someone who has run a business over an extended period of time, and I'm talking about a real operating business, one that sells something other than accredited, professional expertise. Unfortunately, people don't always use the resources available to them. Ken, for one, knew about a guy with a related business, selling trade directories for the film industry. They'd never talked. Subsequently, Ken found out that the guy was selling 7,000 directories a year—after ten years in business. At least Ken's mistake was not fatal. He worked out a deal to repay the printer in full with regular monthly installments of $2,500. The printer was impressed with his honesty and agreed to print the new directory as well. Thereafter, Ken got his business advice from businesspeople. As for the accountant, he did what he was good at: Ken's taxes.

Presumed Guilty

I feel the same way about going to lawyers for business advice. Whenever a good deal falls through or a promising negotiation goes awry, it's usually the lawyers who are blamed, and often they're guilty as charged. Then again, there's always another culprit in the shadows, namely, the client. Nine times out of ten, problems arise because clients allow their lawyers to make business decisions for them—something the vast majority of lawyers are not qualified to do. Smart lawyers understand that and limit themselves to providing legal advice. Not-so-smart lawyers charge ahead and screw things up.

Take the case of a person I know who tried for years to open a retail establishment. Let's call her Polly. She figured that she needed to raise about $1.5 million and had lined up a couple of investors who'd verbally committed themselves to providing the bulk of the capital, but they hadn't even begun discussing an investment agreement yet, and no money had changed hands. Meanwhile, Polly had found a location she considered ideal. When she told the investors about it, they indicated that they wanted a voice in negotiating the terms of the lease. Polly decided to bring one of them to her next meeting with the landlord.

It turned out to be a bad idea. The investor wanted to go over every detail. Among other things, he noted that the place needed extensive renovation. He estimated that it would cost $100,000 to bring the building up to code and insisted that the rent be adjusted accordingly. The landlord bristled and said he would do the work himself for $25,000. The rest of the meeting was equally testy. Afterward, the landlord told Polly, "Next time you come alone. You're the decision maker, right? I don't need to talk to anyone else."

So Polly had a problem. She'd hoped that, by bringing the investor to the meeting, she could reach an understanding on the lease and the investment agreement more or less simultaneously, but that obviously wasn't going to happen. Which one should she take care of first? It was a chicken-and-egg situation. The investors wouldn't give her the money without a signed lease, but the landlord would never sign a lease unless he was confident that she'd be able to live up to her end of it, and she couldn't give him that assurance without the money.

Polly realized that she needed to talk with her lawyer, if only because he would be involved in writing and reviewing any contract she might sign—whether a lease with the landlord or an agreement with the investors. She explained her dilemma. The lawyer said she should take care of the lease first. "You've got limited funds," he said. "There's no point in paying me to work on an investment document before you're sure about getting the lease. If the lease falls through, you will have wasted a lot of money you can't afford to lose." That made sense to Polly, and she was planning to start negotiations on the lease when she came to see me. She wanted to know how I thought she should handle the conflict between the landlord who wanted to get the deal done quickly and the investors who insisted on scrutinizing every sentence in the lease.

I listened to her story and said, "I usually don't tell people what to do, but I'm going to make an exception in this case. Lawyers are not businesspeople. The advice your lawyer gave you is the worst I've ever heard. You absolutely should *not* do the lease first. You should do the investment document first. If you don't, I can guarantee you that this deal will never happen." Polly was obviously taken aback. "Listen," I said. "You're telling me that your biggest potential investor is a guy who negotiates to the nth degree." She nodded. "You also tell me the landlord is a guy who likes to make things simple and get things done." She agreed. I said, "Well, look at this from a businessperson's perspective. You're going to negotiate the lease and get ready to sign it. Then what are you going to do?"

"I'm going to work on the investment agreement and take it to the guys to sign and give me the money," she said.

"You're going to take it to someone who negotiates to the nth degree and expect him to give you the money right away?" I asked.

"No, that will never happen," she said.

"Right, never happen," I said. "He'll want to make changes. I know that I would if I were the main investor. So is your landlord willing to wait thirty, sixty, ninety days while you get the money?"

"Never," she said.

"Right," I said. "He'll say, 'Come back when you have the money.' Even if you get it pretty quickly, you've planted a seed of doubt in his mind. You said you had it, and then you didn't have it. He has to wonder about whether he can trust you to keep paying him for the next ten years. You've lost credibility. Do you get the picture?"

"I'm beginning to," Polly said.

"Your attorney shouldn't be giving you business advice," I said. "It's nice that he doesn't want to waste your money, but he's going to kill the deal in the process because he's not looking at the whole picture and he's not taking into account the character of the people involved. He's saying, 'Why run up legal fees unnecessarily?' That's thinking like a lawyer, not a businessperson. If it were my business, I'd have already done the investment agreement and told the investors, 'Let's sign this, and I'll put the money in escrow pending your approval of the lease. It will be there accruing interest for you in case things don't work out.'

Then you could tell the landlord, 'By the way, I have a million dollars in the bank, subject to the lease being approved. You don't have to worry about getting paid.' A big difference, right?"

"Yes," she said. "I hadn't thought of that."

"What are the investors going to get for their investment, anyway?" I asked. "We haven't discussed it yet," she said.

Then I really knew she'd gotten bad advice. If you've ever tried to raise money, you know that there's a huge difference between a verbal and a written commitment to invest. There's an even bigger difference between a written commitment and the actual transfer of funds. At the last minute, people come up with all kinds of excuses as to why they can't come through with the money they've promised. "I didn't know you wanted it so soon." "I just had a big margin call." "My wife won't let me do it." "My dog ate my checkbook." Getting the capital was the biggest hurdle Polly faced. It was pointless to spend time working on a lease until the investors demonstrated their commitment by putting money in an escrow account. Once they did, moreover, Polly would have other options even if she wound up being unable to get acceptable terms on the building she'd been looking at. She could always come back to the investors and say, "This deal fell through, but I have another possibility if you're still interested—subject to your approval naturally."

Lawyers don't think that way. They're trained to focus on protecting their clients. Businesspeople focus on achieving their goals. Lawyers think their primary duty is to make sure clients aren't exposed to potential liabilities. Businesspeople know that you sometimes have to be exposed to potential liabilities or you won't get anywhere. That said, I can't lay all the blame on Polly's lawyer for the bad advice he gave her. Part of the fault was hers. She'd gone to him asking for advice when she should have been asking for information. She should have inquired about the potential consequences of following this or that course of action, with the understanding that she would then make up her own mind about what to do. Why didn't she do that? I suspect it's because, like many first-time entrepreneurs, she wasn't yet ready to take responsibility for her decisions. Once you really, truly understand

and accept that responsibility, you become very selective about whom you go to for advice—and you don't go to people whose main concern is to keep you from taking risks.

Listen, most business decisions involve risk. That's why the businessperson has to make them. Who else can say how much risk he or she is willing to live with? Unfortunately, some lawyers don't understand that, as this one apparently didn't. It was Polly's responsibility to set him straight and draw a clear line between giving legal advice and making business decisions. By not doing so, she ran the greatest risk of all—losing the opportunity to launch her business.

You have to remember that lawyers are not businesspeople, although many of them would have you believe otherwise. In fact, the practice of law leads people to develop mental habits that are the *opposite* of those you need to be successful in business. I do not mean to disparage lawyers here. I went to law school after college, and I consider it one of the best decisions I ever made. Law school taught me a variety of skills that have served me well in business. It showed me how to take problems apart, analyze them, and figure out solutions. It taught me how to do research, and it forced me to develop a mental discipline that would have helped me no matter what I'd decided to do afterward. Because of my legal background, moreover, I have an edge now in business dealings. I can understand what legal documents say, and I know what's going on when legal issues arise. I also get a certain respect when I walk into a meeting. Most important, I understand how lawyers think— and how that limits their ability to make good business decisions.

Indeed, during the brief time I practiced law, I developed some of the same mental habits I'm referring to. I learned the importance of focusing on the details, of crossing every *t* and dotting every *i*. I learned to look for any and every potential problem that might come back to haunt my clients and to make sure they were protected. When I went into business, I had to develop a whole different mind-set. I couldn't afford to be too detail oriented or to focus too narrowly. I had to bear in mind all the changing factors that would ultimately determine my success or failure, and I had to be willing to make trade-offs in the interest of reaching my goal. I still tried to anticipate problems, but with an eye toward dealing with them, not protecting myself from them. As a businessperson, I learned that problems can be great teachers. They didn't stop me; they inspired me. I got a huge kick out of solving one and moving on to the next.

Luckily, I'd practiced law for a short enough time that I was able to handle that transition. After ten or fifteen years in practice, I suspect, it would be extremely difficult for most lawyers to start thinking like a businessperson. By the same token, I doubt that I'd make a very good lawyer at this point. I've been in business for too many years. My mental habits are too deeply ingrained.

That's why I always get the best legal advice I can before I make a big decision. I need to be reminded of things I might otherwise overlook. But I have a clear understanding with any attorney I hire. I say, "Here's the deal, and it's very simple. What I want from you is good legal advice, period. You can protect me by explaining the potential legal consequences of any decision I might make. I don't want you to tell me what to do from a business standpoint. I have other people I rely on for business advice."

You'd be surprised how difficult it is for some lawyers to follow those rules. I had one lawyer who said I was crazy to spend $20,000 in legal fees on a case that I knew in advance I would lose. He insisted it was a bad business decision. I believed that, in this instance, it was worth $20,000 to make a certain statement—and to avoid having to face similar problems in the future. The lawyer couldn't accept that. I let him go.

But most good lawyers have no trouble with my conditions. My longtime lawyer, Howard, is one of the best. He does exactly what a lawyer should do for a business client. He explains what various legal provisions mean. He clarifies what my legal obligations are and what they would be if I took a particular action. He makes me aware of any risks I'm taking, and he points out the conflicts I might have with other commitments I've made—my bank covenants, for example.

That's the kind of input I believe all businesspeople should get from their lawyers. Yes, there will be times when you need business advice. If so, get it from an experienced businessperson. Not only will the advice be better, but you probably won't be charged for it by the hour.

Ask Norm

Dear Norm:
We want to add experienced businesspeople to the staff of our
small company. We've tried local SCORE chapters, word of
mouth, and some Internet searches—with no luck. What should
we do now?
    Donald

Dear Donald:
I can't offer you a quick, reliable solution, but you shouldn't be
discouraged. It always takes time to find good people. Here's
a tip: the people you want are probably not looking for work.
They may be retired. They may be between projects. They may
just be bored with what they're doing. If they're looking at all,
they're networking with their friends. You should do the same.
Talk to your customers, your suppliers, your bankers, other
businesspeople you know. Eventually, someone will turn up.
    —Norm

The Steady-Income Rule

The need for help from experienced businesspeople doesn't go away
as your company grows, but many of us have a problem getting it on a
day-to-day basis. I was able to solve that problem at one critical point
in the growth of CitiStorage. I did it by applying an important rule of
business. The rule is: you can do almost anything as long as you have
a steady income. The income doesn't have to be as much as you want,
or even as much as you need. What matters is that you can count on it
week after week and month after month. Without that regular flow of
funds, you'll be constantly getting distracted from your goals. With it,
you're free to focus on the things you enjoy most and do best.

    You might think everybody would know that rule, but a lot of people miss it, including some of the smartest and most capable business practitioners around. I'm talking about the type of people most of us would love to have on our payroll. They're executives who've run businesses and done deals and who have the knowledge, contacts, and experience to lift a company to another level—if you can afford them, that is. Most small-business owners assume they can't.

I've found, however, that—with the help of the steady-income rule—you can sign up the kind of talent that would otherwise be far beyond your means, and it won't cost you a dime. How's that possible? Because people of that caliber pay for themselves many times over, provided you give them the space they need to perform.

I'll tell you about Ben Zitron, who came to see me after a couple deals he'd been working on went bad, costing him a small fortune. With tuition payments due for two kids, he suddenly found himself desperate for cash and in need of a job. He wanted to know if I'd hire him. Ben was one of the best deal makers I've even known, a guy who's made millions putting mergers together, helping companies go public, finding capital, and the like. He'd owned and run a variety of businesses over the years. He could sell. He could negotiate. He could do everything I could do, but he'd never learned the steady-income rule. As a result, he was always just a couple bad deals away from disaster.

Now that disaster had finally struck, I was of course going to help him, but I knew right away it would never work to bring him in as an employee, at least not in the usual sense of the term. Ben was a free spirit. Even if I could come up with the money to pay him what he was worth—probably somewhere in excess of $300,000 a year—there was simply no way he was going to devote his full attention to any job I might find for him. Sure, he'd give it a shot, but before long he'd be off working on his own deals, pursuing his own agenda, and I'd be fuming. We'd start arguing. Other employees would start grumbling. It would be a mess.

So I thought it over and came up with an offer. I said, "Look, Ben. I know you. You don't need a job. What you need is a steady income that will allow you to get back to what you love—doing deals. So I'll hire you, but I won't hire you full-time. I'll give you certain projects to do for me. You'll work out of my office, and you can set your own schedule. As long as you take care of my projects, you can do all the outside deals you like. In return, I want a percentage of any deals you close."

I wasn't just being a nice guy here. I knew that—even if Ben were part-time—I'd be paying him an annual salary in the low six figures, and that kind of expense had to make financial sense for the company, or I couldn't bring him in. I'd have to find another way to help him instead.

But it so happened that I'd recently landed a contract with the New York State court system, worth about $250,000 a year in sales. I needed someone to expand our business in that area, someone who could meet with high-court officials and sell our services to other parts of the system. If Ben hadn't come along, I'd have had to hire a salesperson for $50,000 a year. From that perspective, I was overpaying Ben by a substantial amount. Then again, I knew the result I was going to get, and I fully expected that, over the long term, he'd return three or four times whatever we paid him.

He didn't disappoint me. Within eight months, he'd expanded our sales with the court system enough to cover his salary, and he continued to pay us big dividends thereafter. In four years, that part of our business grew from $250,000 to more than $1 million a year, largely through Ben's efforts. Meanwhile, he landed two very big customers and got us our first round of financing. Without him, I'd have had to hire an outsider to do the deal—at a cost of about $50,000. He also came up with more than $800,000 for a new warehouse from a state program to promote employment in the inner city.

Later I used the same approach to hire Sam Kaplan. It was an easier sell with him than with Ben, however, because Sam already knew the steady-income rule. He paid for himself in about five minutes. I asked him what we should do about a new facility we wanted to build but couldn't get financing for. He looked over the plans and suggested a few simple changes. We had a financing deal in two months. Without his input, we'd have had to lease the additional space we needed. Right there he saved us at least $100,000 a year for ten years. You know the rest.

So I wound up with two top-notch people providing the kind of advice and service that would normally cost a company hundreds of thousands of dollars. Granted, it helps to have been in business for thirty years and to have friends like Sam and Ben, but people with similar credentials are all over the place. These days, there are very few parts of the country where you can't find cashed-out company owners who aren't yet ready to retire, or experienced businesspeople looking for a base from which they can do deals.

Those people represent a source of talent that most small to midsize companies overlook. I'm not talking about start-ups and very young businesses here. They need the kind of help you get from a mentor, or maybe a board of advisers. But in established companies of a certain size—for service companies, I'd say $5 million and up—you want executives who can implement as well as advise, and whom you can talk to as insiders about the big issues facing your business. The hard part is keeping them, which sometimes requires you to put aside your own needs and focus instead on theirs. You have to create a situation in which they're going to be happy. They won't stick around out of gratitude or loyalty, after all, or because they need the job. They'll stay only if they're making money and having fun.

Think of them as one-person businesses. When you hire them, you're investing in a company. To get a return, you have to give them the leeway they need to run their business—which you may find difficult. I certainly did. I often got furious with Ben. He came in when he wanted to. He had his own schedule, his own ideas, his own way of doing things, and it drove me crazy. I'd go home and rant to Elaine, "That moron! It's stupid what he's doing." Putting up with his ways was the hardest part of the whole experience. Funny, isn't it? We bring in talented, creative people because we want fresh thinking, and when they offer it to us, we have trouble accepting it.

Eventually, Ben went off to develop his own projects, but by then he had already made enormous, long-lasting contributions to the company. Sam, on the other hand, decided to stick around and become my partner.

The Bottom Line

Point One: When you're struggling with a problem, get an outside perspective to make sure you've identified the real one and come up with a solution that's going to address it.

Point Two: Accountants are good for explaining what has happened in the past, but don't go to them for business advice. Talk to an experienced business owner instead.

Point Three: Your lawyer's job is to tell you the potential legal consequences of a decision or a course of action—not to give you business advice.

Point Four: Yes, your small company can afford to hire world-class executives as long as you're willing to create a situation in which they can make money and have fun.

CHAPTER SIXTEEN

When the Student Is Ready, the Teacher Appears

No matter how far you go in business, no matter how much you learn, you never know it all. Business is an adventure that never quits and an education that never ends. I've had more teachers than I can count over the course of my career. Some of them have been mentors and advisers. Some have been people I've met, and some have been experiences I've had along the way. They've all left me with lessons I've used to improve myself and my businesses.

Take, for example, the routine I follow with people who visit me in my office in Brooklyn. When they have to leave, I put on my jacket and walk them to their cars. Often the visitors will say, "Oh, that's not necessary. You're too busy. I can find my own way."

I say, "No, it is necessary, and I'll explain why on the way down." Then I tell them about my meeting with King Hussein of Jordan.

It was in the mid-1990s, during a trip to Jordan that had been arranged by the Simon Wiesenthal Foundation, on whose board of directors I was serving at the time. The king had invited us to see his country and to meet with him and his wife, Queen Noor. Seven board members—led by Rabbi Marvin Hier, the founder and dean of the Simon Wiesenthal Center—had traveled to Amman, the capital of Jordan. We'd been there a few days, taking tours in limousines provided by our host, when word came that the king was ready to see us.

Our chauffeurs drove us to the royal compound at the appointed hour, and we were shown to a room in one of the buildings on the property. In the center of the room was a large, oblong table, with a chair at the head for the king. As we awaited his arrival, the chief of protocol arranged us in a sort of receiving line. "The king wants to meet each of you personally," he said.

A few minutes later, King Hussein, Queen Noor, and their entourage showed up, and the introductions began. Working his way down the receiving line, the king greeted us by name. "Oh, Mr. Brodsky," he said when he came to me. "You're a businessman from New York, I understand."

I had two reactions. First, I was deeply flattered. It made me feel warm and fuzzy all over to think that the king of Jordan knew who I was and what I did. Second, I was floored. I figured he must have twenty or thirty such meetings a week. Did he prepare for each one as he'd obviously prepared for ours?

Following the introductions, we took seats around the table and for the next hour or so chatted with the king and queen. Finally, the king said, "I'm terribly sorry, but I have another appointment that I must go to now. I want to thank you all for coming. Please enjoy the rest of your visit to my country. Let me show you to your cars."

Now, I'd never been shown to my car by a head of state before. In this instance, moreover, we had a fairly long walk. King Hussein strolled along, talking with us, as we went down a hallway and descended a flight of stairs. Outside, in front of the palace, he stopped to let us take pictures before sending us on our way.

"This is unbelievable," I said to the chief of protocol.

"What's unbelievable?" he said.

"The king walking us to our cars," I said.

"It's only common courtesy," he said.

I thought about that comment for days afterward. If it was only common courtesy for a king to walk me to my car, and only common courtesy for him to find out who I was before we met, couldn't I do as much for people who came to see me? King Hussein had made me feel about him and his country exactly the way I want my customers to feel about me and my company—warm and fuzzy. I want to send the message that I care about them personally. That's how you develop long-term relationships.

So I returned from Jordan with two great business tips in addition to a lot of wonderful memories. Henceforward, when people I didn't know would come visit me, I would make sure that I had some background information about them, just enough to establish a bridge I could use to begin building rapport. And at the end of our meeting, I would walk them to their cars.

That's typical of how I get my business ideas. I pick them up wherever I go. I regard everyone I meet as a potential source of tips to improve the way I do business. Not that I pump people for suggestions, but I watch carefully what they do and how it affects those around them, including me. As a result, I'm constantly discovering new things I can do to reinforce the relationships we have with people inside and outside the company.

Here's another example. A while back, I found myself in Princeton, New Jersey, and I decided to check out a local clothing store. I hate to shop, but I love to watch salespeople in action. It doesn't matter whether they're good or bad. I can learn from them all. I even enjoy going to vacation resorts and listening to the pitches of time-share salespeople. For me, it's pure entertainment.

The Princeton store turned out to be nirvana. The salesman who waited on me was one of the best I'd ever seen. He wasn't pushy; he had a friendly, easygoing manner; he made me feel that he really cared about having me look my best. I'm generally a finicky clothing shopper, but when I get a good salesperson, I'll buy anything, whether I need it or not. In this case, I bought two suits and a sport jacket, which I had shipped to my office. We exchanged thanks, and I left.

Three days later, I received a note from the salesman, thanking me for coming in, expressing his pleasure at helping me, and inviting me to let him know if he could be of service in the future. It wasn't a form letter. It wasn't computer generated. It was a personal, handwritten message from him to me. I showed it to my wife, Elaine. "Isn't this fabulous?" I said. She said, "We have to start doing this." I agreed. Thereafter, Elaine wrote personal notes, by hand, to all of our new customers, welcoming them to the company and urging them to contact either one of us directly should the need arise.

Some people, I know, will question the importance of such gestures. Does it really matter, they'll ask, if you walk people to their cars or send them handwritten notes? Customer relationships are based on price, service, and benefits. If you can't compete on those issues, you're not even in the game. I don't disagree, but there's more to a long-term relationship than the basics. Anyone can match, or beat, your price and benefits, and everyone promises great service. If you want to hold on to customers, you have to do more. You have to give them reasons for staying with you. One of the best reasons is that they like you, trust you, and want to do business with you. There's no magic formula for creating those bonds. It's a matter of doing the simple little things that build loyalty and trust—calling customers, visiting them, caring about them, treating them as well after five or ten years as you did when the relationship was brand new.

Problems, Problems

Problems can be another great source of management wisdom, provided you're willing to learn. Unfortunately, people often deal with problems as onetime occurrences, without looking for the root causes. As a result, they don't learn the lessons that the problems are trying to teach.

Consider an experience Elaine and I had at a fancy seafood restaurant in Dallas a few years ago. Although the restaurant was crowded, and we had no reservation, the maître d' said he thought he could seat us in twenty minutes or so. We went to the bar, and Elaine ordered a shrimp cocktail. Before it was served, the maître d' came over to tell us he had a table available in the balcony overlooking the main dining room.

"I just ordered a shrimp cocktail," Elaine said.

"No problem," said the maître d'. "I'll have someone bring it to your table."

The shrimp cocktail arrived right after we did. Elaine tasted the sauce and found it too spicy. Intending to dilute it a bit, she reached for a bottle of ketchup on the table. As she turned the cap on the bottle, there was a loud pop, and ketchup came shooting out, covering her sweater, her blouse, her skirt, her whole arm. Elaine sat there stunned, drowning in ketchup. Our waitress came running over. "Oh, I'm so sorry," she said, handing us napkins. "Let me help you." She worked feverishly to clean up the mess. "If you bring me your clothes tomorrow, I'll have them cleaned for you," she said.

Ask Norm

Dear Norm:

I've had the entrepreneurial bug since I was in college fifteen years ago. Now I'm happily married with two sons. Those relationships bring joy and meaning to my life, as well as a lot of responsibility. For that reason, I plan to keep my day job as an executive of a Fortune 500 company, but I feel I must also honor my entrepreneurial itch. I have a great deal of experience and knowledge that I feel would be useful to someone launching a new venture. I'm thinking about volunteering in a start-up, donating up to twenty hours of my time per week. In return, I'd ask that I be treated like a partner, but with no salary or equity. What do you think?

    Gregory

Dear Gregory:

I think you should be applauded for making a tough life decision, putting your family obligations first. A lot of people couldn't do that. And yes, I think your idea has a lot of merit. I also love starting businesses, and I've found that I can satisfy my itch by helping other people start theirs. But twenty hours a week sounds way too ambitious. Instead, I'd offer to meet once or twice a week with an entrepreneur to offer advice and serve as a sounding board. You'll be doing a great service and learning lessons you can put to use when you start your own business—after the kids leave home.

    —Norm

The manager showed up a moment later and also offered his apologies. He wiped ketchup off a chair and sat down with us. "I'm terribly sorry about this," he said and gave me his card. "Just send the cleaning bill to me. I'll make sure it's taken care of."

Both Elaine and I were suitably impressed. Every business, including ours, has its share of accidental, unavoidable, nightmarish customer screwups. If we're the customers involved, we mainly want people to act as though they're sincerely sorry and to do what they can to repair the damage. We would have been quite satisfied if the manager had left it at that. But as he stood up to leave, he said, "In a way, you were lucky."

"What do you mean?" Elaine asked.

"The last time this happened, the person got ketchup all over her hair. We had to send her to the beauty parlor. At least you just have it on your clothes."

"You mean this has happened before?" I asked.

"Oh, yeah," the manager said. "It happens fairly often. This part of the restaurant can get extremely hot during the day. We ask the waitresses to loosen the caps of the ketchup bottles, so the pressure doesn't build up inside, but sometimes they forget, and the bottle explodes when the guest goes to open it." With that, he excused himself and walked away.

Elaine and I didn't know whether to be outraged or to burst out laughing. We were dumbfounded. I could think of all kinds of ways to make sure customers don't have to endure ketchup bombs: take the ketchup downstairs every evening; buy a small refrigerator for the balcony and keep the bottles there during the day; put the ketchup in vented containers; serve ketchup only when the customer asks for it. Instead, the restaurant had come up with a solution that solved nothing. The bottles kept exploding; the ketchup kept flying; the staff kept cleaning up and apologizing; and the victims kept telling everyone they met about their experience, thereby turning what should have been a onetime embarrassment into an ongoing public relations problem. That's what can happen when you don't learn from your mistakes.

The ketchup case is an extreme example, but the phenomenon is by no means uncommon. When you're deluged with problems, there's a natural tendency to focus on the crisis at hand, deal with it, and then move on to whatever else is demanding your attention. I know a couple, for example, who had a company that made women's clothing. In order to ensure that they always had enough stock on hand to meet the demand, they would habitually produce more clothing than they needed. Inevitably, they'd wind up with a ton of excess inventory, which they would then sell off at a loss. That was easier and quicker than dealing with the underlying problem, their inability to forecast accurately, and so they kept doing it, year after year—until they went out of business.

The fact is that if you don't eliminate the root cause of a problem, it only goes away temporarily. For that reason, I've tried to introduce a certain discipline in my company by constantly reminding people that there are two steps involved in fixing problems. First, you have to stop the bleeding—that is, deal with the consequences and minimize the damage. Then you have to figure out why it happened and make sure that it doesn't happen again.

I'll give you an example from the early days of my records storage business. We were getting lots of boxes at the time. To keep track of them, we put in a bar-coding system that allowed us to identify each box and pinpoint its location. That way, it didn't matter where we stored the boxes. We could always find them when we had to.

Before too long, however, I began getting phone calls from customers complaining that we'd lost some of their boxes. At first, I was skeptical. I believed our system was foolproof. To me, it seemed less likely that we'd lost the boxes than that the customers had made a mistake in their record keeping. But when we found some of the missing boxes in our warehouse, I knew we had a problem, and so we moved into our two-step problem-solving mode.

First, I put together a team to search for the missing boxes. We had to go through the entire warehouse and scan the boxes in each location, then compare the list to the one in our computer. Fortunately, we had few enough boxes at that time for the task to be manageable. A couple of years later, it would have been much more difficult.

We did in fact find the boxes, and I suppose we could have stopped then and there and hoped it wouldn't happen again. But that wouldn't have gotten to the root of the problem. So I ordered that no new boxes be put away until we figured out what was going on, and I created another team to find the cause and come up with a solution.

It didn't take long. In reviewing our procedures for tracking boxes, I realized we'd made a basic mistake: we had failed to take into account the inevitability of human error. We had no system for double-checking our work. A driver would pick up boxes from a customer and deliver them to our warehouse, where they would be put directly on the shelves. At no point did we stop to count the boxes and make sure the number we unloaded from the truck matched the number we'd received from the customer or that the number we put away matched the number we'd unloaded.

Clearly, we needed to add a step to our box-storing routine. We decided that in the future, when a truck returned from a pickup, we would put all the boxes in a temporary holding area marked by a cone. We would scan the bar codes on the boxes in the cone, as we called it, and download the information into our computer. Then we would move the boxes to a permanent location and scan the bar codes again. When we downloaded the list of boxes in the permanent location, the computer would compare it to the list of boxes in the cone. If the two lists didn't match, we would know right away that we'd made a mistake, and we could attempt to fix it immediately.

With the new system, we put the problem of the missing boxes behind us. We eventually added another safeguard by purchasing equipment that allowed our drivers to scan the bar codes at a customer's location. As a result, we now have checks between the customer and the truck, between the truck and the cone area, and between the cone and the shelving. Yes, it's still theoretically possible that a box might get lost, but it hasn't happened in years.

The point is that you don't really solve a problem unless you attack the cause as well as the symptoms. As obvious as that may seem, most people tend to lose sight of it in the press of everyday business demands. How can you make sure that you keep it in mind? My advice is to get yourself and your people into the habit of asking, "Why did this problem arise in the first place?" And one other thing: the next time you find yourself in a fancy seafood restaurant in Dallas, be careful when you open the ketchup.

Be Prepared

Early in my career, a judge taught me a great lesson that has served me well to this day. I was twenty-three years old at the time and fresh out of Brooklyn Law School. Although I had passed the bar exam, I was not yet a full-fledged attorney. In those days, it took six to eight months to be admitted to the bar after taking the exam. I, like most young lawyers, spent that period working at a law firm, where I received my initiation into the practice of law.

The initiation began during my first week on the job. As I was getting ready to go home at about five-thirty one afternoon, the attorney I worked for handed me a massive file and said I should show up in court the next day to represent a motion he had submitted on behalf of the client. I was taken aback. "You want me to go into a courtroom?" I said. "I've never been in a courtroom."

"Don't worry," he said. "It's nothing. Just be there at 9:30 a.m."

"Nine-thirty!" I said, staring at the file. "You want me to read all this tonight?"

"No, no, no," he said. "You don't have to read anything. Nothing's going to happen. When the judge calls the case, you just say, 'For the motion.' The judge will say something like, 'I'll take it under consideration.' Then you can leave."

"OK," I said, but I was nervous all the same. The next morning, I took a seat in the gallery of a dingy courtroom in Queens, New York. It looked to me as though the other people there were all in their nineties. We stood as the judge entered. He, too, looked about ninety years old to me. I waited until he called my case, whereupon I leaned forward and said tentatively, "For the motion."

At the sound of my voice, the judge put on his glasses and looked in my direction. "Is that you, sonny?" he asked. "Did you say that?"

My stomach tightened. "Yes, your honor," I said.

He pointed a long, bony finger at me and curled it back abruptly. "Come here," he said. I rose and walked down the center aisle toward the judge's bench. I could hear people snickering all around me. The judge waited until I was standing right in front of him. "Now-w-w-w," he said slowly, peering down at me from the bench, "is this your first time in court, sonny?"

"W-w-well, yes, your honor," I said. I heard laughter from the gallery.

"Are you admitted to the bar yet?" the judge asked.

I must have turned bright red. "No, not yet, your honor," I said. More laughter.

"Well, sonny, tell me what this motion is all about," he said.

I stammered and squirmed. "Well, I, uh . . . it's about . . . I mean, we filed this motion . . . well, not we, but the attorney I work for . . ."

The judge cut me off. "You have no idea what it's about, do you, sonny?" he said. "You came into this court unprepared, didn't you? I should deny this motion for that reason alone."

People behind me were now roaring with laughter. I felt so embarrassed I wanted to melt through the floor. "Yes, your honor," I said.

"But instead I'm going to give you your first lesson in life out here in the real world," the judge said. "Never, ever walk into my courtroom unprepared." He glowered at me for a moment to let the lesson sink in, then waved his hand dismissively. "Now scoot, scoot, scoot. Go back and tell your boss that you didn't do so well today."

I turned and walked out with my tail between my legs. Everybody was in hysterics. I heard someone say, "He got another one." I left the courthouse as fast as I could and drove back to the office. When I walked in, my boss had a big smile on his face. "What happened in court?" he asked.

"You know what happened!" I said. He just laughed.

So I'd been set up. I later learned that the judge had a reputation for dispensing such lessons to novice lawyers. The experience had been excruciating, and I swore that I would never allow myself to be so humiliated again. In the following months, I went to dozens of such hearings and said, "For the motion," many times. No judge ever asked me what the motion was about—but I could have answered if I'd had to. I'd read the file. I was prepared.

By the time I went into business, the habit of intensive preparation had become second nature to me, and it proved to be a major competitive advantage. I found that I could close a significantly higher percentage of sales than my competitors simply by knowing more than they did about the customer, its representatives, and every other aspect of the deal. That's still true today. Our closing rate is better than 95 percent among prospective customers who come to visit our facility, and not just because we have nice warehouses, beautiful offices, and wonderful employees (though all that certainly helps). We prepare thoroughly. Before the customer's people arrive, I go online to find out as much as I can about the organization's structure, mission, and history. My salespeople give me a full briefing on the visitors I'm about to meet—what they're like as individuals, who else they're considering, how the decision will be made, and so on. I tailor my presentation accordingly.

Once, for example, I gave a tour to some people who were thinking about switching their company's business to us after many years with another provider. Their biggest concern, my salespeople said, had to do with maintaining access to their files during the transfer. Now, in the course of one tour, I can't tell visitors everything we do, but if I know about a specific concern, I can address it without waiting to be asked. In this case, I made a point of saying, "One of the things we're most careful about is making sure that people have access to their files or boxes during the move. Here's what we do." The prospects were delighted. We closed the sale.

It's even more important to be prepared when you meet with a customer after you've screwed something up. To be sure, you need to apologize and promise that the problem won't arise again, but you should also be able to answer the question that customers always ask: "How did it happen?" That takes preparation. You have to figure out exactly what went wrong, and why, and how you can ensure it won't recur. Then you can say right up front, "Listen, we've researched this incident, and here's what caused it. We're not making excuses. We just want you to understand what happened and what safeguards we've put in to protect you and all of our other customers in the future. The truth is, you've helped us to correct an important problem we were unaware of. We really owe you our thanks for that as well as our apologies." In most cases, I've found, customers will be willing to give you a second chance.

There are no shortcuts here, not even when you're dealing with customers with whom you've had a long-term contractual relationship. You can't assume that you or they know what's in the contract just because you've been operating under it for several years. It's too easy to forget critical details—details that may determine whether or not you keep the business in the future. I remember one account that came up for rebidding after we'd had it for twelve years. The customer was a city agency. Because of our track record and our cordial relations with people who work at the agency, we figured we had a good shot at landing the contract again, but—when the bids came in—we discovered that, on paper at least, our bid was higher than the others.

"What are we going to do?" Brad Clinton, our sales manager, asked me.

"The first step is to read the contract," I said.

He gave me a curious look. "Sure, if you say so, but…" He shrugged.

"But what?" I asked.

"Well, it's not like we don't know what's in it," he said. "We've had it for twelve years."

I couldn't help smiling as the memory of my first day in court flashed through my mind. "Let me tell you a story," I said.

Brad got the point and pulled out the contract. When we went through it, we came across a clause stipulating that whoever got the business could not use subcontractors. That eliminated one of the other bidders, whose people had neglected to read the contract as closely as we did. In addition, we were able to show that the remaining companies had based their bids on unrealistic expectations about how some parts of the job could be done. Instead of doing the research, they'd guessed. When you calculated what they would actually have to charge, it turned out that we were the low bidder after all. So we got the contract again, and I owed it to the judge I encountered the first time I ever set foot in a courtroom.

Ask Norm

Dear Norm:

I've been in executive recruiting for fifteen years. Two years ago, I formed an alliance with one of my clients, and it's working out great. I've had to hire two new recruiters to keep up with the demand. My annual revenues have already gone from $150,000 to $800,000, and we're barely scraping the surface. I see only one thing that can stop us from building a substantial organization: me. I've come to realize that I don't have the ability, the patience, or the know-how to manage and grow this franchise. What should I do?

Bruce

Dear Bruce:

First, don't be too hard on yourself. You're lucky you came to this realization before getting your company in trouble. It took some tough experiences to teach me that I didn't have the qualities required to manage a business, patience being perhaps the most important one. I eventually learned that I can take a company only so far and don't enjoy running it beyond that point. I need to bring in real managers—patient, detail-oriented people. They aren't good at starting businesses, and I'm not good at managing them. We get along just fine. Just remember that you'll need to have a good working relationship with the person you bring in. That means both of you have to be open to learning from each other.

—Norm

Hurry Up and Wait

Without doubt, the most educational experience of my business career
has been my passage through Chapter 11, although I wouldn't recommend that you follow my example. Before the bankruptcy, I was like a
lot of the young entrepreneurs who now come to me for advice. They're
all in a big hurry. They have a tremendous sense of urgency about
achieving whatever goal they've set for themselves—now. Most of them
have already decided on their next step, and they're on the verge of
taking it. What they want from me is encouragement. What they get is
advice to stop and think.

You should never make important business decisions when you're
feeling driven by urgency. I don't care whether the urgency is coming
from your own impatience or from other people putting pressure on
you to decide. If you feel as though you have to make the decision right
away, don't make it. When you make decisions hastily, you don't think
them through the way you should, and there's a very good chance that
they will come back to haunt you.

That isn't an easy rule to follow. Most entrepreneurs are impatient
people by nature. You wouldn't go into business in the first place if you
didn't feel a strong desire to get somewhere, to make things happen.
But that same desire can turn into your worst enemy if you don't learn
how to control it. I, for one, had to get whacked in the head before I
realized the danger of being in too big a hurry to reach our goals.

It was impatience, after all, that—in the late 1980s—led me to
acquire a company with major problems. In my heart, I *knew* it was a
bad deal. My inner voice was saying, "Are you nuts? You need these
problems like a hole in the head. You're putting the whole company
at risk." But you don't listen to your inner voice when you're being
driven by a sense of urgency. You override your good instincts. You
make excuses. You tell yourself what you want to hear. I'd turned
around other insolvent companies before. I knew how to handle salespeople. I could deal with any problem they threw at me. Hey, I felt like
Superman.

So I went ahead and did the deal. You know the rest. (If you don't, go back and read chapter 2.) Over the next three years, as we worked our way out of Chapter 11, I spent a lot of time thinking about what I'd done wrong. There was more to it, I realized, than one bad decision. That decision was connected to some fundamental character traits, one of which was my need for instant gratification. I do things on the spur of the moment, without considering the consequences or consulting with other people. And when I set a goal for myself, I'm single-minded about achieving it—even if it turns out to be the wrong goal. Looking back, moreover, I could see that such traits had led me to make countless other mistakes over the years, in my personal life as well as in business. Somehow I had to figure out a way to control those tendencies. I knew that I probably couldn't get rid of them. They were too deeply embedded in my personality. But I didn't want to go on letting them make my decisions for me.

So I came up with a rule: don't make any major decision without taking a shower.

By *major*, I mean a decision that will have long-range consequences. I'm not talking about routine, day-to-day issues. I deal with those as they arise. But if an opportunity presents itself, or if there's a big problem to handle, or if we have to make some change in the way we operate, I always take a shower before I decide. Understand that, while I do my best thinking in the shower, I don't have time to take one during the day. So I'm actually telling myself to put off the decision for twenty-four hours. That was very difficult to do, at least in the beginning. I *like* to make instant decisions. When people want me to do something, I have a lot of trouble saying, "I've got to think about it. I can't give you an answer right now."

What I needed was a mechanism I could use to slow myself down, and the shower rule served the purpose. It was a way of selling myself on the idea of waiting. It forced me to give myself time to think through the decision, hear what other people had to say, take into account the likely effects of whatever I decided. Often I wound up doing the same thing I'd have done in the first place, but I did it with the confidence of having gone through the right thought process. And sometimes that thought process would save me from a mistake I was about to make or point me to an opportunity I'd have otherwise missed.

My shower rule eventually became a habit. I learned to recognize the sense of urgency and stop it in its tracks. Now, whenever there's a big decision to make, I put it off automatically. My managers accuse me of procrastinating, but they're wrong. What I'm doing is giving my unconscious mind a chance to work on the problem. I'm making sure that my sense of urgency doesn't drown out my inner voice. It's a trait I've noticed in other successful businesspeople, the ones who've been running companies for a long time. Nothing is urgent for them. They don't rush into decisions prematurely. They've learned how to take four steps back, weigh all the factors, and decide calmly how to proceed.

But stepping back doesn't come easily to young entrepreneurs who are eager to get ahead. The fear, of course, is that they'll lose the opportunity in front of them. It's a feeling that smart salespeople know how to exploit. They make you believe that the opportunity they're offering today won't be around tomorrow, and then they use your sense of urgency to push you to a fast decision. With age and experience, however, you learn two things: first, that the world is full of great opportunities, more than you can ever take advantage of, and, second, that real opportunities don't disappear. I can't think of a single opportunity I've lost since I adopted my shower rule.

And, meanwhile, I'm just about the cleanest CEO in town.

The Bottom Line

Point One: There are great business lessons to be learned wherever you go, but you have to remember to look for them.

Point Two: Solving a problem is a two-step process. First, you should stop the bleeding, and then you need to address the underlying cause.

Point Three: Preparation is a crucial competitive edge. Don't assume you know what's in a contract—even an old contract—unless you've gone back and reread it.

Point Four: The harder someone pushes you to make a quick decision, the more insistent you should be about taking your time.

CHAPTER SEVENTEEN

Keeping Up with the Stones

We began with Bobby and Helene Stone, and I'd like to end there as well. I've kept in close touch with them over the years and watched their progress as their annual sales grew from $162,000 in 1992 to $3.2 million in 2007. Looking back now, I can see there were several important milestones along the way.

One of the first came four and a half years into the business, when they reached a turning point that every successful new business goes through eventually. It begins the day you decide you need to have another salesperson in addition to yourself. Bringing on clerical help or front-line people is a different story. You do it because you have to—because you simply can't handle the work on your own. But when you hire a salesperson, you're making a decision to grow, and how you go about it can have long-term consequences for you and your company. Bobby and Helene were approaching that transition in the middle of 1996. At one of our regular meetings, they asked me what it would take to bring in their twenty-seven-year-old son, Steven, as a full-time salesperson. I told them that, like most things in business, it would take good planning.

There are three major challenges you face when you hire a salesperson, particularly the first one. To begin with, you need to make sure that he or she is going to have enough time to succeed. How much time is enough varies from business to business, depending partly on the selling cycle. In my records storage business, for example, it typically takes two years to close a sale. In other businesses, the selling period can be as short as a few weeks. But even in businesses with a short cycle, you need to give new salespeople time to adjust to the culture, learn the products, develop a sales base, and so on. You can't expect them to start making sales—and I mean good sales, with healthy gross margins—as soon as they walk through the door. In fact, it's generally wise to assume that new salespeople won't make *any* sales during the first year. You won't be able to judge their performance objectively if you're counting on their sales to make ends meet.

So I advised Bobby and Helene to put off hiring Steven until they had accumulated enough cash to pay his salary for a full year. Even then, I said, they shouldn't bring him on unless they were projecting the same volume of sales in the next twelve months—without any contribution from Steven—as they had in the previous twelve. My advice was, I admit, very conservative. I wanted Bobby and Helene to have a big cushion. With other people, I might have settled for less. The size of the cushion you need depends to some extent on the level of stress you feel when you're operating without any cash in the bank. I knew Bobby and Helene would have a hard time handling that pressure. So we agreed on some goals that would pretty much ensure their survival even if everything went wrong after Steven came on board.

As it turned out, they hit the goals by the end of the year, which brought them to the second challenge: giving Steven the right kind of training.

When you hire a salesperson, you're making an investment, and you have a right to expect a return on the investment in a reasonable amount of time. Let's say the person costs you $45,000 in salary and benefits, plus another $5,000 for other expenses (telephone, travel, whatever). Suppose also that your average gross margin is 40 percent. The salesperson would have to bring in $125,000 in sales at a 40 percent margin ($125,000 × 40 percent = $50,000) just to cover what you've spent on him or her in the first year.

That's a tough concept for many people to grasp. Most companies don't even try to teach it. But you'll have continual problems with your salespeople if they don't understand how the business works and what you're counting on them to contribute. They'll make bad sales. They won't follow the rules. They'll constantly complain about being unappreciated and underpaid because they don't know what's really going on. Education is the only way around those problems. You need to change the way your salespeople think. You need a process that teaches them the business while they go about their jobs.

Bobby and Helene used the same process with Steven that I'd used with Bobby. They came up with a plan, gave Steven goals for gross margins as well as sales, and got him involved in tracking how he was doing. Having a little competition helped. Steven dug up Bobby's records from his first year and set out to do better. Meanwhile, he and Bobby competed to have the best sales and gross margins each month, with Helene acting as referee.

It took time for Steven to learn. He finished 1997, his first year, with sales well ahead of what Bobby's were in his first year, but with lower gross margins. Although he'd covered his salary, the company still wasn't breaking even on its investment. In effect, Bobby and Helene were carrying him. So we went back and focused on the gross margin issue, and gradually Steven caught on. By August, it was clear that 1998 was going to be a blowout year for him in terms of both sales and gross margins.

Which brought us to the third major challenge: keeping him focused and motivated.

In the fall, Bobby, Helene, and Steven said they wanted to meet with me. They'd come up with a new compensation scheme for next year. Their notion was to motivate Steven by giving him an incentive to exceed the numbers in the plan. He would receive a monthly salary, for which he'd be expected to hit the agreed-on targets. In addition, he'd get a commission on any sales he made above the targets. They asked me what I thought. I told them I thought it was a bad idea.

I don't like commissions, for reasons I explained in chapter 14. I admit that I'm sometimes forced to pay them to new salespeople, but eventually I move the best ones to straight salary. It's better for them, for me, and for the company. With a salary, salespeople work as members of a team. When you put them on commission, you're giving them an incentive to follow individual agendas.

That's what I feared would happen with Steven. Let's say his monthly target was $20,000 in sales. How would he feel if he got to $18,000 with three days left, and Bobby and Helene needed his help to fill mail orders, or they had to go away for a while, leaving him to cover the office? And what if, at the end of the month, Steven found himself with a choice between servicing a high-margin account or going after additional low-margin sales? The first might be more important to the company, but the second would clearly be better for him. Commissions create divisions in a company, and this plan was bound to drive a wedge between Steven and his parents. I asked them, wasn't it better to pay him a salary, adjusted annually to reflect all his contributions to the company? Sure, they could give him a bonus if he did something really extraordinary, but shouldn't everyone be rewarded for doing what's best for the company as a whole? They thought about it and agreed.

So, after seven years, Bobby and Helene had passed another milestone. They'd made it through the start-up; they'd achieved viability; they'd moved beyond critical mass; they'd successfully brought in another salesperson. The company finished 1998 with total sales of $725,000, up from $162,300 in 1992. The average gross margin was 38 percent. The main problem was that—with three full-time people and part-time clerical help, not to mention all the computer supplies they kept on hand—Bobby and Helene were running out of space in their house. They were using a shed in the backyard as a warehouse, and the basement was filled to capacity. Even the children's old bedrooms had been converted to storage. There were no rooms left to convert.

Sooner or later, Bobby and Helene would face a choice: move the business to a new location, or stop growing. They weren't yet ready to decide.

The Internet Opportunity

Meanwhile, the business environment was rapidly changing. The Internet, in particular, offered a world of new challenges and opportunities. While it was obvious, to me at least, that the majority of new Web-based businesses wouldn't survive, there was no question that the Internet could be an enormously powerful sales tool for many traditional businesses, including Bobby and Helene's. In fact, it completely transformed Bobby's and Steven's roles as salespeople.

Ask Norm

Dear Norm:
I have a $3 million business and several paid advisers—
accountants, lawyers, and so on—but I feel alone and, frankly,
confused. Where do I find someone I can talk to who doesn't
have his or her own agenda?
    Henry

Dear Henry:
First, understand that there's nothing unusual about feeling
alone and confused. Entrepreneurs are always alone, and we all
do a lot of groping in the dark. In fact, loneliness is the biggest
challenge we all face. Fortunately, there are many places you
can go to get unbiased advice, including industry conferences,
business seminars, and networking groups, not to mention organizations like SCORE (Service Corps of Retired Executives),
the counseling arm of the Small Business Administration. If
you want one-on-one advice from an entrepreneur still active
in business, look around your town and pick out a business you
really admire. Then I'd write or call the person behind it.
    —Norm

Both of them had grown used to doing their work the old-fashioned
way: prospecting for customers over the phone, setting up appointments, making sales calls, and so on. Then, in 1997, the Stones got an
offer of a free Web site and one month's free hosting, provided they'd
agree to pay $25 a month for the service thereafter. They accepted the
offer and posted their product list, along with the name, address, and
phone number of the company. Within a few days, they had enough
new sales to cover the cost of the site for an entire year.

The Stones were happy to have the additional business, but they didn't really discover the selling potential of the Internet until the following year, when Bobby put up a new Web site (in addition to the original one) and began educating himself in the fine points of Web-based marketing. He focused most of his attention on the search engines, looking for techniques to attract customers to his site by getting it listed among the top choices for the products he wanted to sell. Thus, for example, he figured out how to make sure that their company, Data-Link Associates, would come up first or second when somebody searched on Google for, say, "DLT bar code labels."

As Bobby and Steven improved their Internet selling skills, the company's sales took off, increasing 50 percent in 1998 and almost doubling—to $1.4 million—in 1999. In 2000, they increased again, to $1.5 million. Meanwhile, between 95 percent and 98 percent of Data-Link's new business was coming via the Internet. The only other source of new customers was referral.

What I found most interesting was the effect that the Internet had on Bobby and Steven as salespeople—what they did, how they did it, and the consequences for their company. I could see at least six critical changes that had occurred as a direct result of their move to selling online:

1. More leverage with prospective customers. Instead of going out to find customers, Bobby and Steven would now work on figuring out how to let customers find them. That change had important repercussions. For one thing, it fundamentally altered the relationship between salesperson and sales prospects. As the salesperson, you were no longer the one pestering prospects with phone calls; instead, you were the person answering their questions. That gave you a significant psychological advantage. You could close a higher percentage of sales as a result.

2. More time for selling. By 2001, Bobby could hardly remember the last time he had gotten in his car to go on a sales call. Steven hadn't done any cold-calling in at least a year. I'm a great believer in the benefits of cold-calling, but there's no question that it takes a lot of time. You can spend hours locating decision makers, setting up appointments, traveling to meetings, and so on. By cutting out all those activities, Bobby and Steven had more time to follow up on leads generated by the Web site—answering queries, closing sales, writing up orders. There was also more time to study the sales data and identify trends. Were certain products getting hot? Should the company run a special on something? Did the Web site need to be modified? Did Bobby need to work on search engine placements?

3. Cheaper, faster, easier access to customers. Data-Link's new customers were Internet users by definition, and so—it turned out—were most of the old ones. After putting up the Web site, the Stones discovered that a majority of their regulars liked using it, too. As a result, Bobby and Steven could reach almost their entire customer base faster and less expensively than before. They used to have to spend time and money sending out brochures, doing fax mailings, and trying to reach people by phone during office hours. Now customers could check the Web site to see what was in the brochure or to find out about specials. As for direct customer communication, Bobby and Steven could do a lot of it by e-mail—at any hour of the day or night.

4. An expanded marketplace. Then, of course, there was the Internet's almost magical ability to remove geographic barriers. Before the Web site went up, Data-Link's market was pretty much limited to New York, New Jersey, Pennsylvania, and Connecticut—that is, places within driving distance of the Stones' home. To get customers, Bobby and Steven had to go see them. After going online, Data-Link could sell to customers as far away as Australia, South Africa, Singapore, and the United Arab Emirates.

5. A higher percentage of credit card sales. For a small company, there are no bigger headaches than the ones you get when you're trying to decide about extending credit to customers, or when you have to send out and collect hundreds of little bills. It's almost always better for customers to pay by credit card, but it's hard to insist on that when you're signing them up through cold-calling. A customer who seeks you out through the Internet is another story. Before Data-Link went online, about 1 percent of its sales were charged to credit cards. Afterward, the figure was closer to 20 percent. As a result, Helene Stone mailed out 250 fewer bills in 2000 than she would have had to send in 1997, and she had 250 fewer concerns about collecting.

6. A solution to the onetime buyer problem. Although most businesses want a solid base of repeat customers, it's nice to have some onetime buyers as well, if only because you don't have to offer them the discounts you give to your regular customers. The problem is that onetime buyers are notoriously expensive to find and difficult to collect from. By getting customers through its Web site, Data-Link could find onetime buyers very cheaply, and it could deal with the collection issue by insisting they pay with a credit card or waiting for the check to clear before shipping the order.

I could probably come up with other benefits that flowed from Data-Link's move to Web-based selling, but you get the picture. The changes clearly strengthened the company in just about every respect. And, unlike the folks at, say, Amazon.com, the Stones built their online business while maintaining average gross margins of 32 percent.

Follow the Numbers

As time went by, the Stones' business continued to grow, even as they continued to work out of their home. In 2001, Bobby and Helene's daughter, Jennifer, joined as Data-Link's third salesperson. The following year, the company's annual sales topped $2 million for the first time and kept growing. By the middle of the decade, Data-Link was doing more than $3 million in sales every year.

Meanwhile, Bobby and Helene continued to monitor their numbers closely. Whenever they noticed something of concern, they would give me a call, and we'd arrange a meeting, usually followed or preceded by dinner. One day they called me about what they perceived as a disturbing trend. They told me that, for the previous five months, their monthly sales had been 25 percent to 30 percent lower than normal. Among other things, they'd lost all their "special sales." Those were nonrepeating, high-volume, low-margin sales—exactly the kind of sales that I wouldn't let them accept when the company was small but that had become a nice source of profit for them in recent years.

Now, I should probably say a few words here about why those sales were dangerous in the early days but perfectly fine once the business became firmly established. It has to do with risk. Whenever you extend credit to a customer, you run the risk of not getting paid and being stuck with having to cover the cost of whatever you've sold, plus delivery charges. The bigger the sale, the greater the risk. It's generally a bad idea to take that risk on a large, low-margin sale before your business becomes viable—that is, able to sustain itself on its own, internally generated cash flow. On a $2,500 sale with a 30 percent gross margin ($750 in gross profit), you'd lose about $1,750 if the customer went out of business or just refused to pay for whatever reason. On a $25,000 sale with a 10 percent gross margin ($2,500 in gross profit), you could lose $22,500. Granted, it's tempting to go for the $2,500, particularly when the sale seems like an easy one, but—before your company has reached viability—you have to guard your start-up capital like the crown jewels. You can't afford the risk of losing a big chunk of it all at once. That $22,500 could be the difference between success and failure.

The picture changes, however, once your company becomes viable. Not that you should ever be blasé about the possibility of losing money. It's still important to do thorough credit checks on customers, especially high-volume ones. But if you know you'll survive even if you get stiffed, you can accept some of those high-volume, low-margin sales. You just have to make sure they don't become such a big percentage of your total sales that not getting paid for them could jeopardize your entire business.

As Data-Link's core business of high-margin sales had grown, Bobby and Helene had been able to do more and more high-volume, low-margin sales, and it had paid off handsomely for them. In their monthly income statements, they'd created a separate line for these special sales and kept a close eye on it. Whenever such an opportunity came along, they would decide whether or not to accept it based partly on how their regular low-volume, high-margin sales were doing and partly on how confident they were of getting paid.

Thanks largely to the special sales, they'd grown accustomed to doing between $250,000 and $300,000 a month in overall sales, and so they were concerned when they noticed a significant drop one month. Then again, one month's drop can be an aberration. If it happens two months in a row, you start to wonder what's going on. After three months, it's "Houston, we have a problem." Bobby and Helene were well beyond that point by the time they came to see me.

"Look at these numbers," Helene said, pointing to a spreadsheet for the past few months. Special sales were zero.

"OK," I said. "Why is this happening?"

"We don't know," Bobby said.

"The answer is important," I said. "Maybe you're doing something wrong that you can change."

"How do we find that out?" he asked.

"You can start by calling up customers who've done special sales in the past. Ask them why they haven't come back to you lately. Meanwhile, let's think about what you can do if the special sales never come back."

"That would be horrible!" Helene said.

"No, it wouldn't," I said. "You have a wonderful business. You're making good money on it even without the special sales. But if you lose them, you'll probably want to find another source of revenue." I didn't have to explain. They knew that they'd reached a saturation point in their main line of business. Their regular sales had been more or less stable for four or five years. "While you're investigating the drop in special sales," I said, "think about ways to expand something else you're doing. Then we'll get back together."

When we reconvened a couple of weeks later, Bobby and Helene reported that the special-sales decline appeared to be happening for several reasons. For one thing, there were more competitors offering these products. For another, the Internet allowed customers to shop more and pay less. In addition, one big customer had stopped buying, claiming that some tapes it had bought were defective. That turned out to be untrue, but the customer was no longer placing orders. "Given all this," I asked, "can you get back in the game?"

They weren't sure. The special sales came in via the Internet, and nobody could predict when one would show up. The best the Stones could do would be to improve their chances by upgrading their Web site and working on their search engine placements. But they said there was another opportunity they could go after. A couple of years earlier, they had begun selling cabinets and cases for firearms, adding them to the mix at the urging of a major supplier, a manufacturer of office furnishings that made gun cabinets as well. Recently, the manufacturer had told Bobby and Helene they were missing out on sales because Data-Link was not an approved vendor of the General Services Administration. The Stones had submitted an application shortly thereafter and won GSA approval, opening the door for sales to local police forces and other government agencies around the country. "We're doing a couple thousand a month in GSA sales right now," Helene said. "The average sale isn't as big as the average special sale, and the gross margin is lower, but the opportunity is basically limitless."

"So where are you going to get the biggest payoff over the next five years?" I asked.

"Well, obviously GSA," Bobby said, and Helene agreed. So did I. By and large, the special sales were one-shot deals. The buyer might never come back for another one. The sales to government entities, on the other hand, had the potential to become repetitive. That meant Bobby and Helene could build a business around it over time. In fact, their GSA sales quickly grew to more than $40,000 per month, and— after they did considerable work on the Web site—some of the special sales came back.

But what made me happiest about the episode was the Stones' ability to answer, by themselves, the question of what to do. They could answer it because they knew their business. They had a firm grasp of the numbers and could use them to make smart decisions for the company.

Ask Norm

Dear Norm:

I am a Korean-born female. I majored in sociology as under-graduate and worked as magazine reporter. After that, I spent two years in USA got my MBA at Wharton, and came back to Korea. I did business planning at Citibank Korea for five years. I left due to boredom and joined an established Internet company in Korea. Here is my problem. My husband got a job offer from a Korean-run start-up in Los Angeles. I want to go with him and start my own business in USA but I'm not sure I can be successful, since I have very little connections, knowledge, and some language limitation. What do you think?

   Jeongwon

Dear Jeongwon:

I think you should follow your dreams. To me, success isn't about achieving a specific goal but rather about having the courage to try. Of course, you want to build a successful business, and you probably will. The factors you consider handi-caps are easily overcome in this day and age. Given your background, I'm sure you'll have no trouble with language or connections, and your experience is fabulous. More important than the company you build, however, is the life you lead. If you have a dream and don't follow it, you'll regret it forever.

—Norm

Love Thy Business

Working with the Stones has been as rewarding an experience for me as it has been (I hope) for them. One episode in particular imparted a lesson that I think every businessperson should take to heart. It happened as a direct result of the Stones' creative use of the Internet as a sales tool. Through the Internet, they had developed relationships with customers all over the world, one of which—Bobby learned—was a Canadian manufacturer of high-quality media storage cabinets. As it happened, Data-Link sold such cabinets, but it couldn't afford to carry the Canadian company's products because the U.S. distributor had set the prices too high.

Then, in the spring of 2002, Bobby heard that the Canadian manufacturer was changing its distribution strategy and looking for four or five independent companies to be its U.S. representatives. He immediately called the international sales manager, who said he would be coming to the States to interview candidates. Bobby asked him to include Data-Link on the list. The sales manager readily agreed and made an appointment to stop by. He had no idea what he was getting into.

The sales manager was used to doing business with companies located in office buildings or industrial parks. The rep firms on his list all worked out of suites with spacious offices, modern furnishings, water coolers, and other trappings of mainstream business life. Whenever he arrived for an appointment, he would be greeted by a receptionist who would offer him coffee before leading him to a conference room, where he'd meet with people in suits.

So you can imagine what he must have been thinking as he pulled up in front of the Stones' house in a middle-income, residential town on Long Island, New York. Helene Stone answered the door, holding her then three-year-old granddaughter, Rebecca, in her arms. She said hello and called for Bobby, who came upstairs from the basement, shook hands with the man, and asked him to walk around to the rear of the house, where the business entrance was located. When he got there, Bobby ushered him into Data-Link's basement headquarters.

There was hardly room to move. The place was packed with desks and chairs, fax machines, computer equipment, filing cabinets, storage racks, and boxes of products waiting to be shipped. Bobby was oblivious to the mess. For him, it was simply a by-product of success. The sales manager, however, looked around in disbelief. Winding their way through the clutter, they came to a narrow, steep set of stairs and climbed up to the first floor, where Bobby invited his guest to take a seat in the dining room that served as their conference room.

"He was in shock," said Helene. "I mean, really. He kept looking at us, like, 'What is going on here?' There's Rebecca, dancing her way across the living room, and I'm chasing after her while Bobby is talking. At least Bobby wasn't in shorts. He put on pants and a shirt for the occasion." Most of all, said Bobby, "he wanted to know how we did business. He couldn't believe the numbers we were churning out. It just blew him away that we were running the business out of a basement with no sales force. He had a million questions."

And Bobby was delighted to answer all of them. He loves talking about the business, as does Helene. The business has been an adventure for them, filled with discoveries, challenges, and triumphs. What the Stones lack in trappings, they've made up for in resourcefulness, particularly in the area of sales. Among other things, as I noted above, they've figured out how to use the Internet to turn the traditional sales process on its head. Instead of going out to knock on doors, they've set it up so that customers get in touch with them. Bobby tried to explain to the sales manager how it works—how they get great placement on search engines; how they identify trends and use the information to decide what special promotions they should run; how they've vastly expanded their market and also improved their collections, since a higher percentage of sales are paid for by credit card.

The meeting lasted for about an hour and a half. When it was over, Bobby and Helene showed their guest out by the front door. A week later, he called back: "Welcome aboard," he said. He'd visited some twenty companies and selected five to be distributors. "I'm sure you're going to do a great job."

But the Stones didn't find out what had really happened for another year. Shortly after the first anniversary of their meeting, the sales manager called to say he was coming back to town and would like to take the Data-Link staff out to dinner. He knew the routine by then. When he showed up, he parked his car, walked around to the rear of

the house, and knocked on the basement door. The Stones were waiting for him. He said he wanted to speak with them for a few minutes
before going to the restaurant.

"You should have seen the notes I made after my last visit," he
said, as he settled into a chair in the living room. "I wrote, 'This company is either going to make it big or do nothing at all. I can't figure it
out.'" Back in Canada, he'd told his colleagues all about Data-Link.
They shook their heads and laughed. Then he told them he was choosing Data-Link as a distributor. They thought he was nuts. He said
he'd take full responsibility. There was just something about Bobby
and Helene and the way they talked about what they did that made
him think it was worth the risk. And he'd been thoroughly vindicated.
Data-Link had outsold the other four U.S. distributors in the first year.
"You far exceeded our expectations," he said. Now he wanted to take
the relationship to the next level. He hoped that the Stones would start
promoting a wider range of his company's products. They agreed.

So what convinced the sales manager to go with them in the
first place? At the risk of sounding ridiculous, I'd say it was love—
specifically, the love that Bobby and Helene have for their business.
You can't fake the kind of enthusiasm they have when they talk about
it. Those feelings have to come from the heart.

I have similar feelings about my business. When most people visit
my company and look around one of my warehouses, all they see are
boxes—hundreds of thousands of boxes neatly arranged on shelves
that rise up to the ceiling, almost fifty-six feet above the floor. But
when I look around that warehouse, I see something different. I see a
fabulous business that my employees and I have built from scratch. It
sounds silly, but the smell of cardboard gets my juices flowing.

I don't think it's possible to be a successful entrepreneur if you
don't feel that way about your business. Whatever your company does,
you need to believe in your gut that it's the most interesting, exciting, worthwhile enterprise you could be engaged in at that moment, or
you're going to have a hard time convincing anyone else—employees,
customers, investors, whoever—to make commitments to you. If I
thought storing boxes on shelves was boring, I never would have been

able to attract the great people I work with, and we wouldn't have been able to accomplish what we've done. Fortunately, I've found every aspect of records storage fascinating from the start. I just love showing off our facility to visitors, and I'm sure my enthusiasm is contagious. Enthusiasm usually is. In fact, genuine enthusiasm is one of the most powerful forces in business. It can help you overcome a lot of obstacles, as the Stones demonstrated.

That kind of enthusiasm is worth all the headaches and heartaches that go into building a company. If you don't have it, you probably should find some other pursuit. Life is too short to waste your time—and everybody else's—on things you don't believe in. Then again, if you do have the passion, you'll look at entrepreneurship the way I do: as a fantastic journey and a truly fabulous way to spend a life.

The Bottom Line

Point One: Be prepared to carry new salespeople for up to a year before getting the kind of production that will justify what it costs to hire them.

Point Two: If you want salespeople to make good sales, teach them how your business makes money.

Point Three: Watch your numbers carefully, and—when they change—find out why. There's always a reason.

Point Four: Enthusiasm is the lifeblood of a business. Be generous with it.

Acknowledgments

Before *The Knack*, there was "Street Smarts," the monthly column in *Inc.* magazine that we began writing in 1995. Those articles, and the research behind them, provided much of the material for this book, and we would like to begin by thanking the people we've written about for their willingness to share their stories with a wider audience. Judging by the feedback we've received from readers, you have helped a lot of other people in their entrepreneurial journeys. For that matter, we also want to thank those readers (and especially you, Dr. Philip Leopold). You have kept us going with your observations, comments, questions, stories, words of encouragement, and thoughtful criticisms. Unfortunately, we could not answer every e-mail you sent us, but rest assured that we read and appreciated each one.

Our colleagues at *Inc.* have been tremendously supportive over the past fourteen years, and we are indebted to them all. We would particularly like to thank the magazine's three editors in chief during that time: George Gendron, who guided us during the first seven years; John Koten, who led us through trying times thereafter; and Jane Berentson, who has encouraged and inspired us ever since. Jeff Seglin helped to get the column going. Nancy Lyons, Michael Hopkins, Evelyn Roth, and Karen Dillon all played a role in its development. During the past seven years, we have benefited greatly from the extraordinary editorial talents of Loren Feldman. Some of the best work we've done has come as a direct result of his observations, insights, and suggestions. Of course, we owe special thanks to *Inc.*'s founder, the late Bernie Goldhirsh, for giving us a platform to stand on, and to its current owner, Joe Mansueto, for making sure the platform has remained as solid as ever.

In addition, we are grateful to the many others at *Inc.* who have done—and who continue to do—so much for the magazine in general and for our column in particular. We have enjoyed the support of dozens of people, including creative directors, photography editors, publishers, deputy and senior editors, managing editors, production managers, researchers, fact-checkers, copyeditors, editorial assistants, advertising salespeople, circulation directors, events managers, marketing directors, and on and on. We would love to recognize each of you by name, but that would essentially involve reprinting every *Inc.* masthead for the past fourteen years—and even then we might inadvertently leave some people out. Failing that, please accept our thanks and know that you have our deep appreciation.

We'd also like to acknowledge all the people at CitiStorage and U.S. Document Security who have played such a big role in this book and in our lives. We especially want to thank Brad Clinton, Peter Gunderson, Mike Harper, Bruce Howard, Sherry James, Sam Kaplan, Noelle Keating, Patty Lightfoot, Patti Kanner Post, Louis Weiner, and—of course—Elaine Brodsky.

Thanks as well to Adrian Zackheim, the founder and publisher of the Portfolio division of Penguin, who proposed we write *The Knack*. Penguin's Will Weisser used his tremendous marketing talents to help us refine the concept. The team at Penguin Portfolio—including Francesca Belanger, Courtney Nobile, Joe Perez, and Courtney Young— did their usual fabulous job.

And where would we ever be without Jill Kneerim, our literary agent? She is simply the best. Ever since we first showed up in her office almost ten years ago, she has been unstinting in her support, dead-on in her advice, and indefatigable in her efforts on our behalf. Through her, we have also enjoyed the support of the great team at her Boston agency, Kneerim & Williams at Fish & Richardson, including Hope Denekamp, Cara Krenn, and Julie Sayre.

As readers of this book will surmise, we are both strong believers in putting the life plan before the business plan. Our life plans have been centered around our families. We'd be lost without them. So to Elaine and Beth Brodsky; Rachel and Adam Luna; Lisa, Jake, Maria, Owen, and Scarlett Burlingham; and Kate Burlingham Knightly and Matt Knightly, this one's for you.

—Norm Brodsky and Bo Burlingham

Index